HOW TO MAKE YOUR MAN COMMIT

Also by Zelda West-Meads

The Trouble With You

To Love, Honour and Betray

HOW TO MAKE YOUR MAN COMMIT
AND WHAT TO DO IF HE WON'T

Zelda West-Meads

Hodder & Stoughton

Case Histories
All case histories in this book are based on real people. However, all names and distinguishing details have been changed so that the couples are unrecognisable.

First published in Great Britain in 1999 by Hodder and Stoughton
A division of Hodder Headline PLC

10 9 8 7 6 5 4 3 2 1

British Library Cataloguing in Publication Data
A CIP catalogue record for this title
is available from British Library

ISBN 0 340 71780 7

Typeset by Palimpsest Book Production Limited,
Polmont, Stirlingshire

Printed and bound in Great Britain by
Mackays of Chatham PLC, Chatham Kent.

Hodder and Stoughton
A division of Hodder Headline PLC
338 Euston Road
LONDON NW1 3BH

For Tim and Emily, David and Caroline

Acknowledgements

I would like to thank the many women and men who have agreed to be interviewed for this book, and told their stories of love, heartbreak and fear of commitment. I am grateful for the courage and generosity they displayed in telling their stories. Thank you also to the people I have counselled over the years from whom I have learnt so much and who have also contributed to my understanding of men who fear commitment and the women who fall in love with them.

I would also like to thank my husband, children, family and friends who have given me such love and encouragement in the writing of this book. Finally, thank you to my editor Rowena Webb, whose advice, direction and enthusiasm I have very much appreciated.

Contents

1

He loves me, he loves me not.

Alas! the love of women! it is known
To be a lovely and a fearful thing!

Lord Byron; *Don Juan*

MEN WHO ARE AFRAID TO LOVE – AND THE WOMEN WHO LOVE THEM.

When you have fallen passionately in love with a man who swears he loves you truly, madly, deeply only to find that the next moment he has taken flight, then you have experienced the pain of falling for a man who is afraid of love – a man who can't commit. Some men are so commitment phobic that even if they knew the world was about to end tomorrow, they could not make a commitment for fear of the long-term consequences. But the majority of men who shy away from commitment are capable of forming loving and sustaining relationships. The important thing for you to know is how to be able to distinguish between the worst-case commitment phobic men who will never change and the ones who are able to overcome their fears and make a committed relationship – to you, the woman they have fallen in love with.

Commitment phobic men – CPMs – appear to be looking for love but, once they find it, run in the opposite direction. They are torn in two, with half of them longing for a loving relationship and the other half being terrified of making a commitment. This behaviour is thoroughly confusing for them but even more so for you. You may not hear from them again after a wonderfully romantic first date. They may have pursued you with all the passion of a star-struck lover only to abandon you after the very first time that you make love. The relationship may have been good, lovely and stable and just when thoughts of marriage crossed your mind he suddenly ends the relationship.

For many commitment phobic men the change only takes place once they are married, they are then faced with the thought of being together for ever and find their panic button has suddenly gone into orbit. Then they may distance themselves from you by ignoring your emotional needs. They may become abusive, have a string of affairs or turn into workaholics.

When this sort of experience has happened to you it is an indication that you are dealing with a man who can't commit. What he is running away from is his fear of commitment. He may or may not recognise this fear within himself, but one thing that is also likely to be true is that at the beginning of your relationship with him neither did you, which is why it is such a hurtful and confusing experience.

Are you a Magnet for CPMs?

- Do you feel you are unlucky in love?
- Are you always losing out in relationships?
- Do you go from one disastrous relationship to another?
- Are you constantly attracted to the wrong sort of men?
- Have you fallen head over heels in love, only to find that after a whirlwind romance he is off with someone new?
- Do you find that time and again you think you have met a man who is just right for you, only to find that he loves you and leaves you?
- Do you repeatedly find yourself in relationships with men who won't commit?

If these things are familiar to you the chances are that at some time or another you have fallen for a man who is afraid of commitment. It may have happened just once in your life, it may have become a pattern and you are finding yourself constantly falling for men who won't commit to you or you might be married to such a man.

Are you attracted to unobtainable men?

- Are you attracted to men who you know have a track record of being footloose and fancy free?
- Do you find them a challenge and think maybe they will turn over a new leaf? Do you think you will be the girl who will change them?
- Do you find unpredictable men exciting and quite irresistible? Are reliable and dependable men just a little bit dull as far as you are concerned?

If the answer is yes to one or more of these three questions that may well be because you too have a problem with commitment. Perhaps you recognise this or it may be deeply buried and by falling in love with a man who fears commitment it lets you off the hook. So rather than admit you have a problem you can blame it on him.

Is falling for men who can't commit like a well worn record in the same old groove?

Most of us at some time or another have fallen in love with a man who won't commit, but for some women it has become a recurrent theme in their lives. So they find themselves time and again attracted to men who turn from loving and adorable princes into horrid slippery frogs who dash their hopes and dreams as they flee away from the scene of yet another broken love affair into the arms of another where they wreak the same havoc over and over again.

Do you wonder if you frighten men away?

If this pattern is becoming all too familiar it could be because not only do you keep falling for a man who can't commit, but it may be something that you are doing when you get into relationships with men.

- Do you drive men away because you are assessing whether each new man in your life has the potential as a lifelong partner, while his horizons don't stretch much beyond the next date?

- Do you expect too much from men? Are you over-demanding, or does your jealousy or possessiveness end in too many of your relationships coming to grief?
- Do you try to take over their lives, so that they feel the claustrophobic relationship you want is not for them?

Are you searching for your knight in shining armour?

'Bold bright young women,' says Fay Weldon the novelist, 'have grown so picky, so sure they can do without men, that there are many young men wandering around desperate for a little affection.' Around 25% of women in their thirties are single or divorced. As a young woman nowadays you are likely to be more financially independent, in a reasonable or extremely good job. You may have your own car and a flat, either rented or owned. Most women also have terrific friendship networks, friends they love and trust, and with whom they share their ups and downs. Lovers may come and go, but true friends are there through thick and thin. Many women also have some good male friends who really are 'Just good friends'. They may have been romantically linked to them in the past. The sexual interest has long since faded but the friendship continues. All of this makes for a fairly independent and interesting lifestyle.

Therefore there is far less need than in previous generations to find a man just to fulfil your security needs. Your expectations of what you want from the man you want to marry are far higher than in previous generations. And as you are choosing to marry later than your mother and grandmother you are searching for even more in your potential mate – an equal partner, best friend, good lover, an involved father to your child, a good provider, and faithful partner. You have worked hard to achieve what you have and where you have got to in your working and social life and you want a man who can equal that, or perhaps even outstrip it. Many a man who might have been acceptable if you had met and married him in your early twenties, ten years on fail to interest. The eighties have a lot to answer for. 'We live in a culture where we value only the things that offer status and money,' says Cary Cooper, Professor of Organisational Psychology at Manchester University's Institute of Science and Technology. So although modern women may deny it hotly, you are also looking for your knight in shining armour. So you say to yourself better to have no relationship than to settle into one that you know will only ever be second best.

Do you believe that love and marriage go hand in hand?

Are you in love with a man who loves you to bits but who becomes nervous or evasive if the subject of marriage rears its head?

Do you want to settle down to marriage and children, only to find that the man you love has suddenly planned to throw in his job and travel the world? Taking big steps.

At the beginning of the relationship men who fear commitment make you feel the most desirable woman in the world. You thought it was the start of a relationship only to discover his romantic intentions were no more than a one-night stand. You played hard to get, and he pursued you all the more; when you were certain that you loved him, he lost interest. One moment he wants to spend every waking moment with you, the next you can't see him for dust.

When the plans for the big white wedding reach their peak you find that his ardour has cooled and he breaks off the engagement. He may even marry you but his fear of commitment is so profound that he consistently refuses to try to understand your emotional needs. If these things have happened to you the chances are you know just how painful it can be to fall in love with a commitment phobic man.

WHY THIS BOOK IS FOR YOU

If this is the story of your love life this book will help you to understand what it is about you that is attractive to men who won't commit and why so many of them fight shy of commitment. It will explore the underlying reason why you became involved with such a man. It will help you understand why you are attracted to elusive mates, and help recognise these destructive patterns and understand where this behaviour originated. It will explore why, when you know these relationships are not meeting your needs, you still frequently stay in them, endlessly hoping that in time the man you love will change. Why the loving often becomes an addiction so that you feel you cannot survive without him. Why you may be ruled by fear: fear that you are not really lovable, not attractive enough, not good enough or that if you don't get this man you will never find anyone else. Why you sometimes even convince yourself that you will never fall in love again. These fears can make you stay in relationships that are hurtful, unsatisfactory, even emotionally abusive.

All the rest of the world can perhaps see what you choose to ignore – that you are up to your eyes in 'going nowhere relationships'.

THE GOING NOWHERE RELATIONSHIP

Non-commitment can take many forms but I have chosen the story of Abigail to illustrate the 'going nowhere relationship'. Abigail, a very pretty girl with long blonde hair and blue eyes, very intelligent, lively, socially confident and outward going and extremely popular with all her friends, was twenty when she first met Joe who was a year older than her, and twenty-seven when she finally left him after realising he was never going to marry her.

'We were on a ski-ing holiday with the university ski club when we met – we were both at King's College, London. I'd noticed him immediately when the group met at Victoria coach station. He was dark-haired and very good-looking and he was carrying his own skis so I knew he must be quite good. I saw him looking at me too and he smiled. But he told me later that he was too shy to approach me. When we arrived at our hotel many hours later, I made sure I sat next to him at dinner. He smiled and told me his name was Joe and filled my glass with wine. I knew immediately that I really liked him. Everyone was really tired after our long day and so we were drinking lots of wine and were all getting very giggly and playing word games. I was getting on really well with Joe. He was quite quiet but he seemed very sweet and gentle and when he did speak he was funny. I asked him if he was good at ski-ing and he said, quite seriously, he was brilliant. I laughed, but he clearly really meant it. I said I had only been once before and he said why didn't I come with him the next day and he would try and teach me.

'So I did. He was so patient and good fun. I kept falling over and instead of helping me up, he just took the opportunity to throw snowballs at me. I was helpless with laughter. I remember thinking he was so kind and clever and funny and I guess I fell in love with him then and there. By the end of the week, we had become inseparable and I was so thrilled when he said could he see me when we got back to college.

'So when we got back, we started going out together and that was that. It was great in the early days, there was only one thing that I found strange – he was so quiet which was the thing that I had noticed in the first place. I'm a really talkative person but he would never talk to me. Though he was never hesitant about telling me he loved me he would never really talk about his feelings. If I tried to talk about anything serious, he would just make a joke of it.

'I remember the first time I went to Sunday lunch at his house and I was absolutely astonished. There were Joe's father and stepmother, and his stepbrother and stepsister and me all sitting round the table and nobody talked. They would ask for someone to pass the salt and pepper or talk about the things they had to do that afternoon, but the conversation was interspersed with long silences, as if someone was desperately trying to think of what to say – it was so awkward. It was so different from my own family where everyone talked all the time.

'I was even more astonished by what he told me after lunch though. I commented that he didn't look much like his father and he said: "No, well I wouldn't, I'm adopted." I was speechless. We'd been going out together a whole term by then and he'd never mentioned it, even though I'd often asked him about his family. He'd told me that his parents had got divorced when he was seven and both remarried a few years later but when I'd sympathised about his parents getting divorced, he just said it was no big deal. Now I asked him why he'd never told me he was adopted and he just said the same thing, that it was no big deal. I asked him if he'd ever thought about contacting his real parents and he said: "My adopted parents are my real parents. My mother didn't want me, why should I have anything to do with her?" He sounded so cold and callous when he said that, not like the Joe I knew. Perhaps I should have known then that it wasn't going to work.

'But I didn't of course. We went out together all through the next two and a half years of university and then got jobs. We were very different in our choice of careers. Joe got a first in mathematics and went straight into a top accountancy firm. I got my degree in English and had a harder struggle to find a job, but I did find one that I liked apart from the pitiful salary in a small PR company in London.

'It was his idea to buy a house together and because I didn't want to rent, and because I really loved him, I was delighted. We were both so young then – only twenty-two and twenty-three – that neither of us wanted to get married, let alone have children.

'We were happy together, but I did start to find it difficult that he never really talked about how he was feeling. In my family we all talked about how we felt, everything was expressed, love, compassion, hurt, anger, disappointment, it was never difficult to tell how the other person was feeling, we were just so used to telling each other. But with Joe I always had to drag it out of him. In the main, if we had any disagreements he just used to clam up and refused to discuss it.

'By my mid-twenties, I had started to change. My career as yet had not really taken off, I'd changed jobs five or six times partly because I was not really sure what I wanted to do. But I never had difficulty in finding a job and I was never out of work.

'After we had been together for five years I started to feel I wanted some security in life. I found that at the age of twenty-five I was starting to think about marriage. We had after all been together for five years by this time and I couldn't imagine life without him, so I started to want more commitment. The trouble was I knew that he was really anti-marriage. He'd always said he didn't want to make the mistakes his parents had. My parents were divorced too, but I'd gone the opposite way, I felt I wanted to get it right.

'I said to Joe why don't we get married but he just said that we were fine as we were, what difference would a piece of paper make. He also said that we were too young. I think he thought that would be the end of it, but over the next year or so, I really wanted to get married more and more. I kept asking him about it but he just kept saying the same thing. I don't think he realised how hurt I felt. I couldn't understand why if he loved me and kept telling me that he did, he didn't love me enough to marry me. It really came to a head when a friend of ours, Alex, suddenly got engaged after a six-month romance. Alex said that it just seemed like the right thing to do. I just kept wondering why it didn't feel to Joe as though it was the right thing to do. I felt so rejected, and I started to feel unmarriageable. I felt I must not be good enough to marry.

'But I was also starting to want children. This was even worse because if Joe was anti-marriage, he was even more anti-children. If friends of ours got pregnant, he said he didn't know why on earth they wanted to have children, that it would stop you being able to do anything.

'Whenever I mentioned that I wanted marriage to Joe, he was so dismissive. He just made a joke out of it and said how could he possibly marry me. I was too chaotic to organise a wedding. But when I finally dared mention that I wanted children, he was really quite hurtful. He said I didn't want children, I just wanted something to do because my career wasn't working out. The awful thing was, I believed him. It was made worse because it was the mid-eighties and women weren't supposed to want marriage and families, they were supposed to want careers. I even started to feel guilty for wanting marriage and children.

'Then I had a scare that I might have an ectopic pregnancy and I had to go and have a test. I was fine but I went back to my mother's house afterwards and Joe rang me there. "Are you OK?" he asked. "Yes, I'm fine," I said, and then because I wanted to know what his reaction would be, I said, "It's not ectopic, but I am pregnant." I heard a sharp intake of breath at the other end of the phone and then a long pause. Then I laughed and said I was only joking. He just said "Thank God." I asked him later what he would have done if I really had been pregnant and he said that I'd have had to have an abortion. He didn't even ask what I would have wanted. I'm amazed that I wasn't more hurt by that at the time. Friends have been outraged when I tell them, but I guess that I'd been so brainwashed into thinking that we shouldn't have children I just agreed with him.

'But of course my feelings didn't go away. I was getting

more and more broody. It wasn't that I wanted children right then, but it was the thought of never having them that really got to me. It was getting to the point that whenever I saw small children I would start crying because it seemed impossible that I would ever "be allowed" to have them. I was utterly miserable for the last year of my relationship with Joe because I just couldn't see any future. I thought it would just go on and on like this for ever because he was totally immovable. He didn't want marriage and I did. He didn't want children, I did. But there was never a question that I would get my way – he was totally in control of the situation. I tried to explain that I was really hurt that he didn't want to marry me, but he just kept saying that he loved me but a piece of paper didn't make any difference. Once, he even said if I really wanted to marry him, why didn't I send him an application form with two reliable references stating my case. I thought at the time he was joking, but now I'm not so sure.

'Eventually, I was twenty-seven and I started to think that if he didn't want marriage and children, perhaps I should find someone who did. But I was terrified of being on my own.

'I'm ashamed to say that it took meeting someone else for me to find the courage. Joe had gone away for two months to work abroad and he was only phoning me once a week. A friend of my boss knew he was away and asked me out for dinner. I was so miserable and, though I didn't realise it at the time, angry with Joe, that I went. Over dinner, I poured my heart out and said that I had been going out with Joe for seven years and that he still didn't want to marry me. Brian just looked at me and said: "He must want his head examined. If you were mine, I'd want to just hold on to you for dear life." It was a revelation. I felt all the pain and the hurt coming out. I had felt as though nobody had wanted me for so long, as though Joe didn't really want me. As though no one would marry me. And suddenly, here was someone saying they did. I started seeing Brian while Joe was away and when Joe came back, I met him at the airport and explained that I had moved back to my mother's house and that it was over.

'Joe was devastated and I felt awful. He started crying and saying that he loved me. But I said that although I loved him I knew that he was never going to want to marry me and have children. He said he might have done, eventually, and why wouldn't I just wait. I said I'd waited seven years and I thought that was long enough. He said I'd lied to him about not wanting children and reminded me that we'd both said at the beginning how we never wanted children. I tried to explain that I was really young then, how could I know that I was going to become broody. But he didn't want to know. It was awful. It was the worst night of my life. I went back to my mother's house and just cried for weeks. Though I was the one who had finally left, I had really loved him and I was distraught. I had been so sure I was doing the right thing, but I wasn't prepared for how much I missed him. It was an incredibly bitter split and, even five years on, Joe still won't talk to me.

'Of course, it didn't work out with Brian. I didn't love him, I had just been flattered by being wanted. But I did meet someone about a year later who I knew pretty soon was the man for me. He was so different from Joe, so warm and open and could talk about his feelings. Within about two months I knew it was the right relationship. But I was terrified. I couldn't bear to go through it all again. What if Chris didn't want to marry me or have children either? So I took a big risk. One evening I said to him, "You know I've been hurt before, so please tell me, I have to know. If this works out would you have any objections to getting married or having children?" Chris smiled and laughed gently. "No," he said, "that would be fine, but maybe just not quite yet."

'We married a year and a half later and now I'm expecting our first child. I'm incredibly in love with my husband. I realise how much was missing in my relationship with Joe; I'm sorry I hurt him but I am so glad I had the courage to leave him. On reflection I realise that I should have left much sooner. During the last three years of our relationship we had lots of rows and I was very miserable, but I had loved him and I kept hoping that we could have worked things out. I know now that was never going to happen. He was never really going to open up and talk to me but I didn't really see that at the time. I kept hoping he would change.'

WHY WOMEN STAY IN RELATIONSHIPS WITH 'MR FOREVER ON HOLD'

It is important to learn from Abigail's story how to avoid the same thing happening to you. Because like many women who get involved with men who can't commit, Abigail stayed in a relationship with Joe for far too long. She stayed hoping against hope that he would change his mind, endlessly trying to make something work that patently was not working. This is very typical behaviour when a woman falls in love with a commitment shy man.

We are brought up to believe we are the carers and nurturers. Because we as women set so much store by relationships we also frequently take on the bigger share of responsibility for making them work. So when they go wrong or run into trouble we tend to end up feeling it's our fault and that we need to do something about it, that if we try hard enough we can work it out.

It's a catch 22 situation – we love the man with all our heart and we don't want to lose him, but we don't want to walk away either because we keep hoping that he will change and offer us the commitment we are looking for. But for relationships to work well, both sides have to accept a fair distribution of responsibility for them. By looking at Joe's childhood you will see that he experienced so much hurt and rejection that it made it almost impossible for him to really trust a woman. Men who can't commit frequently have similar sorts of childhood experiences as Joe; understanding the past can frequently explain the present.

HOW THE PAST AFFECTS THE PRESENT

As Abigail discovered, Joe had a history of not dealing with painful and difficult problems. She only discovered several months into the relationship that he was adopted, and that was only because she observed that he did not look like his father. Joe had been adopted at six months old, so that he would have been old enough to have formed a bond with his mother, only to have that broken when she perhaps was no longer able to cope and had put him up for adoption. He felt rejected by her and it was clear he had in turn rejected her. He said, 'My adopted parents are my real parents. My mother didn't want me, so why should I have anything to do with her?' His feelings of loss and rejection increased when at the age of seven his adoptive parents divorced. Yet he described both events as 'no big deal'.

He went to live with his adoptive mother who was cold and had little real interest in him. He was closer to his father who did love him but had difficulty expressing it. When Joe was nine his father remarried. His stepmother was kind but Joe always felt an outsider in the new marriage as he felt further displaced in his father's affections by the arrival of his stepmother and by the fact that she had three younger children. Joe felt unable to talk to anyone about what he was feeling. He also learnt from an early age that it was not really safe to commit yourself a hundred per cent to someone you loved as there was always the fear that if you did, you might lose the person you loved most. He became very emotionally locked up and he carried this forward into his adult relationships.

His attraction to Abigail was because she was very emotionally open. This was something he longed to be but was unable to achieve, so he sought it in her. But he was so damaged by his childhood experiences that he was unable to learn from her. When she tried to help him to express his feelings he retreated into anger or silence.

Abigail adored him when they first met, but slowly over the years he strangled that love. She started to feel that he did not love her enough. Not enough that is to want to marry her or to want her to have his children. His hidden fear, unrecognised by him, was that if he had children of his own they might replace him in Abigail's affection and yet again he feared he would lose the person he loved. He could not risk repeating that cycle of pain. All he knew was that he did not want children. He had little idea why.

Five years on he is still bitterly angry with Abigail because she too eventually rejected him. But that is only part of the picture. His real anger is with his mother, who as he saw it, did not love him enough, and gave him away. The anger grew with his adopted mother who was cold and distant, and his stepmother who married his adopted father and who already had children of her own. So when Abigail the one woman he loved also rejected him, he could not acknowledge this was because he could not commit to her. But instead the full force of his anger with all the women who as a child had let him down was now directed at Abigail.

But Abigail did love him, she had tried endlessly to help him to express his feelings, but he continually failed to do so. His fear of commitment meant he failed to understand Abigail's need for marriage and children and so in the end he lost a woman who had really loved him.

Over the next few years Joe had no problems attracting woman as he was good-looking, clever and successful. He had four or five more relationships all of which started off very intensely with him doing the pursuing, but each time the girls involved realised that the relationship was going nowhere they in turn each left him.

HE LOVES ME, HE LOVES ME NOT?

In interviewing women for this book I was struck by how many had stayed in relationships in the hope that one day the man they loved would commit to them How when they wanted more from the relationship, such as to move in together, marry and have children the relationship had turned sour. How the men had resisted any change to the relationship or had taken flight altogether. Abigail's experience sadly was all too common. Many like Abigail had stayed in the relationship far too long hoping against hope that the man would change his mind, only to find that they had waited in vain. The problem for women in this position is threefold.

- You love him and you think that one day he too will want to marry and have children
- You have got so used to being part of a couple it feels very scary to end the relationship and be single again.
- Even though you have a lot to offer a man, you have been so hurt by the man who won't commit that you fear you will not meet someone else, someone who returns your love in full measure and who wants the commitment of marriage and children.

What is important is to understand that part of a CPM wants a loving relationship and the other part is downright scared of having one. He is torn in two directions. What you need to do is to be able to recognise when you are involved with a man who fears commitment but is able and willing to work at overcoming his fears and the worst-case CPM scenario when the only answer for you is to cut your losses and run.

THE CLASSIC COMMITMENT PHOBIC MAN

Anthony is a good-looking, fit and athletic man, with an easy relaxed confident manner with women. At thirty-three he seems older than his age. He works hard and has a well-paid job in which he uses his quick financial brain to good effect. He plays a lot of sport and drives an expensive fast car. He has had six or seven relationships lasting about six months but most of his relationships until his present one have been very short-term, a couple of months or less and a few one-night stands.

He has known his current girlfriend Gill for about six years. She is small and pretty with a good figure. They have been together for about four years with a break of a year in the middle, when he had another relationship with a girl he met at a party.

Anthony said, 'I like being single but I don't want to be on my own. I like to have a girlfriend as well. But I prefer living on my own and in that context you're making sure you don't commit because that way you've always got your own base.

'When I met Gill she was the mother of a girl I went out with for just a few weeks, but right from the beginning I got on better with Gill than with her daughter. She is fun and very intelligent and we got on very well from the first time I met her. I fancied her very much but it wouldn't have seemed right to do anything about it while I was taking her daughter out. I waited a year before I made my first move. Then I telephoned Gill and asked her out to lunch. I knew she was married, but in some ways that made her safe. I took her to a little French restaurant and we had a lovely long leisurely lunch. She insists she had no idea what was on my mind because of the age gap – she is seventeen years older than me. After lunch I invited her back to my house, saying I wanted to show her a beautiful antique mirror I had just bought, which was true. But I knew exactly what I also had in mind. I had been very flirtatious over lunch and she had been highly responsive. I set out to seduce her. I wanted her very much. We ended up in bed together. It was a wonderfully lustful experience. Sex was fantastic, in fact it still is. Sex is very important to me in relationships. In the past I've tended to get bored very quickly and so I have ended the relationship, but this has not happened with Gill. I think that's because she thinks like I do sexually and is very adventurous. We also get on so well in every other way.

'At the time she was married and living with her husband, so it was just a question of seeing each other once or twice a week. To start with it was purely a lust relationship. It suited her and it suited me. Seeing each other just a couple of times a week was pure excitement. It didn't concern me that she was in a marriage. It was obviously not a good one and in fact she is now divorced.

'After about a year I met another girl at a party. I did not want to be unfaithful but I did want to give this other relationship a go, so I ended my relationship with Gill. She was very upset, I know that. Over the next year we stayed in touch but very distantly and then this girl and I split up and after a few months I got back together with Gill. I can't remember how we got back together but I made the first move. When we split up it was a shock and I did feel guilty. I also felt guilty about getting back together, because ultimately, I knew this relationship was going to end and it would hurt her all over again. When we got back together it seemed the natural thing to do. We both wanted that, so we did it.

'I didn't know what her thoughts were then in terms of permanence. I suppose I had not really spelt it out that the relationship had no future, but I think Gill knows now.

'From my point of view our relationship is better than

ever. Originally I was attracted to her because I thought she was fantastic. I still think she's fantastic, all of her, her attitude towards life, her sense of enjoyment, everything.

'Breaking up with her husband hasn't been easy for her. He moved out about two years ago and over that period it's been quite upsetting for her, going through the rigmarole of divorce. I've never been involved in seeing people get divorced before. But it's all hassle. Very emotional and very upsetting and she hasn't enjoyed that.

'I told her about a year ago that the relationship was never going to be permanent. I thought she was becoming more dependent on me, therefore I'd better make things clear. I can't remember the exact discussion. But it was just to say that I can't see this relationship lasting for ever. I admit it did cause a bit of hassle. I think she knew really but thought as the relationship was becoming more stable that might not be the case. If she was ten years younger my attitude might be slightly different, but I can't see myself committing to someone long-term. I don't want children and to me that is the most important and logical reason for getting married.

'She hates the thought of us not being permanent, I suppose because she loves me and she would like it to be permanent. She says that our relationship is brilliant, but now she also says that she regrets getting back together because she's worried about what will happen in the future. She'd love to live together, be looked after and have a normal life. Then I point out that if we had a normal relationship we wouldn't have such an exciting and great time. We don't, hopefully, take each other for granted. We've been back together about two years now.

'We see each other mainly at weekends, sometimes once in the week. I do a lot of sport and I haven't got time to fit her into my week generally. Gill is fantastic in letting me do what I want. I think she understands that if she tried to be restrictive then we wouldn't be together. A girl of my own age might make a lot more demands on me and that wouldn't allow a relationship to last.

'I dictate the relationship. I'm able to do what I want. Gill accepts that. She would like to see me during the week as well, but it wouldn't suit me. I know I have the control but that is how I am in relationships. Sometimes she says she should end the relationship, but not seriously. Though I do recognise that as we're not going to be together always perhaps we should end it now, because it would give her a chance to get her life in order. Maybe I should help her to do this. But I love her very much so it would be hard for me to do that. Normally people split because they no longer like each other. We have none of that so it would be a bit bizarre to say "right, let's finish."

'The idea of living with someone permanently is restrictive. I've always lived on my own and done my own thing, so the thought of having to be responsible and considerate for other people is not what I want.

'My current relationship is the most intense I've ever had. I've never loved anyone quite as much and so it's a much more emotionally involved relationship. But because I don't see any long-term future I always hold something back in my relationships. Whether that would be the case if I met someone and saw us being together for ever I don't know.

'In a normal relationship you would plan for the future, but I don't do that, not even with Gill. I wouldn't even want to plan a holiday six months ahead because how would I know whether we would still be together then? I like that uncertainty. I can plan something for a week or two ahead, no, really a fortnight is plenty,' Anthony said with a smile. 'Whatever relationship I was in I wouldn't commit myself to saying I was going to do something several months ahead because then I would have to. I don't think I've ever carried the attitude that a relationship is going to be for ever.

'Gill and I don't talk about where our relationship is going very much. When I see that subject coming up I always skirt around the issue. I distract her by changing the topic or suggesting something fun to do. I don't know what to say to her because I haven't got the answer she wants to hear. I also think I avoid that particular conversation because if we discussed it, perhaps it would make it happen. She would push too hard and that would split us up. Because I would have to tell her I am not going to be around for long but at the moment I don't want the relationship to end. I suspect it will happen because she will get so annoyed at me not giving a commitment that she will force the issue. I'm aware that in all my relationships, if a suggestion is made to get permanence into the equation, I will set about planning to end that relationship. I know I shy away if a woman wants to make our relationship more permanent, it's just not my scene,' he said crossing his arms firmly across his chest.

Anthony's parents had a rather turbulent marriage. He has never been sure whether it was a good marriage because as a child he remembers them fighting and arguing a lot. The arguments always seemed to be about money. Anthony said: 'My dad was always a bit dishonest where money was concerned. He used to hide things from my mother to stop upsetting her, and he would never tell her what he was earning. He was always flying around the place trying to find work. At one time he ran a company but that went bust, so there was never enough money to go round.'

So it was his mother who was left endlessly trying to make ends meet, very much running the household, in charge, the dominant force in the household. When Anthony's father died two years ago, Anthony was convinced that he would find out some terrible secrets, like the fact his father had another wife or something. But nothing dreadful emerged, though his father was in debt to the tune of £5,000. The fact that his father appeared so hopeless with money made Anthony very determined to avoid money problems at all costs. And the fact that the woman who was closest to him also controlled him is likely to have set up a strong resistance in him to having a close live-in relationship.

Anthony has compensated for his father's lack of control and fecklessness over money by exercising a very firm control over his own money. He will never get into debt or run up an overdraft, he needs to be in control just as his mother was. In his job as a financial adviser he not only controls his own money but other people's as well. He also takes control in relationships, physically and emotionally. He chooses not to live with anyone so that he can more or less do what he wants when he wants to. He is also in control emotionally when it comes to relationships, but never giving too much of himself, always holding back emotionally, so that he never fully commits to relationships. If the woman pushes too far in that direction, he simple ends the relationships.

Anthony said, 'I do want to control my relationships and dictate how I run them. I like to be precise in lots of things.' But in some ways Anthony is also like his father who found it difficult to be honest with his wife about money. Anthony finds it difficult to be really honest with his girlfriends about the future of the relationship. So he avoids the issue as much as possible or tries to divert the conversation when the subject of commitment comes up.

Anthony admits, 'I'm not dishonest but I keep my thoughts to myself. If I was in a full-time relationship I would have to expose my thoughts more, also there would be less likelihood of escape from difficult questions. If you don't live together it's easier to keep your thoughts to yourself.' This is certainly very like his father who was secretive about money much to his wife's annoyance and frustration, which is probably rather similar to how Gill must feel when she tries to talk to Anthony about her need for commitment.

Anthony, like most commitment phobic men, is very good at the beginning of the relationship. He makes a woman feel very special, that a relationship with her is the most important thing he wants, because at that moment that is exactly how he is feeling. Anthony said, 'If you go out with someone now it's natural and not a taboo thing to jump into bed together. Recently I've thought that it would be nice to go out on a few dates first, but that is perhaps because I've hardly ever done that, which is why it seems appealing. So giving someone a peck on the cheek and saying "good night" is quite an interesting thing to try to do. There would be the added anticipation to compensate. The girl's brain is more important than looks, certainly when it comes to the sexual side. Initially sex can be a physical thing but you need to be on the same wavelength as well.

'I'm not good at ending relationships even when I know I want to. It would be better to make the decision and just tell them straight away, but I've never been able to do that. I actually care about hurting them. So I find reasons to make love less, and to see less of them, then eventually I finish with them, or they get fed up and end it, which is of course what I want anyway.

'What I am finding now is in my age group lots of people have wives and children. You can't get a best mate out on a Friday night because he's got other things to do. So I've now got a number of younger friends because all my older friends are dropping by the wayside. They're all committing. A friend of mine has just announced he's getting married. I know why he's doing it. He wants to have a family. The girl is almost secondary. I think that's awful.'

Another reason for not committing is because Anthony can't envisage himself being faithful to one woman, throughout most of his relationships, even the short-term ones, he has been unfaithful, which is classic commitment phobic behaviour. Having 'a little on the side' is a way of keeping and maintaining a certain distance in a relationship.

Anthony said, 'My view of faithfulness is I would love it if it were achievable. But in my experience it's never been achievable. It's a shining star, a beacon in the distance. I've never been able to get that far. I would not tell my partner and I would be discreet. If I were in a permanent relationship I would try to be faithful but because I've never been in that situation . . . I don't believe you can be with someone for ever. I don't believe it can be achieved.

'I don't want to be responsible to someone, because then I would upset them. By avoiding commitment you can be as selfish as you like, because it's only influencing you.'

WHEN YOU WANT MORE THAN HE IS WILLING TO GIVE

So often the stumbling block occurs with a CPM when you are wanting a major change in the relationship, like agreeing to moving in together, marriage or having children. It is at this point when you think that the relationship is moving towards more commitment that the man who up till then has seemed so much in love with you, suddenly seems to pull back from the relationship. He may become cold and critical, pick an argument over the silliest little thing or end the relationship altogether or threaten to. Anthony is a classic non-committer, because in all his relationships, if the woman pushes for more commitment that is the beginning of the end.

THE PROMISCUOUS NON-COMMITTER

Just as Anthony is a classic non-committer keeping one foot in the door as a way out of the relationship when he grows tired of it, there are also the 'Serial Romeos'. Serial Romeos are men who leave a whole string of broken relationships in their wake. They may be single or indeed married but that does not stop them from playing the field just like their bachelor counterpart. They are often successful, rich and powerful and the adrenaline of yet another beautiful woman falling for their charms, is the ultimate aphrodisiac, as I will show in chapter two. Such men are not of course limited to the rich and powerful like for example President

Clinton, but are to be found among men everywhere, but a large bank balance or powerful position helps.

MARRIED MEN CAN BE COMMITMENT PHOBIC TOO

Lack of commitment is not confined to men who are reluctant to tie the knot. Many men continue to be emotionally uncommitted and unavailable to the women they love even when they are married. I find it is very common in counselling to see marriages where the man still has a problem with commitment.

As a woman ask yourself, are you in a marriage where the man in your life is emotionally unavailable? Do you find that whenever you want to talk he always has something vital to do instead? When you turn to him for support does he complain that you are never there for him? Does he seem more interested in sport, watching television or having a good time than he does in you? Are you always playing second fiddle to his work, his friends, his ex-wife or even his mother?

Many phobic men marry and then start to panic about the long-term commitment that marriage entails. They are torn in two directions. They want a loving relationship but they also fear that they have fallen into that tender trap called marriage. For you it is utterly confusing for here is a man who wanted to marry you, but suddenly he appears to be half-hearted about the whole idea. He does not understand why he is doing it but little by little he starts to sabotage the relationship. Whereas once he loved practically everything about you, faults and all, he now seems to do little but undermine you. It's not pennies from heaven that fall from the sky, but hailstones of criticism that make you feel hurt and uneasy. He is distancing himself from you because inside he is struggling with feelings of panic. He feels caught and trapped and is looking around for ways of escape from these tense and uncomfortable feelings. He feels too close for comfort and he blames it on you. In his mind you have changed from the woman he wants to spend the rest of his life with to his gaoler or keeper. You've become the ball and chain. So he starts making you feel unloved or insecure to relieve his anxiety about being in a relationship from which he fears there may be no escape. That way if he does decide he wants to end the relationship he has already demonstrated that you are wrong and therefore it's easier to say the whole thing is a big mistake.

JANE AND HARRY – A MARRIAGE WITHOUT COMMITMENT

Jane's husband Harry had promised marriage several times only to retract that promise as the serious business of making wedding plans started to hot up. He went back on his word several times. It was only when Jane said she'd had enough and was deadly serious about ending the relationship that he begged her to give him one more chance and they were eventually married. The first few months were a mixture of good time and bad times: first Harry was tender and loving and then for no reason he would became cold and distant. Then Harry was offered a good job with an advertising company in Australia and they both agreed that they would go there as they felt it would be the making or breaking of their relationship. They had two really good years out there, enjoying a relaxed and active outdoor lifestyle and made lots of friends. Jane said, 'We were on our own together on the other side of the world far away from family and friends – it was difficult leaving all that behind. But his job went well, I also got a job that I enjoyed and we found a lovely little flat to live in. Our lifestyle was pretty good. Having to stand on our own feet meant we became a unit, it was very good.'

Three years later when Jane wanted to start a family the whole scenario started all over again, with Harry agreeing to have a child and then saying he did not want children. 'But this time,' said Jane, 'I recognised the signs and though I won't pretend it was easy we were able to talk about it much more. I think I understood that it was not me he was running away from, but the fear of the commitment of having children and the responsibility that entails. We now have two children and he adores them both.'

When he was a child neither of Harry's parents had shown much interest in him. He was the youngest of five, and his parents frequently referred to him as a mistake. His mother was well into her forties when he was born and there was a ten-year gap between him and his older brothers and sisters. Shortly after his birth his fifty-year-old father had a stroke. Harry's mother had to spend all her time looking after his father and all too little looking after Harry. From an early age Harry had felt very responsible for both his parents and after his father died when he was fifteen his mother had leaned very heavily on him for emotional support. As he explored his fears about having children it became clear to him that so much responsibility had been heaped on his shoulders at an early age, that this was making him reluctant to take on any more, which was why he went into panic mode at the prospect of marriage and later repeated that pattern when Jane wanted to start a family. Understanding why he was feeling the way he was enabled him to make a commitment to Jane, because he realised that it was not that he did not love Jane but his fear of commitment that was getting in the way of that love.

FOOTLOOSE AND FANCY-FREE

When we fall in love in our early to mid-twenties we are not necessarily seeing it as a life-long commitment, in fact quite the opposite. Falling in love is a wonderful, passionate, romantic head-over-heels experience, so why limit it to just once or twice before we walk up the aisle? There is plenty of time for that and the world is full of men. We are single and fancy-free to enjoy whatever relationships we want, so why cramp our style by settling down to nest-building with one man?

It may also be that we are bounding up the career ladder that is giving us enormous satisfaction, or we are struggling to find one that does. All of which takes up our time and energy. So we are not looking for the 'happy ever after' type of relationship from men at this stage in our life.

Nowadays the average age of marriage for men is twenty-nine and for women twenty-seven so what has happened is that the emotional and biological time clock to find Mr Right is set several years later than it was ten years ago. For many women, once the thirtieth birthday has been reached they start to feel that the single life is no longer quite so attractive and desirable. On top of this we are older and wiser and more discriminating in our choice of men. This makes finding Mr Right that much more difficult, especially as a man in his early to mid-thirties may well choose a woman a lot younger.

IN SEARCH OF MR RIGHT

There comes a time usually in your thirties when you start to want a more committed relationship. It is much more accepted by society that a man should be footloose and fancy-free, whereas for a woman, once you are thirty-something and without a man, you are often still seen as something of an enigma. Surely you must be in search of a man, your mother, your father and your smug married friends imply.

Yet if we are truly honest with ourselves, most of us would admit that in our twenties and thirties much of that time was spent in a relationship with a man, getting over the break-up of a relationship or in search of a new one.

By the time we reach thirty-something most of us want a committed relationship if not marriage. When the big three-0 is behind us rather than ahead, marriage and children are very much on our minds. Why has Ally McBeal, the intelligent successful American thirty-something lawyer in the sitcom of the same name, struck such a chord? She is frequently seen fantasising about falling in love, marriage and babies. These desires are frequently at odds with the hopes, dreams and behaviour of the men she meets.

One intelligent, attractive and single woman of thirty-seven who admits she is looking for a man to share her life with said: 'There are certain things people say when you're over thirty and single, like "Don't worry, your prince will come," or "Cheer up! Your luck will change."' Her mother who means to be kind and reassuring is constantly saying to her, 'Never mind darling! There's someone nice just around the corner.' Driven to distraction by her mother and a string of broken relationships she replied exasperatedly: 'There's probably someone horrid just around the corner. In fact, I can almost guarantee that there's a right bastard who's going to get me to be very interested, waste an awful lot of my time, and then sod off leaving me back at square one.'

There are thousands of Fleurs out there as the phenomenal success of *Ally McBeal* and Helen Fielding's creation *Bridget Jones – A girl in search of Mr Right* show. They are both searching for that very special man to spend the rest of their life with, but asking themselves where have all the husbands gone.

ARE YOU HAPPY TO BE SINGLE?

At one level the virtues of singledom are extolled. It's wonderful to be single and free, you can pursue your career just as men have always done. You are more financially independent than your parents or grandparents. There is much more to life than marrying and having children, you do not need to be part of a couple, you are proud to be single, footloose and fancy-free.

But, and there is a big but . . . is that really so? Are we really so happy to be thirty-something and unattached? It might be fun for the twenty-something, but that biological clock has a funny way of tripping you up when you least expect it.

Those careers you strove for, the material advantages

you fought so hard to get can somehow seem just a little bit empty. The fact that you have your own flat or house, your own car, good holidays, the freedom to do what you like when you like, suddenly seems to have lost its appeal. This is frequently reinforced by your dwindling set of single friends, whose weddings you attend with growing envy rather than nonchalant disdain.

Being a little older than your twenty-something sister you are more choosy, more discriminating. So that many of the men you meet are not really the sort of man you want to fall in love with and have children with or they are already married.

CIVILISING THE MALE OF THE SPECIES

Ideally I think you would agree that if you are going to have children you would choose to bring them up in a loving relationship, with the emotional and financial support of a man you can trust and rely on. A man who is a loving partner and a responsible father. Laureen Snider a lecturer and researcher in the department of Sociology at Queens University, Kingston, Ontario says (in her research paper 'Towards safer Societies' published in the *British Journal of Criminology*, Winter 1998), 'Being assigned the primary responsibility for children in most cultures has made it essential for women to find ways to control the labour and actions of males, since patriarchal cultures make women dependent on men for sustenance and protection. The ability of women to be financially and therefore materially independent of men is a new and still fragile phenomenon.'

She suggests that it can be argued that men have suffered more than women in the civilising process since they represent the more aggressive sex. She writes, 'The classic male dream of freedom involves escaping wives and children (deemed responsibilities), pursuing lives where sexual gratification and job labour are casual, impulsive and commitment free.'

Much of popular culture and literature she points out is aimed at young men. 'The Easy Rider, going down the road. The frontier where "a man can be a man" – all these images celebrate men's independence from the demands of women and civilisation.'

I know from my counselling that these thoughts of escape from commitments are not confined to the young. The not so young man's dreams particularly around mid-life are frequently about leaving all responsibilities behind him and taking off into the blue. I need to find myself, I need some space, they tell their perplexed spouse or partner. This is not just the stuff of dreams. Many men put it into practice.

FALLING IN LOVE AGAIN

The desire to fall in love and have a committed relationship is not limited to when you are in your mid to late twenties and thirties of course. Many women in their forties and fifties and beyond who have been married or living together and who are now single again, are also looking for a new man and a new relationship. Your partner may have left you, or you may have chosen to divorce him – 70% of divorce petitions are filed by women. But once the wounds have started to heal over most of us want another chance to have a loving and permanent relationship but sometimes find ourselves wondering where all the desirable men have gone.

WHOSE PROBLEM IS IT ANYWAY?

Which brings me to another very important point – fear of commitment is not just a male phenomenon. Many women are also wary of commitment. Not in such great numbers as men, but at an increasing rate. Many women admit openly that they are not interested in a committed relationship, that they see marriage as a dead end or an outmoded arrangement. They feel that marriage is about the control and servitude of women, and not about loving and sharing and being equal partners. They want to bring up children on their own, and don't want any interference from a man.

However, many women fear commitment but fail to recognise this in themselves. Like men who are commitment phobic, part of them wants a loving relationship and the other part fears it. The reality is that many women who have a secret fear of commitment get involved with men who also fear commitment because rather than recognise this trait in themselves, it is easier to blame the man for what they can't accept about themselves.

DO YOU SECRETLY FEAR COMMITMENT TOO?

It may be that the fact that you have failed to recognise your fear of commitment frequently means that you project this fear on to men. You do this by getting involved with a man who for example has a track record of broken romances or a man who is unavailable because he is married or gay. So he lets you down, does not leave his wife for you or resists all your attempts to turn your friendship into a sexual relationship. This then allows you to blame the man for not wanting a committed or close relationship. By doing this you are setting up a relationship that is destined to fail, as a way of avoiding your own buried fear of commitment.

When you have been badly hurt by relationships that have gone badly wrong that is when you can avoid getting into new relationships. Where relationships are concerned you stick to the shallow end for fear of falling once more into deep emotional troubled waters or you avoid relationships altogether.

As a woman, if you fear getting too close to someone because of your own unresolved fears of commitment, it is often easier to destroy the possibility of closeness rather than pursue it. If you explore your own behaviour and understand why you act in a certain way, you are then opening up the possibility of change, which many of us struggle to avoid. We tend to want to change others, rather than ourselves. It is easier to keep repeating unsatisfactory but familiar patterns than to have the courage to create new ones.

WHEN HIS PROBLEM BECOMES YOUR PROBLEM

The majority of women who become involved with commitment phobic men blame themselves when the relationship runs into difficulties. What I hope this book will show you is that in the main it is not you who is at fault but the problem is that you are or have been involved with a commitment phobic man. It wasn't that something went wrong in the relationship, it's the very fact that the relationship was going really well that scared him. What was wrong is that the man who seemed to want you so much can't make a commitment. If you have experienced this it is totally confusing as he seems now to be giving you quite different messages. Whereas once he seemed to want you more than anything else in the world, now he is distinctly cool, has stopped pursuing you, and he may well be running in the opposite direction or has disappeared off the face of the earth.

USE THIS BOOK TO:

- Help you recognise the commitment phobic man, so you can assess whether you are in a going nowhere relationship and, if so, have the courage to end the relationship, as Abigail did.
- Protect you from repeating the pattern and avoid getting involved with a man who can't commit.
- Recognise when the man is a worst-case commitment scenario and unable to change.
- See how by changing the way you relate to him you may enable him to overcome his fear of commitment and allow him to have a committed relationship with you.

We can't change someone if they are determined that change is not for them. But we can look at our own behaviour and see if, by changing things about ourselves, that can enable those around us to also adapt and change. Change is possible but we have to recognise that change can rarely take place without some experience of loss and pain as well as the desired things we hope to gain. Which is why we frequently jump through hoops to avoid changing how we behave. Behaviour that is familiar to us is like a security blanket to a young child. Something to hang on to, something that makes us feel safe, but as time goes by it becomes increasingly unsavoury and unhealthy. If we take the blanket away from a small child, put it through the washing machine or try and replace it with a wholesome new one, it causes temper tantrums and screams and complete uproar. The reality is that as adults we often behave in much the same way as children with regard to change, because it is easier to stay in a world we know, one that we are familiar with, rather than branching out into new ways of behaving and relating to others.

This is never more so than with men who can't commit. They may not necessarily find happiness being the way they are but it can seem to them easier and less scary than discovering new horizons and new ways of relating to the women in their lives.

If this is all too familiar to you I hope this book will show you how you can break the fatal habit of falling for men who won't commit. Both the men and women who are involved in these types of relationships are playing their part, it takes two to tango. It is possible for things to be different, to change these destructive patterns of behaviour. It is not necessarily easy and it can't happen overnight. The first step is to recognise there is a problem and then be prepared to do something about it.

2

The Love-Rat Roll-Call

Sigh no more, ladies, sigh no more,
Men were deceivers ever;
One foot in sea, and one on shore,
To one thing constant never.

William Shakespeare

THE RICH AND FAMOUS WHO SHY AWAY FROM COMMITMENT

Men who fear commitment are everywhere. When I was writing this book and people asked what the subject was, as soon as I said 'Men who fear commitment' there was an instant response – from a smile of recognition, to gasps of frustration and anger and outrage. It was something nearly every woman I talked to had either experienced at first hand, or she had been around to pick up the pieces when someone close to her either in her family, or a good friend had fallen in love with a man who feared commitment. And what was the men's response, did they deny it, or claim that was how other men behaved? No, far from it: they smiled, they laughed, they joked. One man said speaking for many, 'Men who can't commit, that's me. Why commit yourself, I've got a girlfriend, two children, the eldest will be seventeen next birthday. I am happy as I am.' 'Is your girlfriend happy with the arrangement?' I asked Bill. 'No, she gives me hassle from time to time, but I ignore it.' 'You mean she wants to marry you,' I persist. 'That's right.' 'Is the reason you choose not to marry because it leaves you free to have other women?' Bill roared with laughter.' You've got it in one,' he replied.

Men who can't commit are not limited to the everyday working man, far from it. Among the rich and famous they are as numerous as confetti. The lives and loves of such men are littered with the woman they have loved and left.

SERIAL ROMEOS

Men who can't commit break countless hearts. They use their charm, looks, status, and power to pursue the women they desire. They are wonderfully good in the art of seduction, they make the women they pursue feel that they are special and desirable. Men such as these love the chase, and the exhilaration of a new love affair. They are charming, attentive, difficult to resist and lethal.

If a woman plays hard to get she becomes even more attractive to them and they step up their efforts to win her over. These are the secret weapons of seduction in their armoury and they use them all to good effect.

One of the world's best known commitment phobic men is James Bond – 007. He is famous for seducing all or almost all of the beautiful women he encounters. Unfailingly they fall for his irresistible charm. Even if they have been sent to kill him, his seduction technique we are led to believe is quite impossible to resist. At the end of each Bond film he is seen on some impossibly romantic location sailing off into the blue with an exquisitely beautiful woman at his side. It is made very clear that it is not marriage that he has on his mind as he gathers her into his arms. He always turns up in the next film as free as air, with Miss Moneypenny still desperately hoping that one day he will notice her and propose marriage, but he never has.

Pierce Brosnan, the current dashingly good-looking James Bond – 'licensed to kill' – is also said to be reluctant to take out a licence to marry. His long-standing girlfriend Keely Shaye Smith by whom he has a baby son, is said to have given him an ultimatum. 'Marry me or leave,' she has told Brosnan. He has denied that she is putting pressure on him to marry and he told the inquisitive press, 'We have no plans to marry. We are quite happy, Keely is great. She is beautiful, and now I have a partner I love and adore and with whom I enjoy sharing my life.'

Brosnan was devastated by the death of his first wife Cassandra and is known to have said he would not marry again when she died of breast cancer six years ago. Maybe he thinks if he married again it would be unfaithful to her memory. Alternatively it could be that he is afraid of marriage, because maybe he associates marriage with risking losing the woman he loves and he could not bear that ever happening again. Though Keely may understand how he feels it may be rather hard to accept the reality. I suspect she has been giving him hassle about his reluctance to put a ring on her finger. Though she knows he loves her, the fact that he won't marry her makes her feel that she is not loved quite enough or worse not as much as he loved his first wife.

A SERIAL DUMPER

Daniel Day-Lewis, one of Britain's most interesting and brilliant actors and the star of many films such as *My Beautiful Laundrette*, *My Left Foot* and *The Crucible*, has shied away from commitment all his life. Then a couple of years ago at the age of thirty-nine he secretly married Rebecca Miller (the actress daughter of the playwright Arthur Miller, former husband of Marilyn Monroe), forgetting, it seemed, that at the time he was sharing his house and his bed with another girl. Until his marriage he was notorious for not only unceremoniously dumping his girlfriends, but was so commitment phobic that it was nothing for him to be running between two or three girls at the same time.

His name has been romantically linked with a long line of beautiful actresses, Isabelle Adjani, Tilda Swinton and Greta Scacchi. Among his first loves were the delicious actress Juliette Binoche and the Irish singer Sinéad O'Connor. He is a man women have abandoned other men for. Winona Ryder walked out on Johnny Depp and Julia Roberts fell for Daniel's charms, so she ditched her lover Jason Partic and spent thousand of dollars on first-class flights and telephone calls to Ireland, but in the end she too was dumped by him.

It is said that Madonna invited him up to her London hotel suite when she was looking for someone to father her child.

Minnie Driver the young British actress who first saw him when she was a schoolgirl at Bedales, one of Britain's top public schools, and incidentally Daniel Day-Lewis's old school from which he ran away as a teenager, said that he was the most handsome man she had ever seen.

He has also been described rather less favourably as 'a rather likeable ice lolly' and as 'the British Warren Beatty' a man who compulsively beds every beautiful woman on sight. He is so secretive it is claimed that not even his partners know whether they are having a proper romance with him or whether he is just having a fling.

When Day-Lewis discovered his girlfriend of six years, the beautiful actress Isabelle Adjani, was pregnant he dumped her. He did not have the courage to tell her face to face but he sent her a fax when she was seven months pregnant telling her the relationship was over.

The next woman to share his life and New York apartment was Deya Pichardo, a twenty-six-year-old fitness trainer who fell madly in love with him. They had been living together for a year when Daniel, unknown to her, married someone else. Adjani his previous girlfriend inadvertently broke the news to Deya. She had heard that Daniel Day-Lewis had married. Assuming that Deya was the bride she rang her in New York to congratulate her. But Deya knew nothing of a wedding until that telephone call – then she read in the papers that he had secretly married Rebecca Miller. Deya said, 'He never told me a thing, not a call or a letter. He told me he had moved to New York to be with me.' She continued sadly, 'He told me, when he met me, it was just like a scene where everything in the room stops, and there's a spotlight shining on me.'

Deya made the very common mistake of not realising that someone who was prepared to dump the mother of his child by fax might in turn be equally brutally prepared to dump her. So many women choose to ignore that if someone has a history of treating other women badly the chances are high that it could also happen to them.

There are clearly some important factors in Daniel's background which drive him to behave in this way. His father was the Poet Laureate Cecil Day Lewis, a hugely powerful and successful man, who was part of the famous pre-war quartet of poets which included Auden, Spender and MacNeice. Like his son he was very ambitious. He liked to live life in the fast lane, he was a good sportsman and he loved fast cars. He was a communist in the thirties and a champagne socialist in the sixties. He died in 1972 when Daniel was only fifteen. This had a far-reaching effect on Daniel who soon after ended up in hospital after an overdose of migraine tablets.

Daniel had a lot to live up to on both sides of the family. His mother was the beautiful and volatile actress Jill Balcon, who was the daughter of Sir Michael Balcon one of Britain's best known film producers. Both his parents had explosive tempers and the atmosphere in the house was often highly charged. His mother's passion for his father, friends say, at times made her rather neglectful of Daniel and Tamsin his elder sister by three years. This was not made any easier by the fact that she also had a successful career of her own.

Sean Day-Lewis, Daniel's half-brother by a previous marriage recalls that Cecil Day Lewis was a remote father. He also said, 'It didn't appear to me that Jill, his mother was any less so.' His mother admitted that her absorption with her husband meant that she did not like the children to come between her relationship with their father. She said, 'Maybe I was guilty of excluding the children from my relationship with Cecil.' Children who do feel excluded by the intensity of their parents' relationship, can spend much of their adult life desperately seeking and trying to find that intensity of love for themselves, and when they see or imagine that intensity is lessening, they cannot bear it, so they move on to seek it elsewhere. They are addicted to those heady heights of two people when they first fall in love.

This relationship with his parents was not made any easier by the fact that for much of his early life he was brought up by their very proper nanny, Minny Bowler. She imposed an immensely strict routine on Daniel and Tasmin. She instilled what she called 'the three Ps' Punctuality, Politeness and Presentation. His half-brother recalls the two children were presented to their parents at teatime looking very 'spick and span'. So much so that Daniel at five would refuse to go out without wearing a tie.

At six Daniel came home one day to find Nanny Bowler had been replaced. Even if you have had a nanny who was a strict disciplinarian, to suddenly lose someone who had been a constant figure and the one who was with you all your life, would have been traumatic. As a child you can't understand what is happening, but what you have learned is that it is not really safe to trust someone, because if you do, they too might suddenly leave or abandon you. If this is never resolved as a child you can carry this damage with you into adult relationships, as Daniel seems to have done. Daniel himself is repeating this pattern of ending relationships without telling the person who loves him that he is leaving. He avoids telling them face to face.

It is likely that Daniel chases and seduces a series of beautiful actresses as a way of trying to get the love and attention he craved as a child from his emotionally unavailable mother. Because he also has a problem trusting women, he has more than one on the go at the same time as an emotional insurance policy. If one woman leaves him there is still another there waiting in the wings. Rather than risk rejection he dumps his women, avoiding any possibility of them doing that to him.

The fact that he left Isabelle Adjani when he discovered she was pregnant with his child could have been due to his subconscious fear that if she had a baby he would no longer be the most important person in her life. Whether he will settle into a lasting marriage with Rebecca Millar only time will tell. Eve Arnold a long-time friend of Rebecca's mother says of Rebecca, 'She is absolutely lovely, and really talented. She paints, she directs, she's wonderful.' She is also the daughter of one of the most outstanding playwrights of our time so he has married into another literary family.

Maybe he can learn to love and trust her enough not to let her down like her predecessors. Simon Dunstan a one-time flatmate and friend said, 'I don't think Daniel can do commitment.' Let's hope he is proved wrong.

'I'LL BE FAITHFUL TO YOU DARLING IN MY FASHION'

The love rat roll-call of dishonour is long and for the women who love such men it can be heartbreaking. High on this list must feature Mick Jagger. Though married to the incredibly glamorous and outspoken Jerry Hall his name has been constantly linked to numerous other glamorous women including model Carla Bruni, actress Uma Thurman and more recently Jana Rajlich.

Jagger has always run a mile from commitment, frequently having more than one girlfriend at a time. During his five-year affair with Marianne Faithfull in the sixties he was also enjoying a clandestine affair with Marsha Hunt, star of the 1960s musical *Hair*. She had posed naked for photographer David Bailey and her image was of the bad girl on the block. Jagger called her one night and invited himself over on the pretext of using a photograph of her for his new record album. He gave that familiar old story that women seem to fall for and that men have used down the centuries – my wife/my girlfriend doesn't understand me.

He told her how lonely he was, and how difficult it was coping with Marianne Faithfull's drug taking. It is a much travelled road down which women who are attracted to commitment phobic guys fall. It sounds like an intimate conversation, when so often what the man really means is, 'I think you are incredibly sexy and shall we go to bed?' So Marsha listened sympathetically, and very soon they became lovers.

After five stormy years Marianne Faithfull eventually told Jagger that their affair was over. He could not believe that she dared to end it, despite his own infidelities. He did not spend long on his own, and he soon had Marsha installed in the house he had been sharing with Marianne.

Jagger's pride was very wounded by Marianne leaving him, and when he discovered that she was staying at her mother Baroness Erisso's house with her son Nicholas from a previous marriage and her new lover Mario Schifano, he turned up unannounced. There was a major confrontation between the two men, which must have impressed Marianne because it was Jagger with whom she spent the night.

She returned with him to his house in Cheyne Walk, Marsha Hunt having obligingly moved out. But Jagger's fear of commitment remained undimmed and he continued his visits to Marsha. He even persuaded her that he loved her and wanted her to have his baby. When she did finally become pregnant he told her that there was a new woman in his life called Bianca, and that she would be accompanying him on his next tour. Bianca was good at fending off other women, but she was totally unprepared when one day the telephone rang and it was Marsha Hunt calling Jagger from her hospital bed, to tell him that he was now a father. Jagger perhaps not surprisingly had failed to mention his relationship with Marsha to Bianca, perhaps thinking it would spoil a beautiful friendship.

It was more than a week after the birth before Jagger turned up to see his new daughter. Though he came bearing gifts and champagne he took little interest in his daughter. Marsha was getting increasingly angry with him for his uncaring attitude. She was devastated when he told her that she was a fool if she had imagined he had ever loved her. So often at the beginning of a relationship a commitment phobic man does everything to woo and win the woman of his desires, only to toss her aside once they have cooled.

Despite his involvement with Bianca, when Jagger returned to England from his home in France by chance he met Marianne Faithfull in the King's Road outside the 'Granny Takes a Trip' boutique. He embraced her and they talked.

Then he suggested that for old time's sake they had sex, after which they dressed and parted with a kiss.

Jagger flew back to France with a beautiful bracelet for Bianca's birthday and a week later he collected two wedding rings. He married Bianca Pérez Morena de Macías, the Nicaraguan model, on 12th May 1971. Marianne spent Jagger's wedding night drying out in a London police station. Five months later Jagger became a father for the second time when Jade Sheena Jezebel Jagger was born.

Commitment was still not Jagger's forte, nor were demanding, emotionally difficult women even if they were his wife, and he was soon up to his old tricks again. Bianca's Latin temper was becoming legendary and it did not improve matters when she said on a TV chat show that 'Mick doesn't think much of women.'

When he first met Jerry Hall, the twenty-year-old Texan model with an amazing mass of long blonde hair, he was instantly attracted to her. She and her fiancé, Bryan Ferry of Roxy Music fame, had gone to one of Jagger's concerts. He went out to dinner with them afterwards and though on that occasion she flirted outrageously with him, and Ferry stormed off to bed, this sobered her up and she asked Jagger to leave which he did reluctantly.

Six months later he found himself at a dinner party sitting next to Jerry Hall with Warren Beatty, another well known commitment phobic man on her other side. The competition for Jerry Hall was intense. Jagger won and they spent the night together. Eventually Bianca had had enough of Jagger's philandering and she filed for divorce.

Jagger began his life with Jerry by buying a house for them both in New York. Jerry knew that Jagger was scared of commitment but perhaps she made the mistake of thinking, as many other women have done before her, that this time he would be different. But she too had to come to terms with being hurt and humiliated when she read of him being seen with other women. Often when away working she rang home to find the telephone answered by unfamiliar female voices. When she returned home from some of her modelling assignments she would find other women's jewellery carelessly left around the house they shared in New York.

Once when she could take no more Jerry Hall left him for racehorse owner Robert Sangster, but he begged her tearfully to return. And as all good cads before him, he promised her he loved only her and that he would stop his womanising. What won her back was that he ended by proposing marriage and so she returned. But it was only after many more such partings and reunions, several years and two children later that Jagger finally relented and tied the knot. On 21st November 1990 in Bali with only their two children and their chauffeur present they were married. Within months Jagger's name was being linked with the beautiful Italian top model Carla Bruni.

When Jerry gave birth to their third child Georgia in January 1992 Jagger took her flowers but twenty-four hours later he flew to Thailand, for, it is alleged, a romantic reunion with Carla Bruni. Jagger swore to Jerry that the stories were untrue. Women who fall in love with men who can't commit often pay a very high price for their love.

In 1996 Jagger was exiled by Jerry to a London hotel while she consulted top divorce lawyer Anthony Julius about the future of their marriage. Yet again he had humiliated her with his well publicised indiscretions with Czech model Jana Rajlich.

It seemed that once again she had finally had enough. She was perhaps sending a strong message to Mick Jagger that she was just not prepared to put up with him two timing her any more. A friend of Jagger's said, 'Mick felt that Jerry was calling his bluff, that she was just incredibly angry and wanted to call him to heel.' It seemed to work and he was soon back in the family home in Richmond, Surrey. A few months later the triumphant Jerry Hall was pregnant again with their fourth child.

It is not easy when you know that hundreds of woman are just queuing up to jump into bed with your rock star husband. Jerry Hall once said, 'Every so often I had to go and sort of kick some girl on the shin.' She went on, 'I always hoped that one day he would outgrow these things. You know, we always live in hope.' She added rather poignantly, 'There is nothing more humiliating than loving someone so much that you forgive their infidelities.'

It is said of Jagger that it is not so much having sex with different woman that attracts him, it's the chasing of women not their capitulation that excites him most. The talk among his entourage is that 'What Mick really enjoys is the thrill of the chase, getting to the point where he knows he could have her if he wants her. After that it does not much matter what happens.'

If you have beautiful women constantly throwing themselves at you, therefore making instant satisfaction readily available, the act itself becomes less important, the pleasure is now in cracking the difficult case, the woman who does not fall easily into your bed. If there is no challenge life becomes dull.

Psychologist Oliver James explained this when he said, 'Jagger is a ludic lover for whom sex is a game. It's not about intimacy or love, but doing anything to get power over that person.' He revealed, 'Somebody I know felt exactly like that when Jagger slept with her, it was just another notch on his organ. Crucially though, these people get very little satisfaction from sex. They've won and suddenly they feel empty.'

THE PRINCESS AND THE PLAYBOY

Diana, Princess of Wales, was not a good picker when it came to men. She sadly had more than her fair share of men who could not commit and who let her down badly. Prince Charles with whom she fell very much in love at the age of nineteen, was for much of their marriage in love with another woman, Camilla Parker Bowles, whom he had met when they were both in their twenties.

'There were three of us in this marriage, which was rather crowded,' Diana said in that hauntingly tragic BBC *Panorama* programme. What Diana was really looking for in marriage was a man who could love her just for herself and make up for that inner pain and deep insecurity that plagued her throughout her childhood. What she got was a man who loved another woman.

To be loved totally for herself would have gone some way in making up for the pain and hurt that she had experienced as a small child when her mother Frances left her father Earl Spencer for another man, wallpaper heir Peter Shand Kydd, in 1967. The last thing she needed was for the man she loved most in the world to prefer another woman to her. It was a pattern repeating itself all over again. It would not only have hurt her as a woman but it would have also rekindled all the pain she experienced when her mother, as it would have seemed to Diana's young eyes, chose to live with another man rather than with her own children.

On top of this trauma Earl Spencer who was not closely involved with or really aware of the needs of his children remarried another woman, Raine Lady Dartmouth, whom Diana disliked and who she felt replaced her to a large degree in her father's affections. None of the four young Spencer children liked their new stepmother and she was know by them as 'Acid Raine'. Diana admitted on the *Panorama* programme that with her marriage crumbling around her she had had an affair. She said of James Hewitt, the army officer she fell for, how much she loved him, but he also let her down.

He entered into her life when she invited him to teach the two young princes to ride. She was disillusioned with her marriage and desperately seeking love. Hewitt behaved like the cad that he was and with behaviour unbecoming an officer and a gentleman, when he spilled the beans of their affair to Anna Pasternak for her shoddy book *A Princess in Love*.

Diana continued to fall for men who could not commit by becoming involved with other women's husbands. There was Oliver Hoare the art dealer with whom she had a close friendship, and whom it was claimed she telephoned obsessively, much to the fury of his wife. Then the England Rugby Captain Will Carling whose wife Julia left him after she discovered his close friendship with Diana. As married men they may have enjoyed their relationship with her, been flattered by the attention of a beautiful and vulnerable princess, but they could not give her the commitment she craved.

After her divorce from Prince Charles, Diana was searching for a new direction in her life which it seemed that she was just beginning to find, with her campaign against land mines. She declared her desire to be 'the Queen of hearts', to want to give help and support to people in need which she did so outstandingly well, and they in return loved the people's Princess. She was also looking for a new man to share her life with. A man she could trust and who would just love her for herself.

Perhaps for those all too brief few weeks in the summer of 1997 she had found true happiness. Diana had certainly never looked happier or more relaxed than in the pictures taken of her in St Tropez and on the beautiful island of Sardinia which she left one sunlit afternoon to fly to Paris and that terrible car crash in the early hours of Sunday morning the 31st August 1997. But Dodi the man she had fallen in love with came with a track record of broken romances.

Dodi Fayed who was romancing Diana when they were both so tragically killed, has been linked to many of Hollywood's attractive stars. Some say that he was not ruthless enough to have full-blown playboy status, being perhaps rather too sensitive with his deep insecurity and vulnerability never far away. But his easy success with women certainly gave him the credentials associated with most playboys.

As a young rich man, his powerful multi-millionaire father gave him the perfect entrée to Hollywood. As a film producer it allowed him marvellous access to a whole range of beautiful actresses and models. The list of his romances is long and varied: Koo Stark (the one-time girlfriend of Prince Andrew), Britt Ekland, Brooke Shields, Tracy Lynn, Marie Helvin, Tina Sinatra (daughter of Frank), Lynsey de Paul and Kelly Fisher, the American model who was unceremoniously ousted in favour of Diana. Fisher threatened to sue Dodi for breaking off their engagement. He admitted he had given her a ring but denied that they were engaged.

Dodi, like Diana, was riddled with insecurities. He felt he did not really belong anywhere because of his mobile childhood and because of the break-up of his parents' marriage when he was only two. His uncle, arms dealer Adnan Khashoggi, one of the world's richest men, said on CNN news shortly after Dodi's death that, 'Dodi was a sensitive boy, you could see it in his eyes, because he didn't grow up between a mother and a father, you know, the same way normal children would grow.'

The Arab custom is for the father to get custody. His father Mohammed Al Fayed, the owner of Harrods, loved the young Dodi, but he was an ambitious businessman with little time to spend with his young son. So for a little boy to be separated at such a young age from the mother he loved to be replaced by a father who was frequently absent would have affected him deeply. Dodi saw little of his mother and his father was too busy amassing his great fortune to see much of him either. Earl Spencer, Diana's father, was given custody of Diana, her two elder sisters and younger brother after a bitter court battle with his wife Frances who left him for Peter Shand Kydd when Diana was only six years old. A childhood torn apart by the loss through divorce of their mother was something that both Diana and Dodi had in common. This experience left them both in their different way searching to replace that love and inwardly shy and insecure.

Dodi's childhood was spent in a fairly nomadic manner. He moved around schools attending St Mark's school in Alexandria, Egypt, and then the Le Rosey school in Switzerland, a playground for children of rich parents. His holidays were spent behind high-walled compounds and villas in Dubai and Alexandria or on luxury yachts surrounded by bodyguards, uniformed staff and surveillance cameras. It is not surprising that as an adult he was obsessive about security and the protection of bodyguards. They were probably in some bizarre way like substitute parents and for him, represented the security that his parents were unable to give him which is why they played such an important part in his adult life.

Dodi's security obsession baffled his friends. Robert Hanson, son of financier Lord Hanson, said, 'It used to amaze me. Dodi always had a bodyguard and, I think, a bullet-proof car. But who needs a bodyguard for dinner in Soho? It was something I didn't ask him about, but it puzzled me. He kind of liked the James Bond image.'

Jack Martin a showbiz writer and friend of Dodi's since his teenage years said, 'Dodi was a good friend but he was a difficult person to get close to. You got more out of him talking over the phone than in person.' Dodi was for most of his life in a tightly buckled emotional straitjacket.

Dodi's separation from his mother was to haunt all future relationships with women. A little child who has had to learn to cut off and suppress his feelings of pain and loss from such a young age, is understandably not going to find it easy to trust enough to commit himself fully to a woman in his adult life. If he loves too much how can he be sure that it won't suddenly be snatched away from him?

Marie Helvin, the model and wife of David Bailey, remembers that Dodi always said of his mother 'She was so beautiful.' As an adult he became very close to his mother once again, and he was totally bereft by her death from cancer in 1986. To have her snatched away by death would have been a cruel blow for Dodi. It was this which probably catapulted him into his only and very short-lived marriage with American model Suzanne Gregrad-Quilici. They had been together on and off for two years, but within a year of his mother's death he asked her to marry him, the wedding was hurriedly arranged in two weeks but it was short-lived and ended in divorce after only ten months.

After his divorce Dodi dated one girl after another. He found women less threatening than men: 'Women were his confidantes,' said his friend and photographer Terry O'Neill. They perhaps compensated for the loneliness that his friends say surrounded him so much of his life, something else he shared with Diana who despite her many friends was often alone and isolated in Kensington Palace.

Dodi's best man Andrew Wainrid said that after his divorce, 'Dodi became a chick magnet – pursuing a string of models and actresses.' A former girlfriend described him as 'Suave, elegant and very good company, but then he has had a lifetime of dating beautiful women.'

After his marriage broke down he went on to date Tina Sinatra. Then back in London he fell for the beautiful model Marie Helvin. That affair ended when he started seeing actress Brooke Shields, but by May 1990 he was involved with Mimi Rogers estranged from her husband Tom Cruise. Then followed an intense relationship with former child model Tracy Lynn, fourteen years his junior; friends expected them to marry but a year later there were rumours of a romance with Susannah Constantine, former girlfriend of Viscount Linley. He was soon back on the town escorting Julia Tholstrup sister of Mogens, who owns the Chelsea restaurant Daphne's.

Dodi was known for always having another girl lined up before he finished with the one he had – a true sign of a man who fears commitment. While seeing Julia he turned his attentions to Jane Rolfe a successful fashion designer and so the string of beautiful women increased, but none of them tied him down.

Dodi had his own seduction routine according to the MP William Cash's son Bill Cash. A teddy bear was always placed on the back seat of the limo that would pick the girl up from the airport, and extravagant bouquets of flowers would be delivered after each date. After a few weeks he might drop by at Asprey's or Repossi's in Paris where he was so well-known he would only have had to sign a chit for Diana's £130,000 diamond ring that he gave to her the night she was killed. But somehow, it never seemed to work out. When boredom loomed, the girl would be sent home with a one-way ticket, which friends called 'Air Dodi'. This of course rather famously happened to American model Kelly Fisher who was with him in St Tropez when he started romancing Diana who was staying with his father and his second wife at their villa. Kelly Fisher was sent packing and protesting back to America. Interestingly, Diana, according to Andrew Morton, also tended to jump into unsuitable relationships and then equally suddenly would abandon them.

A close friend and showbiz writes Jack Martin, said, when contemplating Dodi's constant stream of beautiful women, 'Dodi loved being in love, but when it came to the nitty gritty, he often shied away. Even when there was a girl of the moment there was always another one lined up behind.'

But underneath his playboy image, said Claudia Christina with whom he had a platonic friendship over many years, 'He was searching for the mother to his children and was wanting one day to be a father. The reason why women fell in love with Dodi is that he took such care of them.'

That of course would have been very appealing to Diana who longed for a man to take care of her and discovered all too often that men exploited her. She had also, I believe, wanted to fall in love again, with a man whom she could settle down with for the rest of her life. She utterly adored William and Harry but I believe she also longed for more children and particularly a daughter. This longing for children is something that would also have drawn them to each other. For Dodi, as Claudia Christina said, was looking for a woman who could be the mother of his children.

One of Diana's greatest gifts was that she had incredible empathy with people who were hurt and in emotional turmoil. She knew what it was like to feel pain and as such she could identify and relate to it in others. It was something that made her very attractive but also very vulnerable. In those short few months she and Dodi had together, this would have been a very strong bond between the two of them.

Diana's close friend Rosa Monckton, wife of the *Sunday Telegraph* editor Dominic Lawson, who had spent a carefree holiday with Diana in the Greek Islands only days before Diana's final and fatal last holiday with Dodi said, 'Diana had a unique ability to spot the broken-hearted, and she could zero in on them.' Rosa added poignantly in her tribute to Diana after her death that Diana had said to her, 'I just wanted someone to be there for me, to make me feel safe and secure.' Looking at those pictures of Diana in St Tropez and in Sardinia's beautiful Costa Smeralda, a paradise playground for the rich and famous, she looked as if she had found it.

I suppose the whole country wanted to believe that the wedding of Charles and Diana would mean that like in all good fairytales the Prince and Princess would marry and live happily ever after, but it was not to be. I fear that if Diana and Dodi had married that too in the end would have been another fairy story with an unhappy ending.

Men who fear commitment are frequently addicted to the lovely, exciting, heady feelings of 'being in love', but after a while boredom sets in and they are searching for a new love. Dodi idealised his mother, and when men grow up idealising their mothers, they tend in their adult relationships to put the woman in their life on a pedestal. The internalised idealised mother is a hard act to follow for the women who fall in love with such men because inevitably they will fall from grace. The pedestal eventually topples and the woman is seen with all her human frailties and the man falls out of love. The longing to love and be loved is always with such men, so when disillusion sets in they set off in search of another woman of their dreams.

A MAN DOES NOT HAVE TO BE A NON-COMMITTER ALL HIS LIFE

Don't despair because a man is a non-committer; it does not mean he is always going to be that. Men are able to change, and with your help plus his wish to change it is possible. It starts with his desire to be different, to move away from the non-commitment mode. For Eric Clapton the guitarist and rock star that change was possible. Previously his name has been linked with a long line of women: his ex-wife Patti Boyd and the mothers of his children, Yvonne Kelly by whom he has a thirteen-year-old daughter Ruth, and Italian beauty Lori del Santo. Their son Conor was tragically killed when he fell from the fifty-third floor of his mother's apartment block in New York. Clapton, distraught with grief, said of himself: 'I went off the edge of the world for a while.'

There have also been innumerable lovers, alleged lovers, girlfriends, and dates. There was Alice Ormsby Gore, daughter of the fifth Baron Harlech, who died a squalid junkie death in a bedsit in Bournemouth, not long after he had helped her through a rehabilitation treatment. Paula Hamilton, Michelle Pfeiffer, Stephanie Beacham, Susannah Doyle, Sheryl Crow all fall into one category or another. Nearly a quarter of a century ago he was quoted as saying he had slept with a thousand woman. So one would assume it's considerably more by now.

But it is important for you to recognise that non-committers do not have to remain so all their lives – of course some do, but not all. If they choose it they can change their own behaviour. Eric Clapton feels he is now at a different stage in his life and takes the idea of marrying and particularly having children very seriously. In a recent interview (for the *Times Magazine* of 28th February 1998) he was asked if after all this liberty would it not be hard for him to settle down and get married. Clapton said, 'No, I think I could. I could probably adapt to just about anything. I still feel flexible. Yes, I value my solitude and privacy and boundaries, but I now feel better able to make those known to someone. In the past my problem was that I wouldn't know how to tell someone I needed to go out or be on my own. My way of interpreting that was to say I can't be with someone. And that's of course not true. I can. I've learnt more about respecting my needs. So I probably could do it quite easily if I found someone who'd done the same amount of work in that area as I feel I've done.'

What Clapton is saying is very important in all relationships, but particularly so if the man involved is wary of commitment. So often a man with this fear will see committed relationships as 'you' taking them over, they fear that you will be depriving them of their personal space and freedom, so they literally see themselves as being trapped.

But if you as a woman are sensitive to their needs and even more importantly the man can articulate his needs, as Clapton was able to do, you can arrive at a balanced relationship that meets the needs of both of you.

When Clapton realised it was quite possible to express to the woman he loved his need for his own personal space, and that she could accept that, he also realised that he could stop running away. He could have the committed relationship he wanted. You will find that if a man is prepared to take time to explore why he is afraid of commitment he too can frequently learn to overcome his reluctance, his fear or his phobia.

The high status and prestigious lifestyle of many rich and famous CPMs allow them to give full rein to their reluctance to commit. Firstly because so many women are attracted to powerful and successful men; as Henry Kissinger the American politician once said when talking about why women are attracted to him: 'Power is the great aphrodisiac.' So they are frequently surrounded by attractive, beautiful, intelligent and available women. Society also seems to be more tolerant of famous CPMs behaving badly, almost as if it is expected of someone who has all that wealth and power at his command.

3

Running away from Love

In former days we'd both agree
That you were me, and I was you.
What has happened to us two,
That you are you, and I am me?

'In Former Days', Bhartrihari (7th Century), trans. *John Brough*

WHY THERE ARE SO MANY COMMITMENT PHOBIC MEN (CPM)

A man can, if he chooses, have a sexual relationship with a woman without any strings. He can fall in love with as many women as he wants with absolutely no need to formalise the relationship by marriage. Gone are the days when as Oscar Wilde cynically said, 'The price men paid for sex was marriage, and the price women paid for marriage was sex.' Rather than saying women can 'have it all', meaning the opportunity to juggle a career, husband, children and running a home resulting in terminal exhaustion, is it not rather the case that it's men who are 'having it all'? Is not this sexual freedom to dip in and out of relationships with women with no requirement of commitment a 'paradise for men'?

James is one of those men that nearly all women find attractive, tall, slim, utterly good-looking and highly intelligent, with all the confidence that a secure, rich, upper-class family background and a good education can give you. A trace of arrogance but not overbearingly so. Women flocked around him, men liked to spar with him intellectually while secretly envying his easy, relaxed and successful way of relating to women. He adores his wife and has been happily married to her for nearly thirty years. The dinner party was going well: people had arrived at the stage in the evening where they were relaxed with the combination of good food, good wine and amusing company. They had drunk enough to be interestingly expansive, and not enough to be abusive or boring.

The conversation moved round to men and women and relationships. James was explaining that his daughter's relationship with her boyfriend had just ended, and that he and his wife were left trying to help her pick up the pieces. Those of us around that table who were parents of daughters knew the feeling all too well.

One moment his daughter was tearful and upset, and despairing of ever meeting the right man and the next she was swearing that life was better without men. She was never she declared going to let another man into her life, they all let you down in the end. She was twenty-eight and she had decided she was going to concentrate on her career, which as it happened was going rather well.

Oliver her boyfriend had ended the relationship. He was four years older than her and she had been more or less living with him for the past three years. James's daughter Lucy had wanted more commitment, like marriage and children at some point in the future. But Oliver was happy with how things were, he could not commit himself about where they might go on holiday that year, let alone whether they would be together this time next year or might one day get married.

He was always telling Lucy he loved her. Surely, he said, that was enough, why did she want to tie him down to promises about the future? James said: 'Sometimes I think I have failed her as a father. Over the last few months I have felt that I should pin the man in question down, and ask him why, as he says he loves Lucy so much, is he messing around with her emotions. I didn't confront him, but perhaps I should have done.' He paused. 'Harriet,' he said, glancing at his wife, 'told me how foolish that would be, and how Lucy would not thank me for interfering, and I know really she is right, but I was very tempted. You see, nowadays men can have everything, the girl, the sex, the companionship, sharing a home, a joint bank account, the lot and all they have to say is "I love you." When I was young a man knew to have all that he had to propose marriage, to be prepared to walk down the aisle, slip a ring on her finger and say "I do."

'The reality is,' James continued, 'however much a man loves a woman, however much he wants marriage and chooses to be true to just one woman, he would also like to be free to enjoy the delights of many women throughout his married life. But because of the love and commitment he has for his wife he tries to stay faithful to her,' he said smiling across the table at his wife. 'My generation of men did make committed relationships, but not so the present generation,' he said scowling and thinking of the feckless Oliver and his daughter's broken heart.

As women, we have wanted the freedom to embark openly on love affairs which did not mean disgrace if we had no ring on our finger. We have wanted equality with men, we have wanted the freedom to move in and out of relationships with men without being seen as a loose woman, as a woman behaving badly or being labelled a nymphomaniac.

Nowadays if a couple are dating, it is not usually a question of should they sleep together or not, but much more one of when they will sleep together. Will they choose to do this on the first date, after just a few nights out together, or not until they have been seeing each other for several weeks or months? Will it be when they agree that they are 'an item' and that neither one of them is involved with someone else? There are no guidelines. Nowadays each couple negotiates and makes its own decisions.

It caused some speculation, and a few negative comments from former Conservative Prime Minister Margaret Thatcher and others, when William Hague the newly elected Conservative party leader shared a bedroom with his then fiancée Ffion Jenkins at the 1997 Tory party conference in Blackpool. An unmarried couple sharing a room together at such a high-profile event would have been unthinkable twenty or even, I suspect, ten years ago.

If William and Ffion had said that they were 'saving themselves for marriage' that would have filled many more column inches in the newspapers than being open about the fact that they were having a sexual relationship.

This new sexual freedom is perhaps good because it acknowledges that women as much as men are free to enjoy a sexual relationship with the man they love. But there is another side to this particular coin. It does have its disadvantages as well as its advantages. It makes women more vulnerable in their relationships with men. The reality is nowadays men are much more able to 'have it all' and they can walk away from that relationship whenever they choose. There is no angry father insisting that they make an 'honest woman' of her.

THE NEW SEXUAL FREEDOMS

So men can now enjoy sexual relationships with no commitment and so can women. Or can we? I would suggest that women have been caught out in this particular relationship rollercoaster and we are now questioning whether this aspect of sexual relationships with men is really what we want.

In an age where striving for equality has been the name of the game, many of us have thought that we wanted what men had, the ability to slip in and out bed or in and out of relationships with no strings attached. But there is a backlash, because what most women have discovered is that we are not nearly as good as men at compartmentalising our emotions. In the main, if we go to bed with a man we are not really looking for just a one-night stand, a brief encounter with a man we hardly know or do not care about. We are not looking for a relationship where we both agree that all we want is to have great sex together with no commitment to each other, though sometimes this can be the case. For most women a good sexual relationship is usually a combination of our minds and our bodies, we are not necessarily looking for a lifetime's commitment but we do want more than just sex from a man we like enough to have sex with.

'I JUST COULDN'T HELP IT – IT'S IN THE GENES'

I now think it's time to explode some myths about men that are usually invented by men. Many male anthropologists and indeed many men perpetuate the theory that non-monogamous behaviour by men is a biologically natural part of their being. They suggest that men are programmed to go forth and scatter their seed as a way of ensuring that their offspring rather than other men's children will be the ones to populate the world in forthcoming generations. Men are in constant competition with each other to make sure that the woman is carrying their seed not that of their competitors; they want to ensure that their genes will be carried forward into future generations. We now have claims that there is a homosexual gene and an IQ gene, so why not in this brave new gene bank 'an unfaithful gene', as some male scientists are already suggesting, only to be found in the male of the species naturally. Then they can back up the theory that 'a man can't help it'. It was just 'nature taking its course' or they were only doing 'what comes naturally'.

I do not think that men are naturally programmed to sleep around and women are programmed to be faithful to one man; I think that when we find a man really attractive we are just as tempted as men. But I do think there are gender differences here. Whether it is nature or nurture is debatable. Most men can have sex with a woman just because they think she has a great body, they fancy her, she is available, or they would like a little sexual variety in their life – they may even be prepared to pay her for sexual favours. Despite the influence of the women's movement and increased sexual freedom, though some women enjoy sex with no strings attached, most women who sleep with a man only to find they are yesterday's woman feel hurt, humiliated and rejected. Most women like to feel that sex is part of a relationship not just an end in itself.

'IT DIDN'T MEAN A THING – DARLING'

Alain de Botton, a journalist and writer of many books, including *Essay in Love* which has been translated into sixteen languages (and who writes a weekly column on books in the *Sunday Telegraph*), was one of the guest speakers at 'The Eve and Adam lectures' at the RSA (24th March 1997). He said 'that a man, be it for biological reasons or otherwise, can be in love with a woman but nevertheless be quite happy about going off to sleep with a whole range of other women, and feel that this doesn't really conflict with his love for one woman in particular.'

He acknowledges that this is very hurtful for women and he admits that 'it is a very awkward fact for a lot or relationships.' But he maintains, 'Men often feel sexually frustrated in a monogamous relationship, in a way that women never do when they are in love in a monogamous relationship.'

In my opinion he is wrong. As women, we may not be

particularly interested in meaningless sexual encounters. Just because we are in love with our husband or partner it does not mean that we are never attracted to another man. Just like a man we can feel sexually frustrated by the constraints of a monogamous relationship and indeed like men we can be tempted into affairs. As women we do have affairs with men we have no intention of leaving our marriage or relationships for. This was widely documented in *The Erotic Silence of the Married Woman* by the American writer Dalma Heyn, who interviewed thousands of women who were doing just that. When the book was publicised she was disbelieved and derided by many male interviewers on her book promotion tour. They did not want to accept that women could be reasonably happily married and yet at the same time stray outside their marriage vows.

In a recent American research study students were approached by an attractive stranger of the opposite sex who said, 'Hi, I've noticed you around town lately, and I find you very attractive.' Then the students were asked one of three questions: a) 'Would you go out on a date with me tonight?' b) 'Would you come back to my apartment with me tonight?' or c) 'Would you have sex with me tonight?'

50% of the women approached by an attractive man agreed to the date. 6% agreed to go back to his apartment, but *all the women* refused to have sex with him.

Interestingly, when it came to the men, 50% agreed to date the attractive woman, 69% agreed to go back to her apartment (obviously they were hoping for more than just a cup off coffee!) and *75%* agreed to have sex with her.

This reminds me of a man who was walking round the office with a smile and a confident step. When asked by a woman colleague what he was looking so pleased about, he said that he had been told that someone had written what a good lay he was on the wall of the ladies' loo. The woman colleague replied with a smile, 'No, Colin, what it actually says is that you are an easy lay.'

As women, we may not be looking for life-long commitment from a particular relationship, but we are rarely interested in relationships with no commitment at all. We do want to feel some emotional involvement with the man we go to bed with. Though men also want this, most men can enjoy sex without any need or any desire for any emotional involvement. They are undoubtedly better at compartmentalising their lives than we as women are.

A man is not plagued with doubts if you do not call him 'the morning after the night before'. A man does not agonise about whether you will think less of him because he was so willing to jump into bed with you on your first date.

In Helen Fielding's amusing book *Bridget Jones's Diary* the author has struck a chord with the thirty-something woman in search of a man. Bridget's obsession is about getting a man who wants a committed relationship or even marriage. As a result she is obsessed with how much she eats, drinks and smokes, and it is directly related to the state of her love life. The worse it gets the more she takes comfort from these 'three vices'.

Most women can identify with the scene in *Bridget Jones's Diary* where Bridget has just been to bed with the delectable Daniel, a man at work whom she fancies madly. Afterwards she agonises about having slept with him – will she ever hear from him again? As the rosy cloud of euphoria begins to disperse she starts to feel alarmed. She realises that no romantic little dinner for two has been mentioned, he has made no plans for them to meet again. So once more she is waiting for the telephone to ring. She recognises that in times like this the situation between the sexes after a first night remains so unfairly imbalanced. It feels to Bridget as if she has just sat an exam and is awaiting the results, only a lot worse.

More than a week later when Daniel still has not rung, Bridget is discussing her agony about what has happened over several glasses of wine with her two friends Jude and Sharon. They all agree that 'he has behaved like a complete bastard'.

Jude introduces the concept of Boy time – as portrayed in the film *Clueless*. Five days during which a new relationship is left hanging in the air after sex does not seem an agonising lifetime to the male of the species, but a normal cooling-down period in which to gather his emotions, before proceeding. But this is not how women feel.

Daniel, argued Jude, was bound to be anxious about the work situation and other pressing problems so give him a chance, just be friendly and flirt. Reassure him that you trust him and are not going to become needy (which strikes terror in the heart of most men) or fly off the handle.

But Sharon, who in general has a far less sympathetic view of men, says, 'It's inhuman to leave a woman hanging in the air for two weeks after sex and Bridget should tell him exactly what she thought of him.'

As women, most of us would feel vulnerable if the first time we make love with a man we care about he does not call for several days or, worse, longer. This behaviour is not just about a man being insensitive to a woman's needs, but it may be an indicator of how he sees the future. That is with him dictating his needs, he establishes the future of the relationship on his terms. He finds you sexy, interesting, intelligent, fun but he does not want to be too close, or too committed. This type of behaviour can be the early signs that this is not a man who is ready or truly interested in a committed relationship. Learning to recognise early on the behaviour of a man who can't commit can save later heartbreak.

The double standards attitude still prevails which is also why as women we mind if the man does not call after sex. Men who sleep around are seen as studs, Casanovas, 'doing what comes naturally'. Whereas it is expected that as women we will have fewer partners than men before finally settling down. If we are very promiscuous and really do sleep around we get a bad reputation. We are described as a nymphomaniac, a slag or slut, or an easy lay. Men rarely feel the need to lie about the number of partners they have had, in fact often quite the opposite; they actually boast about it. The same does not apply to women. The majority of us are economical with the truth when the man we love asks us how many men we have slept with, this is particularly so if the numbers exceed ten or more. It is rather like that exquisite little black number you bought the other day – when he asks the price, you subtract a few pounds or more if it was really expensive.

One of the differences between the sexes when it comes to intimate relationships is that men find it easier than women to separate out their emotional and sexual lives, which means that it is easier for men to have a relationship with a woman with relatively little commitment, rather than the other way around.

ATTITUDES TO LOVE

Some interesting research has been done by American psychologists Cindy Hazan and Philip Shaver and others that shows that men's and women's attitudes to love tend to fall into one of three main patterns. Which of these attachment styles do you think applies to you?

1. I find it relatively easy to get close to others and I am comfortable depending on them. I don't often worry about being abandoned or about someone getting too close to me.
2. I find that others are reluctant to get as close as I would like. I often worry that my partner doesn't love me or won't want to stay with me. I want to get very close to my partner, and this sometimes scares people away.
3. I am somewhat uncomfortable being close to others: I find it difficult to trust them completely, difficult to allow myself to depend on them. I am nervous when anyone gets too close, and love partners often want me to be more intimate then I feel comfortable being.

Now think about which of the above descriptions fits your partner (or a previous partner) best. The CPM is likely to come into the last category – The Avoidant

Obviously thcse patterns are not totally set in stone, some traits overlap but most research seems to indicate that people's way of loving and relating to each other seems to fall into these three distinct categories. They are labelled as follows:

1. **Secure.** You find it easy to get close to others and trust them. You feel comfortable depending on others and don't fret about the possibility of being abandoned.

2. **Anxious.** As an 'Anxious type' you want to get under the skin of the person you love. You become obsessively preoccupied with them. You worry that they don't love you or that you aren't loved enough. Your love sometimes can feel so claustrophobic that it can scare the loved one off.

3. **Avoidant.** You are uncomfortable with intimacy and closeness. You find it hard to trust anyone completely and you find it hard to allow yourself to depend on them.

The non-committer whether a man or a woman tends to fall into this last category. One of the classic things about a man who fears commitment is an underlying fear of close intimate relationships. That does not mean he does not want them; it's much more to do with the fact that he does not know how to handle them.

Research done on mothers and their children has shown that the same three patterns have been found in infants' relationships with their mothers.

Children who are 'Securely attached' have mothers who are consistently sensitive and responsive to them.

Children who are 'Anxious/Ambivalent' have mothers who respond to them inconsistently. They are sometimes neglectful and unresponsive, and at times intrusive. So the child becomes extremely preoccupied with the mother's availability and feelings towards him or her.

Children who are 'Avoidant' have mothers who are rejecting; when they need comfort they do anything but run to their mother, as they cannot trust her.

Hazan and Shaver were the first to test if the three patterns found in children could also be found in adult romantic relationships, and their research found that indeed they can.

These may well be linked, for most research shows that

there is a connection between childhood behaviour and how we relate to others as adults in our close personal relationships. After all, the first place we learn about relationships is within our own families, therefore it is not so surprising that this is likely to influence how we behave in our adult family relationships.

As we grow up other people and other things will influence how we behave as an adult. How we relate to each other is not forever fixed, and the experiences and influences that we are subjected to in later life and the insight we gain can shift and alter childhood patterns.

So for example if a man is an Avoidant type, if he understands the cause of his fear of commitment he can change. Given the time and the motivation he can shift from being uncomfortable with closeness and intimacy towards more secure, loving, and trusting relationships, where he is able to trust the person he loves and where he can feel that he is a lovable person and therefore deserving of being loved in return. The damage of childhood experiences can be healed or partly healed in loving adult relationships.

Matchmaking – Attachment Styles.

Psychologist Dr Marion Tysoe, in her book *The Good Relationship Guide*, says that mismatching of these types of style spells trouble.

She quotes a study by American psychologists Lee Kirkpatrick and Keith Davis, who looked at 300 dating couples, of what sort of partner you are likely to choose depending on your own attachment style – Secure, Anxious and

Avoidance. Interestingly the researchers found no Avoidant-Avoidant, or Anxious-Anxious pairs, perhaps because the first were too intent about not forming relationships and the second too anxious about each other to do so.

The researchers found that nearly half the Anxious women were with an Avoidant man. They were therefore in just the situation they were most afraid of. Most of the Avoidant woman had a Secure partner. Three quarters of the Secure woman chose a Secure man, the perfect recipe. The last quarter were equally spilt between the two insecure types.

Their research shows that people's attachment styles can change – that one person in four alters their attachment style in adulthood, mainly becoming more secure. This would indicate that though a man may well fear commitment, if he wants to change he can. He can learn how to handle the feelings of rising panic and how not to flee from the chance of forming successful, loving, and happily committed relationships.

4

How to Recognise a CPM

'How could you believe me when I tell you that I love you when you know I've been a liar all my life.'

HOW TO IDENTIFY A 'WORST-CASE CPM'

There are certain patterns and characteristics that men who fear commitment have in common and as a woman it is possible to learn to recognise the danger signs.

The reason it is so difficult to identify a man who fears commitment is because at the beginning of the relationship he is so intent on making you feel how deeply attracted he is to you. He is so determined to win your interest and attention and love that he pursues you ardently. Even if you resist him it only seems to intensify his passion. So you are seduced and coerced into a false feeling of security because he seems to be so sure of what he wants and that is you. If you find him attractive his behaviour is without doubt very seductive stuff.

His attraction to you is instant, your eyes really do meet

across a crowded room, and when you turn around there he is at your side. 'This was such a boring party until you arrived,' he says looking intently into your eyes. He is wonderfully romantic, so easy to talk to, he hangs on your every word, you are swept off your feet. You step aboard the lovers' merry-go-round, as it whirls around and around, but many of these passionate relationships can end as quickly as they began. For reasons you can't define they fizzle out all too soon. The man who once seemed to utterly adore you now seems to be losing interest. It's like he is two different people, and what is more it is utterly confusing. You don't know what is happening to him or why he seems to have changed.

'Where have I gone wrong?' you cry, 'Why has he changed so?' But he is not there to answer you or if he still is around he seems as confused as you and often seems to have no understandable answers to your very understandable questions. What you need to understand is that it is not something you have done wrong, it is not your fault. The change is within him, but what has happened does of course affect you both.

If this is happening or has happened to you one of the most important lessons you need to learn is that there is probably nothing wrong with what you were doing. But it is how what you were doing made him feel. You were responding in a normal loving way to what you thought he wanted from the relationship and what you wanted to give. The problem is, it is what is going on inside him that has changed. He wanted you and the relationship but now he has you he is feeling scared about quite how deeply he is involved. It is this fear that makes him change from pursuer into a man who seems to be pulling back from you, or perhaps he has already ended the relationship. Either way you are left feeling unhappy and confused. What makes it so confusing is that at the beginning of the relationship he seemed madly in love with you and now he seems the exact opposite.

The fact is a commitment phobic rushes into relationships because at that point he is not worried about the long-term future, what he is interested in is the short-term gain. He is a man who plans for today. He is not necessarily thinking about tomorrow. The problem is that he is so passionate and intense about the way he feels about you, it is easy to misinterpret these feelings as expressions of long-lasting and undying love.

Falling in love in the main takes a little longer, and even if a man is totally bowled over on first meeting you, he is going to hold back a little. He wants to take time getting to know you, to find out if you really are what you seem, what your interests are, how much you have in common. He needs to think about whether he wants a committed and loving relationship with you before he declares his true feelings. The commitment phobic man on the other hand is not thinking of any long-term future so he leaps in, frequently short-circuiting the getting to know you stage. He could run a master class in seduction, he is skilled at sweeping you off your feet, being your knight in shining armour, and the more you resist the more he pursues you. It puts even more steel into his determination to win you. It is this very fact of being swept off your feet that clouds your vision, and you miss the warning signs that you are entering dangerous waters because at the time it feels more like the path to paradise. But there are signs if you wish to see them.

BEWARE OF TURNING A BLIND EYE

On the 2nd April 1801 Admiral Horatio Nelson (1758–1805) was standing on the deck of his ship HMS *Elephant* during the Battle of Copenhagen. The battle was in full cry when he received a message from the Admiral of the fleet Admiral Sir Hyde Parker. The message from the Admiral to Nelson was 'Discontinue Action' but Nelson chose to ignore the signal.

He said to his fellow officers who were standing around him, 'I have only one eye. I have the right to be blind sometimes.' He then took the telescope from under his arm and lifted it to his blind eye and said, 'I really do not see the signal!' and so ignored the Admiral's command and all the danger signs around him and continued with the battle. On this occasion he went on to victory but if you turn a blind eye in relationships you rarely come out unscathed.

Of course you can get badly hurt when you go into relationships with both eyes open. Love like war is a risky and unpredictable business. But if you have been hurt by a man who won't commit, or if it has happened to you many times you are very likely to have ignored some early warning signs. When we fall in love it is such a marvellous, heady and highly exciting romantic feeling that we tend to see only what we want to see. The object of our desire has usually many attractive qualities of their own, but when we fall in love we frequently invest in that person the qualities we want them to have as well. The nearer they come to our idealised imagine of a perfect loved one the deeper we fall.

If you have ever been tempted to turn a blind eye and ignored those little niggling doubts that arose in the early part of the relationship with a commitment phobic man or are doing so at this very moment you will probably know what it feels like to be badly hurt. Ignoring potential danger areas is all to easy to do if we are blinded by love.

TELL-TALE SIGNS OF A CPM

In the initial stages of a relationship when we are not in quite so deep, it is easier to spot those early warning signs. By being more aware of what to look for, it could help you to be more prepared about what you are likely to encounter and give you more understanding of how to handle such relationships. Alternatively, with more insight you may decide not to get in too deep. If you are already involved and the man in your life is causing you more pain than pleasure, it could also help you to have the courage to recognise what is happening and cut your losses and end the relationship.

TWELVE QUESTIONS TO ASK YOURSELF SO THAT YOU CAN IDENTIFY THE WARNING SIGNS OF A CPM

1. He has barely met you yet he only has eyes for you. He makes it quite clear that he finds you devastatingly attractive. He hangs on your every word. He concentrates so much on you that others around you feel they are intruding or superfluous and they drift away.

2. He makes you feel that you are special. He drops hints

that he has never felt quite like this before. He treats you so well that you feel that he is looking for a deep relationship, not just a brief affair.

3. He is romantic, he loves romantic gestures, flowers after the first date, unexpected little presents to show he is thinking of you, phone calls late at night just to wish you good night, dropping everything just to be at your side.

4. He has a track record of broken relationships, which he keeps quiet about. He is evasive, somehow his past is clouded in mystery, you can never quite pin him down.

5. He tells you about his broken love affairs, but you get the impression that these women were never quite right for him. Somehow they blotted their copy book, he might have been the one who left them, but really they had it coming to them with their unreasonable behaviour.

6. He is soon introducing references to the pronoun 'we': We will dance all night, we will gather mushrooms in the morning dew, we will walk on a beach in the moonlight. He tempts you with references to the future, a weekend away together, a romantic boat trip up the Nile. The message is that we are a couple, we are an item, our relationship has a future.

7. He tells your friends that you are completely fantastic, so they can reinforce his message of how desirable you are and of how much he loves you.

8. He woos you with everything he has: if he is rich he showers you with gifts; if he is brilliant at his job, he lets you know how successful he is; if he can write poetry he writes a poem just for you; if he has been hurt he shows you how vulnerable he is feeling, so that you feel he needs someone who really cares for him and, as the song goes, 'it has to be you'.

9. He pushes the relationship along, sometimes perhaps faster than you would like. His enthusiasm, the intensity of his feelings, his determination to have this relationship with you is hard to resist.

10. Alternatively he seems to adore you but he is unreliable, evasive or elusive. He says I'll phone you tomorrow, at the weekend, next week – but doesn't. He ignores his promise, or makes an excuse. I was so busy, something came up at work, my greatest friend unexpectedly flew in from Canada and I had to help him out in a crisis.

11. He says in a jokey sort of way:

I can't believe it, all my friends are falling by the wayside and getting married.

I love the unexpected, maybe I'll chuck my job in and go and find work in Australia next year.

Do you know, four out of ten marriages fail, that's not very good odds is it?

12. He tells you what a fantastic relationship he has with all his ex-girlfriends and how they only have to call and he will drop everything for them, he may well but that could include his date with you.

Some of the above of course can apply to a man who simply adores you, so don't immediately jump to the conclusion that he is a CPM. But if you recognise four or more of these particular traits, stand back and take a good look at the relationship. Don't ignore those little doubts or feelings of unease because you may well be involved with a man who genuinely does fear commitment. If that relationship was in the past, think back and see which of these applied, that way you may avoid getting hurt the next time around, being forewarned is forearmed.

HIS INDECISION IS FREQUENTLY PART OF THE PACKAGE

I have also found with men who fear commitment that it is not only relationships that they find they have difficulty in committing to. They have difficulty making a decision or once it is made they have difficulty sticking with it. They have no sooner settled for one thing than they change their mind and decide on something completely different. This habit is a real warning sign that is worth being aware of when you are trying to recognise a commitment phobic man.

Chelsea, an advertising executive in her early thirties, said about Barry her long-standing CP boyfriend, 'If we went to a restaurant Barry would be very indecisive. He'd order something and when the waiter turned up he'd change his mind and want something different. He would even change his mind again after that.

'If we were driving somewhere he would stop and say let's go somewhere else. It made me feel insecure because one moment you're going there and then suddenly he wants to go somewhere completely different. We used to joke about his indecisive nature. He couldn't make up his mind because he was always torn in two directions. In the end it became a trait I grew to dislike in him.'

ARE YOU IN A RELATIONSHIP WITH A MAN WHO YOU THINK IS COMMITMENT PHOBIC?

If so try this exercise. Alternatively think back to a relationship where you think this was a problem and check it out.

What are your particular Blind Spots.

1. I suggest that you do this exercise with a trusted girlfriend, preferably who knows you both.
2. Make a list or several if there has been more than one man who was reluctant to commit, and see if you can identify your particular blind spots – for example:

He never calls when he says he will. He never introduces you to his friends or family. He has a track record of broken relationships. He puts you down or criticises you too often. He breaks dates, constantly turns up late, does not telephone when he says he will. He says marriage is for wimps, an outmoded idea.

Discuss this with your girlfriend. If the list is more than two or three things, take a hard look at the relationship: Is it what you want? Is it moving in the right direction? Are you the one in the partnership who is constantly sacrificing your needs? Are you able to talk about all of this with him? If those warning signs are going through the ceiling, you need to think seriously about whether this is the relationship for you, but if not you are probably at a stage where you want the relationship to move forward, but you need to proceed with your eyes wide open.

A WORST-CASE CPM

Where you really do need your eyes extremely wide open is if you are involved with a 'worst-case CPM'. It is not always possible to identify the worst-case CPM but it helps if you can. He has all the traits that I have been describing in this chapter but to an even more extreme degree.

Four Identifying Signs of a Worst-Case CPM

1. The more removed he is from any insight into his problem the more severe the problem is and the less likely he is to want to change. Many men who fear commitment are prepared to struggle with their fear because they accept they have a problem. Whereas the worst-case type tends to have little insight into his problem, and, more usually, he denies it completely. If he is into total denial he is then more able to continue to believe his own lies.

2. He is at number nine or ten on the Richter panic scale of a CPM. He panics very easily and that is when he will feel driven to disrupt or destroy his relationship with you. So he either ends the relationship or starts to find fault with you. Blaming you or your behaviour for the change in his feelings lets him off the hook. It enables him to abdicate responsibility for what he has contributed to the relationship breakdown, because he sees it as your fault, and he wants you to see it the same way. He is then free to move on to pastures new, leaving a succession of broken hearts in his wake. He will then repeat this destructive pattern all over again.

3. The hotter the pursuit at the beginning of the relationship the more likely it is that his passion will grow cold. He is breathlessly romantic. His urgency and need to posses you is overpowering; he is looking for his soul mate, the one wonderfully perfect woman in the whole wide world just right for him – and that is you.

4. He has a track record of broken relationships, they are usually short-term, and he has ended them abruptly or cruelly and usually both. In fact commitment to anything is difficult, he moves jobs a lot, he rarely settles in one place for long, he even finds it difficult to make decisions and stick with them.

Many CPMs though they fear commitment also know that they do want to form a loving and lasting relationship with a woman so there comes a time when they are prepared to work at their problem. The 'worst-case CPM' is unlikely to unless he is prepared to get help to overcome his fears.

THE CONFUSED WORLD OF THE CPM – TOO CLOSE FOR COMFORT

The good news is that the majority of CPMs do not fall into the worst-case scenario, but the bad news is that most CPMs are pulled in two directions. Part of him wants to be in a good relationship, he does want you, but the other part of him is afraid of feeling trapped, of making a commitment. Because of this confusion it is likely that if you are in a relationship with a CPM you too will become confused by his contradictory behaviour. But if you can understand what is happening you will be more able to deal with it. There is also more chance that you can help him to recognise what his problem is, which may help him overcome his fear of commitment.

A CPM ADMITS HE HAS A PROBLEM

All the women Hugh fell in love with ended up hurt and confused until eventually, and many broken hearts later, rather than blaming it on them Hugh was able to admit that he was the one with the problem. I have described Hugh's story in detail as he is a very typical CPM. I hope that this and the analysis at the end will help you to recognise the warning signs of an involvement with a commitment phobic man. The problem may be his, but the fall-out of such a relationship effects you both.

Hugh is someone you would notice if he walked into a room. He is thirty-five, very good-looking, six foot three inches tall, with an athletic figure, blond hair, lovely eyes and a very easy and outward-going manner. He adores women, he likes being with them, he likes the way a woman moves, the way another one smiles, he loves to have a woman at his side. He is interested in them and what they have to say, he can also talk very freely about his feelings and theirs. So it is no surprise that he has no problem in attracting them. His problem is that though he starts by adoring them, he ends up by finding something wrong with them, something he dislikes and that for him is the end of yet another love affair.

Hugh said, 'I love women. I have a weakness that I sleep with them too soon. I get too involved. I've got mates who prefer the company of men. They're married but they don't like being with women. I prefer to go out in mixed company. Occasionally it's nice to be just with the lads. But having a woman around, whether it's just my girlfriend or someone's wife is really healthy and good. I have this need to be loved, or get attention. I've never ever said no to a woman, never ever; it doesn't matter how tired I am, there's always some energy left for sex.

'I'm also a flirt, my eyes constantly get me into trouble. Up until about twenty-four I didn't realise that women found me attractive. Then I suddenly realised that with my height and my eyes I could go into a pub and flash my eyes and I'd frequently get a good response. It's attention-seeking, wanting to be loved. And wanting to pull I suppose.

'I remember at college I slept with a whole load of women and I'm sure they must have put the word out that if I was drunk I'd sleep with anyone. I didn't mind. I thought it was quite nice really. It didn't matter if they weren't all that attractive, but I wouldn't have wanted a relationship with any of them. I didn't sleep with anyone until I was nineteen so I had some catching up to do,' he said with a smile. 'I'm a Catholic and I'd have these phases of religious attacks. I suppose it's the guilt trip thing but it does not last. I have slept around quite a bit, probably with forty to fifty women, and perhaps double that if you count not going quite all the way but everything but. But since my mid-twenties I have been more discriminating.

'Once I've slept with a women I have this real bond with them. Even when it's been a one-night stand it's more than just a physical act for me. I feel I need that contact, not just for sex but to have a woman next to you, for that affection. It's an emotional need being filled. To feel wanted and be accepted for myself, even if it's only for a night, a few weeks or a month or two. In recent years I have had three or four long-term relationships which each lasted about two years. With two of them I think I even mentioned things like marriage and at the beginning of each relationship I did feel really committed.

'I don't have any doubts about my ability to love. I'm really loving. That's why I find this commitment thing so frustrating. I know I have so much to give and yet I've discovered I can't really let go and allow myself to totally commit to one woman. All my long-term relationships have started and ended in the same way. At the beginning I go in head first. I think they are wonderful and lovely, it's always a strong attraction. If I'm attracted to them and I know they are to me I get really frustrated if they won't sleep with me. So I go all out to get them. If I really like them I guess I can't bear to be rejected and yet in the end I'm the one who ends up rejecting them.

'I know when I want to end a relationship, but I am not good at it. In fact I know I do it really badly. I do care about hurting the woman involved if it has been an important long-term relationship. Yet I have ended them all messily. I don't feel very proud of that. There is a pattern and I repeat it each time which is why I decided to have some therapy. I wanted to understand what I was doing. There comes a point in the relationship when something inside me changes and instead of seeing her as this wonderful lovely woman I find myself starting to find fault with her. I start to look for excuses for why I am not quite as in love with her as I thought I was. It's nearly always some physical imperfection. It can be something very small that never worried me at the beginning of the relationship.

'Maria was very slim and like a little doll with this amazing auburn hair. She was great fun and very lively. We met at a marvellous Irish wedding. It was instant attraction and I danced with her all night. When I got back to England

I called her up and she invited me to come over, as she said that she wanted some advice on doing up her flat. She knew I had worked as an interior decorator for several years.

'We spent a long time talking about how she wanted the flat to look, and then she cooked a lovely meal, it was wonderfully relaxed and we just talked so easily and I really did fancy her. It was getting late, and she said "Do you want to stay?" She knew that I did so she continued, "you can either sleep in the sitting-room, the spare room or in my bed." Well, it was not a very difficult choice,' he said smiling warmly, 'and that was the start of our relationship. Our first year together was very good. I did make some mumbling about marriage to her. She was a really nice person, really warm-hearted. She would never criticise me.

'But then after we had been together for about eighteen months my feelings towards her started to change. I don't understand why, as we were getting along really well. She had a birthmark on her arm, it was only a little one, but I just took a dislike to it, and from then on I was always finding fault with her. Where I had once been reliable I was often cancelling dates at the last moment, or saying I would call, and then somehow I would just forget. Eventually I got very drunk and slept with a girl I worked with. I told Maria, because I guess I knew that would be the final straw and that she would end the relationship which is what I wanted. I know I hurt her badly.

'My relationship with Amber also ended badly. We had been together about a year and I wanted to travel around the world. She said she wanted to come with me. It seemed quite a nice idea at the time. But then we were together twenty-four hours a day. After a couple of months I could not stand that any longer, she was really getting on my nerves. I don't think I was very nice to her and she realised I wasn't happy with the relationship. So at my suggestion she agreed that we would continue to travel together as friends instead of as lovers. It was quite awkward really but I could not just abandon her halfway across the world. This time it was her weight I objected to, which was the same as when we started going out together, but suddenly she seemed too plump. I was always getting at her for it. That was just an excuse really to end the relationship. But it really got to me and I just did not fancy her any more. I could see that as a long-term partnership it wasn't going to work because our interests were so different.

'I have had several short-term relationships since then, all of which I have ended. Then about two years ago I fell in love with Caitlin. I was besotted with her. She's very pretty and has a lovely sense of humour and beautiful blue eyes. I find both these things irresistible in women. That's a fatal combination for me. I adore blue eyes. But one thing about her that I found really difficult was that she never really showed her emotions. I am very open with women so I did not really understand it. I was never really sure how much she loved me.

'Thinking back, I think she may have had a problem with commitment. I had not encountered that in a woman before. The first time we met we went to bed together and then she refused to see me again as she was going out with someone else. Then a year later she was with a group of friends and we all went on a skiing holiday together. She was still with this same guy. I really wanted her and made quite a play for her, which worked and we ended up in bed together which was great. She was very good at expressing her emotions sexually. She wanted to keep very quiet about it because of her boyfriend, but he found out. Naturally he was furious, so their relationship was over and he has not spoken to me since.

'Right from the beginning she was reluctant to get involved with my friends or my family. I am very close to my cousins and my aunt who live in France. I wanted to take her to meet them but she could not make up her mind whether she wanted to come. It was the same with my brother's wedding – she only agreed to come at the last moment. She just did not seem able to make a decision.

'I wanted her so much I allowed her to walk all over me. That is not a part I usually play in relationships. I dropped my friends just to see her. My work suffered. I play a lot of sport and I stopped much of that as well. I was a nervous wreck, like a little dog jumping to her command. Anything she said I would drop to be with her because I wasn't sure about how much she loved me and I was trying to make her love me. I felt totally insecure in the relationship. She told me it was only because she was playing hard to get that I wanted her. It was only after the relationship had ended and I went into therapy that I realised she was very similar to my mother who walked all over me too.

'We went on holiday to Italy. She had left me to do all the organising. She was telling me on the plane about a friend of hers whose boyfriend was messing her around and who didn't even love her. I thought that sounded like me, being messed around by someone who doesn't actually love me, and that is when the rot set in.

'I told her on holiday that I wasn't happy with the situation and it felt like unrequited love. It was then, when Caitlin saw she was losing me, she started to chase me. Then suddenly the boot was on the other foot, and this problem over her appearance raised its head as it had done in previous relationships. I'd decided I'd found a physical fault with her. She bit her nails and they were all worn down and ragged, I really disliked that. I got very critical of her just like my mother was with me. All the women I have loved have wondered what's wrong when this happens, but I can't tell them. It must be awful for them, very confusing and it's really horrible for me as well.

'We then went through quite a bad time with lots of rows and things. So I decided to go to France on my own this time. I ended up in a whorehouse with a couple of friends. When I returned Caitlin found lots of scratches on my back. I said I had scratched it helping out in my aunt's garden with whom I had been staying, but she did not believe me. She demanded I told her the truth, so I did. She was really, really upset and said "That's it, it's over." Which was understandable. But I was really pleased it was finished. There had been so much grief. It wrecked me for two years. Pursuing her, chasing her, striving to be loved, from a woman that can't offer love. I realised eventually that she was just like my mother.'

The Birth of a CPM

Hugh explained, 'My mother did not really want me. She was very young, lonely, depressed and living in a foreign country. My father was a rather distant and remote figure who was away for weeks on end.' Hugh can never remember his mother cuddling him; she told him that he was an unresponsive child, but she also admitted that she gave him little love and attention in those first few years.

The way his mother saw it, Hugh was a child that did not want to be cuddled and so she gave up trying.

A little child whose mother rejects it or gives it the minimum in terms of time, attention and affection, at first desperately yearns for what it is not getting. But if that child is not responded to it tends to shut down those needs and withdraws or becomes inwardly despairing. A child who has experienced too little attention as it grows older either becomes very clinging or in turn rejects those close to it. This reinforces the mother's view that she has a child who spurns affection and, as a result, the mother often gives up showing physical affection.

After Hugh was born his mother had two stillborn girls. Then four years later his younger brother arrived. Hugh remembers his mother showering his brother with affection and that made him feel even more excluded. Two years later his mother had another little baby girl who was born dead.

Hugh said, 'There's a comment my father made when I was six which I will never forget. He said to me one day: "Just make sure you don't die before your mother."

'That made a real impact on my life and that's why I always wanted to please her and why I've always wanted to please women, but why I also find them so difficult to trust.' In all his relationships with women Hugh starts by loving them but ends up criticising them just as his mother did with him. His relationship with Caitlin was just a repeat performance of his relationship with his mother. Striving to give her love when much of the time she was rejecting him, yet when she did change and seem to want him he could not trust her and so he then rejected her.

So Hugh developed this pattern of 'Anxious Attachment'. As a child longing for his mother's affection but also fearing rejection. He became the naughty child in an attempt to gain her attention, but even though it was the wrong sort of attention, in so much as it was reprimanding, irritated and critical it was better than no attention at all. He even developed a technique of having a nose bleed to get her attention. Hugh said, 'I just concentrated and it would happen. I did it at school too if they gave me something I didn't want to eat. But in the main I had a reasonably happy childhood running around with my friends.

'I love my job as an interior decorator but my mother is still critical of what I'm doing. She thinks there is no future in it. She pushed me through further education when I didn't want it. It was a typical middle-class approach. I had to succeed.

'I am self-employed and relatively successful. I don't have to take shit from anyone. I can do what I want to do. If any of my girlfriends start telling me what to do it's bad news. It's bye-bye girlfriend.

'I've never lived with a woman. I think it would scare me because it would be a step closer to real commitment. I wonder whether I'm capable of a long-term relationship and suppose I am afraid of making a mistake.

'I don't trust myself to be faithful, to stick to one woman. But if I did marry I believe in faithfulness. I am also worried by the responsibility of marriage and particularly children, to think you have them relying on you for the next twenty years or so.

'As I see it there are two types of women once they have reached the thirty-five age bracket. Those with an ex-husband and children and those with "excess emotional baggage", and I don't know whether I'm ready to take on either of those.' Then he smiled mischievously and said: 'I think I have met the woman I want to marry but she lives in Argentina, so it's safe to say that.'

Hugh has admitted to himself that he has now reached a point in his life where he wants to overcome his fear of commitment. So he has taken the plunge and he has been looking at himself and his problem in counselling.

FIVE CPM PROFILES

1. The Romantic Romeo

Josh is undoubtedly a worst-case CPM, he should have had commitment phobic emblazoned across his T-shirt in large letters. Time and time and again attractive and desirable girls would fall for his charms, only to find that once he had bedded them he soon lost interest in them. Every summer he would take three months out of his job in Britain and jet off to a popular Greek holiday island which abounded with British tourists. He said that the British and Scandinavian girls were the most susceptible. 'I have friends out there who own several speedboats. A group of us have set up a water-skiing club, for tourists. It is a wonderful way to seduce girls and I get a holiday in the sun and a good tan into the bargain.'

'Teaching water-skiing is wonderfully tactile and what other job can you do with so few clothes on,' he said arching an eyebrow quizzically. 'You see,' he continued, 'you have to stand behind the girl, both of you scantily clad, while you teach them how to hold the skis, how to balance, the right angle for their arms and legs. Then of course there is a lot of falling into the water, especially when they are just learning, so that you are constantly pulling them up into the boat, and offering to dry them off. You could say it's like a long drawn-out foreplay.'

Josh had a fairly simple but successful method of attracting his prey. 'I would go to the airport and watch for the new arrivals. I would only pick out the attractive ones, and then check out to see if they were travelling on their own or with a girlfriend, if they had a boyfriend with them I left them alone.' He continued, 'Then I would look at the labels on their cases to see which hotel they were going to. The island I stayed on was quite small so all the hotels were fairly near to each other.

'I never approached them at the airport; that was too obvious. I would wait a couple of days then I would casually turn up at the hotel. As they were not with a man they were usually down by the beach or the pool quite early, trying to get a suntan. It was not difficult to just chat to them in a friendly way, nothing forward or too pushy to scare them off. The best sort of hotels were ones that were situated on the beach. I would arrive in my speedboat with all the skiing equipment on display. That way it was fairly easy to interest them. Girls like the idea of a man with a speedboat,' he said smugly. 'Once I got talking to them, I would mention that I gave water-skiing lessons. Then I would drop into the conversation the fact that I had noticed them at the airport, implying that was because they had caught my eye, and they are usually flattered by this. I think I got rather good at telling the ones who were likely to respond well to my advances. In fact I can still tell if I see a girl walking down a street, or in a wine bar or disco, whether she is going to be friendly and fun and responsive.

2. The long-distance CPM

It is very typical behaviour for a commitment phobic man to get involved with a woman who lives some distance away. The long-distance love affair gives him the ideal opportunity to be really loving and romantic but at the same time it enables him to feel OK about his relationship with you because you are being kept at a safe distance. The distance relieves his anxiety because he feels it gives him the emotional space he needs. So he may spend hours on the telephone, write romantic love letters, even talk about how lovely it would be to see more of you, how much he misses you. All of which may be true and how he is feeling, but then he knows he can withdraw and have his time and his life which does not include you.

Right from the beginning he has built in a safety net which is the distance between you and because of that he can give free range to expression of his emotions. All goes well until you try to move the goal posts. Perhaps by suggesting that you move your job to be closer to him. Maybe that you should meet every weekend rather than once a fortnight. Whatever it is, it panics him and he suddenly does not feel quite as safe. It begins to dawn on him that physical distance does not represent the safety net he thought it did. He might have little understanding of what is going on in his head, but what he does know is that a relationship that once seemed ideal now feels a little bit threatening. If he starts to realise that the relationship has got to a stage where you are wanting more of him than he is prepared to give, he starts to draw back from it. Suddenly he finds fault with you about things that he had previously liked or which had never until now worried him, or he sabotages the relationship altogether.

He has to avoid falling into the modern-day sexual trap of thinking that getting to know someone comes through jumping into bed together. In long-term relationships that is putting the cart before the horse. You need to take time at the beginning of a relationship to get to really know each other. If you rush that stage of the relationship, the satisfying of those powerful sexual feelings often stops you both seeing each other in a more honest and realistic light, which if you are looking for a loving and committed relationship is very important.

It is only when a commitment phobic man learns to understand why he behaves the way he does that he can start to make changes. In Hugh's case he has to learn not to rush into relationships so quickly. His desperate need for love and approval stops him taking time to assess whether this particular woman really is someone he could have a truly loving relationship with. He needs to realise that a deeper belief in himself and his abilities has to come from within. It is not something that he has to constantly seek from his relationships with women.

3. Mamisma Man

Be wary of the older thirty-something man who still lives at home with his parents, in comfort and style as his mother still does everything for him. In Italy they call him 'Mamisma Man'. One Italian lawyer of thirty-six was proud of still living at home. He said that it made his mother still feel useful; he was fulfilling her need to look after him. When his mother was asked to comment she said much as she loved her son she wished he would leave home. She had plenty of things to do with her life rather than spending time looking after him, and anyway she would like his room for a studio to do her sculpting. But it was a wonderful excuse for that lawyer to use when the current woman in his life put the pressure on him for a more committed relationship. Men who are still living at home well into their thirties and forties have got very used to that idea and rarely change, that is until their mother dies. Then often they go in search of a wife, but unless you are planning to be his replacement mother, and take on where she left off when it comes to looking after him, this is a relationship to avoid.

4. He is not a hundred per cent committed to heterosexuality

There is a less common reason why some men are wary of commitment. Some men don't want to accept their homosexuality, they keep hoping that these feelings will go away, or remain sufficiently suppressed to enable them to make and maintain heterosexual relationships. Some gay men want a relationship with a woman because they can't come to terms with their sexual orientation, others because they want to be a father, or for some it is because they feel that society is still so prejudiced that if they 'come out' they will be ostracised for the rest of their lives. They hope that if they fall in love with a woman they can suppress their sexual orientation. They are deluding themselves and perhaps deceiving you. But their ambivalence means that part of them wants an intimate relationship with a woman while the other half resists it because they are terrified that if they get too close their secret will be discovered.

This was the position that Robert was in, he is forty and married for a second time. He wrote to me saying:

Dear Zelda

I find myself in a desperate situation due to my refusal to face up to myself. My problem is that I lean towards homosexuality and it's causing me a great deal of grief. I have had a number of gay relationships before and between my marriages but never during them. I love my wife but we have had no sex for three years now. I know this hurts my wife very much. The fact is that I find myself repulsed by the thought of sex with her or any woman for that matter. She has complained to me that I treat her more like a sister than my wife. I have been seeing a psychiatrist for depression but I have not been able to tell him that I am gay. I can't go on like this, I fear I will do something stupid.

A situation like that is heartbreaking for Robert and for his wife. He can't make her the commitment she wants, he is deeply distressed and she knows that there is something wrong. I hope that Robert can find the courage to face up to his problem, to talk to his psychiatrist and also to be honest with his wife.

5. Other Women's Husbands

'Darling, I love you. I will leave my wife for you, and then we can be together always.' A million mistresses or more have heard these words, only to discover that this fairytale does not come true. If as a man you want to create an emotional distance in your marriage, or you are experiencing marriage as a trap there is no easier way to sabotage the marriage than by having an affair, or becoming a serial adulterer. Your wife may or may not find out about the affair. In many ways you don't actually want her to know, because the affair itself has suited your purpose. You have created some distance and space for yourself and are feeling less trapped by marriage. So once again you can relax and feel OK about being married.

The chances are that a Married CPM will not want to be any more committed to the 'other woman' than he is to his wife, in fact probably less so. So the same pattern will emerge. He will set off in hot pursuit, only to cool rapidly if and when you the mistress make any emotional demands on him. Or worse still in his book, when you start to have expectations about him leaving his wife for you.

'Never wear mascara when you love a married man,' sings Shirley Maclaine, in the film *The Apartment*. If you have ever been the mistress of a married man you will probably know what it's like to be in love with a man who can't commit. The married CPM pursues you as ardently as his single counterpart. He makes you feel very special, utterly desirable. But you will also know that it's you that sits around waiting for his call. It's you that cannot telephone him in case his wife answers the telephone. If he suddenly finds himself with a couple of free hours, he expects you to be prepared to drop everything – your friends, your previous engagements, whatever it is just so you can be together.

Equally he will always feel able to cancel his appointments with you at the last moment. His wife wants him to babysit, one of the children has to be collected from Brownies, 'her' mother has arrived on an unexpected visit – the list is long, and it is pointless you making a fuss, for how can he explain where he is going to be, when pressured by his wife? So it's you who cries buckets as you think of him with her and his children around the family Christmas tree. It's you without him every weekend just thinking of them being together. You who holiday without him, while he is living it up with family and friends on holiday in Italy. While you sit at home alone, or contact your girlfriends to complain about how unfair life is, or you return for a weekend with your parents, who ask you 'why you can't bring a nice young man home'. You are reluctant to tell them that the problem with the man you love is that inconveniently he is married to someone else.

Sophie first met Nick when he came as part of a small team to do some work for the company she worked for. She found him very attractive, but also found out that he was married, so she tried to resist his interest in her. But over the next few months they were engaged working together on the same project. He was so attractive, and they had lots in common and he always made it very clear that he found her irresistible. He would ask her out for lunch, for a drink, to go to a concert with him, and she would refuse. But he kept up his persistence. She said, 'I knew I was beginning to weaken and he really did seem absolutely besotted with me. We were both at a meeting and when the others crossed the room to get some coffee he turned to me and said looking into my eyes with a mixture of laughter and passion, "I can no longer make love to my wife, because all I can think of is making love to you. You are in my thoughts from the moment I wake up in the morning, through every moment of the day to when I go to sleep at night. I desire you only." That evening I agreed to have dinner with him and that was the beginning of our affair. I thought I could handle it, an affair with a married man that is, but I fell hook line and sinker. That was three years ago. For the last two years he has been promising to leave his wife, but he has never quite managed it and when I threaten to end the relationship he always begs me not to and says he is utterly committed to me. I have given him an ultimatum now. Either he leaves her before their annual summer holiday which is in August this year, or the relationship is over.' Have you given him an ultimatum before? I asked her. 'Yes,' she said, smiling ruefully, 'I have, but they have come and gone and he has not left her, but this time I really mean it.'

This is an all too common story. Many a married man feed you stories of how the marriage is going through a rough patch. He tells you that he and his wife are no longer having sex together. That he loves you and he wants to have babies with you. That he is only there for the sake of the children and once they are older, have done their A levels, gone to university, left home – the list grows – he will leave his marriage, and then you can be together for ever. While you may be seeing the relationship as him one day leaving his wife for you, he is torn with being unable to fully commit to the marriage, but neither is he able to leave his wife for you. So as he wants both of you but cannot fully commit to either of you, he stays with his wife and children but he continues to sweet-talk you into continuing your affair with him.

If you are the other woman and you are really in love with a married man, it's very easy to convince yourself that it's his wife's fault. She does not love him enough, she is no good in bed, she is too involved with the children. Maybe she is some of those things, but just as likely she is a woman who is also in love with this man and she like you is trying to have a relationship with him, and by setting up this eternal triangle the man in question can continue to resist fully committing to either of you. What does a sensible woman do in these circumstances? She does not waste her time on ultimatums but ends the relationship. Make yourself – not him – your No. 1 priority, ~~and~~ get on with the rest of your life, because if you wait around for him to make a decision you could cry oceans of tears while the years just slip away.

SO BEWARE

'What am I doing wrong?' Is this a question you find you are constantly asking yourself in your current relationship? As women, we so often seem to be conditioned to look at what it is that we have done wrong when relationships run into trouble. So quite likely you will start to wonder what it is that you are doing wrong now. What is it about you that is making the man you love or are very smitten by suddenly behave differently towards you?

The chances are that it is not you who has changed, but him. He is not reacting to anything you have done, but what he is reacting to is his fear of commitment. He is not a man who is afraid of you but he is suddenly terrified of what you represent. He is afraid that the love he feels for you represents what he fears most, real commitment or worse still those dreaded few words 'They were married and lived happily ever after'.

As you do not know what his fear is the chances are that you will try everything to make things all right. You will try to change your behaviour, to make him feel more loved and wanted, to try and meet his needs. You may imagine that if you were younger, older, slimmer, rounder, prettier, more intelligent, more amusing, had different friends, enjoyed different hobbies, had a more interesting job, he would love you more. But whatever hoops you try to jump through you are likely to increase his fear.

He may well see the very act of you trying to please him as a way of luring him into a togetherness that he fears the most. How far he withdraws from you depends on how deep his fear is. If it is not too severe he may put a little emotional distance between you, telephoning a little less often, being just a little more involved with his work, spending more time with his friends and less with you so that you see less of each other. But if his fears run very deep he may start a barrage of criticism so that nothing you now do seems right. Where once he had been wonderfully reliable he may become irresponsible, arranging to meet you, and then forgetting, or cancelling at the last minute. He may even take another girl out, two-time you, embark on an affair, finish the relationship altogether or behave so badly that you finish with him.

DON'T RUSH IN WHERE ANGELS FEAR TO TREAD

So let's go back to look at how these relationships start. The common thread that runs through the commitment phobic personality is his 'hot pursuit' at the beginning of the relationship. He pulls out all the stops. He is passionate, eager and romantic, he seems to desire you more than anything else in the world. What you have to remember is that he is also being totally unrealistic, he is not thinking clearly or logically, he is not thinking about the future. His concerns are about the here and now, so why go at a slower pace? He wants you and he feels that he must have you – and he must have you now. He wants to sweep all caution to the wind and, what is more, he wants you to do the same.

The fact is that a CPM can afford to act in this way precisely because he is not thinking about tomorrow, with no long-term plan in his mind. What he is intent on is satisfying today's needs without any really serious thoughts about tomorrow. Even if in those early days he mentions marriage that's an airy-fairy romantic sort of thought. He probably has little concept of the reality of marriage.

So the golden rule is never to be seduced by his romantic ideas of whirlwind relationships. They are just as likely to fizzle out as suddenly as they began. If your relationship is going to have any chance of a future, it is up to you to set the pace, and that is going to be at a much slower rate than he would like.

Katherine Hale, creator of Orlando the Marmalade cat, a very sprightly ninety-four-year-old, said when interviewed on Radio Four's *Desert Island Discs* by Sue Lawley (31st

June 1998), that she met the painter Augustus John when she was a young woman. She was struggling in some dead-end job, but knew that what she really wanted to do was to paint. He found her attractive and amusing and was very encouraging and complimentary when she showed him some of her work. On the spur of the moment he asked her what she did, then much to her amazement he invited her to be his secretary, which she gladly accepted.

Katherine Hale said, 'When he came into the room there was always a frisson between us. He was such an exciting person to be with, though for me it was not sexual and I never had an affair with him.' She described Augustus John as a tremendous flirt who was always falling in and out of love. When he wanted to seduce a woman he really fancied Katherine said he would say to them, 'I would like to knock a baby out of you.' Katherine herself thought that this was a rather silly approach and did not take him seriously when he proposed that to her, but she said that many women fell for this very direct request. Perhaps they assumed that if he wanted them to be the mother of his baby, he must be very smitten. But he probably knew it was the way to many a woman's heart and bed. The trouble was that he was thinking of the delights of the next few hours or days or weeks, with the enjoyment of making love to a beautiful woman completely obscuring any thoughts of the long-term responsibilities of fatherhood.

What is important is to understand that part of a CPM wants a loving relationship and the other part is downright scared. He is torn in two directions. What you need to know is how to handle such a man. That way you will have a chance to establish some ground rules enabling you to have control over your life and at the same time allowing him to stop running away from the woman he loves, if that is what he truly wants.

Guidelines: Five Golden Rules

Golden rule one: Be realistic – don't join him on his romantic merry-go-round of love

As a woman it is up to you to be realistic because that is certainly not something he has any intention of being. He hardly knows you, yet within a short time of meeting he is making you feel wildly attractive, desirable and irresistible. It is all very heady stuff and he knows it. He wants you to respond to him so he will pull out all the stops, he may shower you with flowers, write poetry, send you tapes of romantic music, telephone all the time just to hear your voice, take you to fun and exciting places. But you need to keep your feet on the ground. Here is a man you have just met, who hardly knows you, yet all these strong feelings and desires are tumbling out. It is flattering and appealing. Even if at this stage in the relationship you are not particularly interested in him, it is difficult not to be at least a little intrigued.

Being realistic means reminding yourself that he really knows nothing about you. What he is wild about is his fantasy of you, he has not as yet had time to check out the reality. I am not saying that you are not lovely and desirable but the plain facts are he can't possibly know you, he has no idea what you are really like. In his book he does not need to really know you because what he sees is what he wants. He is into instant gratification. As Hugh said (in Chapter Four) about the woman he wanted a relationship with, 'I used to feel really irritated if she resisted going to bed with me.'

At the beginning of the relationship you do have a great deal of control so don't throw caution to the winds and join him on his merry-go-round of romantic illusions.

You are in a high-risk relationship, so recognise it. It could be that is part of the fun, maybe you are a romantic at heart, perhaps the excitement of all those adrenaline-charged feelings is drowning out the warning bells. Don't be tempted to be swept along at his pace, it is very exciting stuff, but it is also just tinsel. He is being unrealistic. Don't collude with that, because if you do and he is commitment phobic then sure as night follows day if things between you move too quickly he will start to panic and withdraw from the intimacy of the relationship.

If you are looking for a more long-term relationship, then that needs to be built on firm foundations. It takes two of you to do the building work, and if the early stages of a relationship are just skated over, eventually it will all come toppling to the ground.

Golden rule two: Resist rushing into a sexual relationship, however tempting

Don't be taken in by his amazing need to take you to bed. In all areas of his emotional life a commitment phobic man expresses his needs with great intensity. This is particularly so where sex is concerned. Most men know that if a woman agrees to go to bed with him, it is because she feels something for him. So he will go all out to make you feel very sexually desirable, so that his sexual desire for you can be satisfied. He is expert in making you feel that his passion is so intense that he cannot possibly survive without you. Don't be taken in if he tries to convince you that his desire for you is more intense that any other man you have met. Remember that this man is expressing such strong needs because he is concentrating on what he wants in the next five minutes, that evening, the following day, next week or maybe even a little bit longer.

So look before you leap if you are on the brink of making it a sexual relationship. Certainly not on the first few dates but quite a lot longer. Make sure he understands if you did go to bed with him quite how much of a commitment that would be for you. Have conversations about how you feel for example that if you are going to have a sexual relationship that is not something you want unless it is part of a loving relationship.

In the book *The Rules – Time tested secrets for capturing Mr Right* by Ellen Fein and Sherrie Schneider – Rule 15 states – 'don't rush into sex'. The authors say 'Don't be surprised if he gets angry when you kiss him good night in the hall rather than invite him up for a drink. He has probably been spoiled by other women who have slept with him on the first or second date and now he feels he is being denied this pleasure. But don't worry, anger indicates interest.'

You might say that you don't mind having sex with him on your first date, you are a modern woman and that is what equality is all about. It's all right if he doesn't call again because you both had a good time, and you can cope with never hearing from him again. But I know from the hundreds of woman I have spoken to that most women who say that are lying to themselves.

The fact is that deep down inside it's not okay with you if you sleep with a man and you never hear from him again. Nearly all of us want the man we have just slept with to call us. Hopefully if we agreed to have sex with a man it is because we really liked him, and not because we drank too much, gave into his pressure for sex, or because we feared losing him if we didn't.

If he doesn't call you again because you refused to go to bed with him, you can be fairly certain he would not have called once you had slept with him either and that would be far worse. So why take that risk when you don't know whether he is going to behave like a gentleman or a cad?

Golden rule three: Listen to your basic instincts.

Be aware that if there is an initial attraction, even just the tiniest beginnings of one, it is difficult not to be just a little bit flattered by his interest in you.

If a man is going all out to capture your attention, if he is in hot pursuit, this is just the time when you should be listening to your instincts. Don't be so caught up in his highly romantic approach to you that you brush aside things about him that worry you or that you are not quite sure about.

This is the time when you should allow your basic instincts to have their voice. Because he makes you feel so accepted and appealing it is all too easy to brush aside those warning voices. But if we look back on relationships that have run into problems it is often those little early niggling worries that later come back to haunt us. The seeds of doubt that were around at the beginning of that relationship are frequently what really bug us later on. For example, you rarely meet his friends as he says he loves you so much that he can't bear to share you with them, he just adores it when it's just the two of you. Five years later you realise that he has hardly any friends as he does not really bother with other people, or he resents the fact that you want to see your friends and tries to control how often and how much you see them. Or he lists all the many failings of his previous girlfriends, and what a difficult time they gave him and how wonderful you are compared with them. Once you have been married a few years, he is ultra-critical of you, and he makes it clear that you are the one at fault, not him. It's your behaviour that has to change, his naturally is just fine!

Golden rule four: Find out about his track record. 'Getting to know you, getting to know all about you.'

So sang Deborah Kerr in *The King and I*. In the early days of getting to know someone that is the time when you need to find out as much as possible about them. This is never more so than when you meet a man who wants to sweep you off your feet. One of the most tell-tale signs of a man who is afraid to commit is his past history. Does he have a trail of broken romances? Are his relationships with women mainly short-lived? Have all the women in his life failed to come up to his expectations? Does he have a reputation for treating women badly? Don't allow yourself to be sweet-talked into believing that he will be any different with you. If he is evasive or positively secretive about his past life, it would not be foolish to assume that he has something to hide. He knows he has a track record of broken relationships, but he wants to forget that fact. If he is into blaming the other women for why all his relationships went wrong, listen carefully to what he is saying and see if you can detect a pattern. They may have been really sweet girls just like you. So don't be taken in but proceed with your eyes open and let him know that you know it takes two to mess up a relationship.

Golden rule five: Keep your feet on the ground – Don't be tempted to throw caution to the wind

One way to a woman's heart is when the man goes out of his way to make you feel that you are very very special. He indicates in subtle little ways that he has never met anyone quite like you. He finds you so easy to talk to. He feels he can trust you, that he can pour out his heart to you. Don't be taken in if he can do that so early on in a relationship, the no-holds-barred approach. He has probably played this card before with many other women. He has learned that talking about feelings and being emotionally open with a woman is a very seductive tool. He knows it creates intimacy and closeness. He knows that it's a good way to a woman's heart.

SO THE FIVE GOLDEN RULES TO REMEMBER ARE:

- Don't rush into a relationship because he seems wild about you. You set the pace.

- Refuse to jump into bed with him. He won't die of unrequited passion. If he gives up on you because you resisted his sexual advances, he would have done so anyway once you had been to bed with him. Which would have hurt more.
- Listen to your basic instincts – keep in mind the things about him that worry you.
- Look at his track record. If it is one of broken hearts don't assume that he will be different with you.
- Don't convince yourself that because he seems so emotionally open, that he really understands himself or for that matter you. He probably doesn't.

It is essential in a relationship with a CPM that you set the guidelines for the relationship, by following those rules and making sure that you are slowing the pace of the relationship, so that you both take time to really get to know each other.

5

The CPM Syndrome

I am not now the man I was before.
I'm sorry I don't like her any more;
What right have you to ask me to pretend
That all desire for her's not at an end?
The unexpected movements of one's soul
Arise completely out of one's control.

R.D. Laing, 1979

THE CPM'S FIGHT OR FLIGHT BEHAVIOUR

If you have already had your heart broken by a CPM you will know that men who are afraid to love have a similar and identifiable pattern to their behaviour. Some may recognise that they fear commitment but others are oblivious. The majority of men who recognise their reluctance to commit rarely understand why. They move from relationship to relationship causing havoc and heartbreak in their wake.

Understanding a CPM behaviour will give you a clearer picture of quite how a commitment phobic man acts when his alarm bells start to ring. Imagine a cat walking in a sunlit garden feeling happy and content with life, when suddenly he encounters another cat who emerges from the bushes and stands in front of him. Suddenly the cat is on his guard, he senses danger, he is no longer happy and relaxed, and his behaviour changes. He arches his back and hisses at the intruder which gives him time to assess how much danger he is in and what reaction he will take. If the danger feels very acute he may screech and turn tail and run. He might back away slowly and as soon as he feels he is at a safe distance flee, creating as much distance as possible between him and the other cat. If the other cat pursues him he will run all the faster, as pursuit by the other cat increases his sense of danger. He takes flight, and only when he senses that he is out of danger does he stop running. Alternatively the cat's reaction might not be to run away, but to stay put and prepare for a fight, so he advances slowly towards the other cat lashing out at him and so the fighting begins, with squeals and yelps and fur flying in all directions. Eventually the other cat has had enough and runs away or the first cat feels he has gained back his control and he can either leave or continue the fight at some future date. It is natural behaviour when an animal feels threatened. It is basic instinct, an act of survival.

Humans also have a sense of preservation and indulge in flight and fight behaviour when they feel threatened. It is legitimate behaviour when faced with real danger but when it comes to personal relationships it is very destructive. When the commitment phobic man feels threatened by the idea of making a commitment, panic sets in and his anxiety levels go through the ceiling. So he has two options, he either takes flight and finishes the relationship, or he stays and picks fights, which hurt you and undermine the relationship. He is aiming to create distance in the relationship, and he will continue to do this until he feels less threatened and back in control of his fears. But the problem is the person he fights with is you, the one who at the beginning of the relationship he seemed to want so much. So now you end up feeling totally confused about what is going on, and to make things worse the chances are he is likely to be feeling just as confused as you.

The problem is that a man who fears commitment is often very confused about his own feelings and behaviour. He often does not recognise what he is doing or why. He is a man torn in two directions, and he cannot balance the two. Part of him wants the relationship he is involved in, but the other part is scared stiff of getting in too deep or he fears that he has already done just that. So when he feels the fear, panic and anxiety take over he either takes flight or stays and fights. Whichever, it is confusing and distressing because there does not really seem to be any understandable explanation. Alternatively he has taken flight so quickly that he is not around to explain his behaviour, and even if he is he may not understand it himself.

TORN IN TWO DIRECTIONS

The fact that he is torn in two directions comes to a head when you have arrived at a point in the relationship where he seems to want you to make a commitment to him. Where he appears to want you to learn to trust him, to want this relationship as much as he seems to want it. So you now feel committed to him. It is at this point that a man who fears commitment begins to get anxious or even starts to panic. It is when he perceives that the relationship has reached a stage where you expect more of him than he is prepared to give that he starts to panic.

In the beginning all he could think about is how much he wanted you and now what scares him rigid is just how much you may want him. When you really know that you fancy him, that you want the relationship as much as you thought he did, or even that you are in love with him, that is when you start to notice a change in him. As you feel able to trust him and give him what you thought he wanted – your love and commitment – he seems to be changing. He is somehow different, a little more elusive, a little bit critical, a little more distant. It may be slow and subtle changes that you notice, like the way he looks at you, taking longer to return your calls, little things about you that he starts to criticise, or he may change with breathtaking speed. You had enjoyed some terrific dates but he does not call again. The relationship was close and sex had been fantastic but suddenly you find him making excuses not to see you. You are a couple and have been going out together for several months and now he is suddenly saying you are not right for each other. You have been living together and the subject of marriage comes up, so many of your friends have been getting hitched lately you gently hint, only to find he is talking of ending the relationship.

It depends quite how fearful he is feeling, as to whether his fear of commitment may slowly creep up on him, or descend out of a previously clear blue sky like a great big black cloud leaving him running for cover. Which ever it is he starts to panic and to withdraw from you. It understandably leaves you feeling puzzled, confused and hurt. You are caught in a spider's web and you may well be in far too deep to get out of the relationship emotionally unscathed.

Blowing Hot and Cold

If you are a woman involved with a man who blows hot and cold it is also thoroughly confusing. One moment he was pursuing you intently, always wanting to be with you, talking about things you would do together, even telling you he loved you, and the next moment you are encountering this stranger. He is cold or distant, he breaks his promises, he seems to have forgotten how much you had in common, how much you had enjoyed doing things together. You feel there is something wrong with you, that he no longer wants you, that he does not care for you, or that he has fallen out of love with you. You tend to see it as something you have done but the truth is that it is not that you have done anything wrong, but that he has hit his own particular panic button. What has happened is that he has come to a point in the relationship where he realises that the relationship has to move forward as it is at a stage where you are looking for more commitment than he is able to give. Some form of real commitment is expected of him – so he panics and sabotages or ends the relationship. It is his point of no return. He either has to move forward or to take flight. Why it is so confusing is because this usually happens just at a point when things seem to be going so well. Whether it's a perfect first date or a relationship that has been going on for some time. As a commitment phobic man he is suddenly too afraid of where the relationship might be going to let the relationship move forward.

That is the beginning of the end of the relationship. It can vary in how long the end is in coming. It can happen abruptly. He does not call or telephone, he cancels a date, he says you were not meant for each other, it is all over between you. Alternatively the relationship can drag on for weeks, months and sometimes even years while he hovers between his desire for a loving relationship and his terror of it.

A sudden end to the relationship can be devastating but so can the commitment phobic's ability to blow emotionally hot and cold. One moment he wants you, the next moment he has suddenly changed his mind. Just when you are despairing of anything ever being right between you again he starts to woo you all over again. That is because he is torn between wanting you and the relationship but struggling with his deeply held fear of committed relationships.

Once he has established the emotional distance he needs and starts to feel safe again, that is the point at which many commitment phobic men then want the relationship to continue. So he tells you that he is sorry that he has hurt you, he does not understand why he is behaving so badly towards you and seems confused about it. He tells you he is frightened that he might have lost you altogether. He will then beg you to forgive him, or be desperately sorry for how much he has hurt you. All of this is classic behaviour of a CPM.

CONSTRUCTIVE JILTERS

A very typical way for a man who fears commitment to end a relationship is to behave so badly that you get fed up and leave. Such men call it 'constructive jilting'. The idea is to make you think that you are dumping him. It is common for men who can't commit to also have problems when it comes to extracting themselves from relationships. For some it's far easier to just let things linger on. That way it is you who has to make the difficult decisions not him. A constructive jilter would rather slowly kill the relationship by his own bad behaviour. Becoming unreliable, constantly finding fault, dating another woman. To be on the receiving end of this behaviour feels anything but constructive, in fact it is positively destructive.

Sean Langan, a journalist and a self-confessed constructive jilter, admits that this is a cowardly way to go about things. He says, 'I would justify my constructive jilting, as letting the other person down gently. I would tell myself I was just too soft-hearted to give it to them straight.' But he admits, 'You end up breaking women's hearts bit by bit, slowly but surely.' He speaks for many men when he says, 'Actively rejecting someone means having to talk about your inner feelings in an open, direct and honest manner. And that's far too frightening an option: far better let inertia ruin the day.' Then he adds something that women in their relationships with men experience all too often. 'When a problem arises in a relationship men prefer to ignore it. When she wants to talk, he wants to sleep. When she opens up, he closes down. Until she can see no way forward apart from out the front door.'

The constructive jilter is not up front, he does not tell you that the relationship is over. But because he was so lovely at the beginning it can take you quite a long time to realise that he no longer loves you or wants the relationship. This is why you frequently hang in there thinking you can make it all right again.

WHEN HE IS IN TOO DEEP AND THE PANIC SETS IN

Men differ as to when their own particular panic button is pressed. It can happen after the first date, after the first time you have sex or after many months into the relationship. It can be once they have popped the question and been accepted, a few weeks before the wedding, or at the very steps of the altar. For many it is triggered by the marriage itself. It is then the problems really begin. They suddenly feel trapped, they panic at the thought of having committed themselves to one woman for the rest of their lives. So they look for ways of finding fault with their partner to justify their desire to leave the marriage or relationship. If a man is torn between his desire for a relationship and his fear of commitment it is very confusing for the woman in his life. As a woman you have made a commitment to him, you long for closeness and intimacy but the man you love is declaring undying love one minute and the next he seems to be wanting to run in the opposite direction.

In most relationships when couples indulge in flight or fight behaviour it happens when relationships are in trouble, when they are going through difficult times, or on the verge of breakdown. But with the commitment phobic man the flight or fight behaviour hits the relationship just when everything is going wonderfully well. So it feels like a bolt from the blue which leaves you, the recipient, reeling in confusion, hurt and disbelief.

When a man runs away from love

There are identifiable times when a man is most likely to run away from love. If it has happened to you, it probably left you in total confusion, not understanding why now, why when things were going so well, why, when we were feeling so close, why, when we were so good together. And that is just the point when a man runs; it's because he has hit a point in his relationship with you when he feels too close for comfort. He knows the relationship is good but something also tells him that more is going to be expected of him. He is in too deep for his own peace of mind and that is when he starts to think in terms of flight.

AFTER THE FIRST DATE

Some first dates are disappointing, others fun and amusing, some interesting and flirtatious, others you wonder how you are going to make it through the evening and you are looking for the first possible chance to escape, others feel good and you want to see the man again, but occasionally that first date is special, wonderful and fantastic from the moment you meet. The next day you wait for his call, and the next and the next, but it does not come. You tell yourself that he has lost your phone number, been called abroad on business, you did or said something dreadfully wrong or stupid. You can't understand it as you were sure he felt the same way about it as you did.

The problem is that is just what he did feel. The feelings he had were strong, they were different from usual, they were more intense, deeper, he might even have perceived that he was falling in love. He saw that this relationship had real potential, but for the ultra commitment phobic man, that's when he has to get out, because he senses danger ahead.

'I was returning from three months working in North Africa,' said Caroline. 'My skin was glowing from the sun, and I felt happy and relaxed and slightly sleepy from the long journey. The English sun was streaming into the carriage of the train I was travelling home on. After a little while I noticed a man I'd seen on Waterloo station and whom I had thought looked very attractive, was sitting further down the carriage. I felt him looking at me rather a lot, and as the trained pulled into the station, a few stops before mine, he got up and gathered his things. As he passed me he bent over and appeared to pick something up from the floor. He smiled and said to me, "I think you have dropped this." I took it and looked up but he was gone and the train was pulling out of the station.

'It was a little note written on the back of his business card, saying, "Forgive me for the intrusion, but I think you are lovely and I would be delighted if you would consider accepting an invitation to lunch when you are next in town." He suggested that as he did not know my name or telephone number I should telephone him. His card showed he was an army officer at the Ministry of Defence. I had several cousins in the army, so though I had never been out with someone I did not know, I did not think I would be taking too big a risk if I did accept his invitation. Anyway, I tend to be quite a risk-taker. I had gone to Africa on the rather slim chance of a job materialising, and it had worked out marvellously.

'The next two weeks I was incredibly busy with work commitments, but I kept thinking about him and I had liked the look of him very much. I suppose I also thought his approach was rather romantic, so eventually I telephoned. He sounded absolutely delighted, we talked for ages on the phone and we arranged to have lunch the following week. It was a perfect occasion, he was fun, entertaining, we had so much in common, he had lovely eyes, and I adored his voice – something that is very important to me. He told me I was beautiful, and that from the moment he had seen me on the platform he had wanted to meet me.

'We lunched at a little Italian restaurant in Soho, and talked so much that we were the last people to leave. When we parted he looked down at me and gently brushed my hair from my eyes, and said, "You're lovely, quite lovely, I want to see you again. I'll telephone you."

'I thought he might ring that evening or the next day, but nothing. I kept picking the receiver up, to check that the telephone was working. Over the weekend I tried to avoid going out in case he telephoned. A hundred times I nearly called him but just about managed to stop myself. I spent hours going over our conversation trying to think what I might have done or said that had upset him. I could come up with nothing.

'So in the end I called him. I think by then I had convinced myself that he had lost my telephone number. He was friendly but I felt a coolness that had not been there before. He said he was just going into a meeting and that he would call. He never did call. Though it was only one meeting, I think I knew in the end it was something very special for me at least and I thought it was for him. Perhaps he was afraid of commitment. I guess it was better to find out sooner rather than later but it was extremely painful.'

AFTER SEX

A classic time when men love you and leave you is after the first time they had sex with you, as Josh did with the pretty female holidaymakers he seduced with his promises to teach them water-skiing. It happens when the man is more interested in the chase, the excitement of the conquest rather than the relationship that follows. Your initial resistance only encourages him further.

One Don Juan said, 'It's the thrill of the chase. Once I've gone to bed with a woman the lust for blood has been satisfied, so it's all over. I call off the hounds and find another vixen to pursue.' Are these sorts of men insatiable cads or as some psychologists say sad 'Mummy's boys' trying to achieve a magical state of oneness with a perfect someone – the sort of unity they felt with their mothers as babies? Perhaps it is just a state of insatiable lust or simple insecurity. The phraseology used by that particular man is interesting, all the people in his fantasy are animals. Perhaps somewhere deep within him is a recognition that he is a user of women so he has to dehumanise them to justify his callous and juvenile attitude to those foolish enough to be taken in by his charms.

A night of passion does not necessarily mean the beginning of a Beautiful Friendship

Leona was a very good example of this. She had been divorced for three years and had put all her energies into bringing up her three children of six, eight and twelve. She was extremely successful at her job but the combination of being a single parent and a career woman had taken its toll in the relationship stakes, in that she had not had a chance to have any. One day she decided to change this and answered an advertisement in her local paper from a man who had also been so committed to his career that he too was missing out socially and emotionally. She telephoned him and they talked for some time. After one or two conversations on the telephone they arranged to meet for a meal, with all the safety nets in place of meeting for the first time in a public place. She and Alan hit it off straight away. They had lots in common and were both good-looking and successful people. Anyway she ended up in bed with Alan that night and sex was fantastic. In the morning he was very caring and made her a lovely breakfast and he took her to a little country pub for lunch.

The next day she felt as if she was walking on air, but that feeling soon faded, as Alan did not call her that day. In fact he did not call for five long days. Five days may seem no time at all to a man but if a woman has been to bed with a man she likes, it's an eternity. It certainly seemed so to Leona. But eventually Alan did call and they met again the following weekend. This time her children were staying with her mother, so Alan stayed the night with her. As he was leaving the next day he said he was going to be away on business for ten days but would call her on his return.

Leona had gone to bed with him because she really liked him, and she was hoping that it was the start of a new relationship. And maybe it was, but by rushing in too soon, she had no idea what Alan was really wanting from the relationship. And it was far too soon for either of them to have any idea about any long-term plans for the relationship.

By talking through what had happened in counselling she was able to see how she could take back some of the control in the relationship. Alan did call her when he returned from his business trip and Leona was able to see that for the time being she could pull back a little on this relationship in that she could go out with him more, and to bed with him less. That would then enable them to get to know each other better and to be able to both have much more idea of where the relationship was going. She would have a chance to have some of her needs met which she felt had been ignored because of jumping into a sexual relationship too soon.

She wanted Alan to call her if they had made love or spent the night together. She also wanted to know when they parted when they were going to see each other again. That way she was not left in the air waiting for the telephone to ring, or refusing other engagements because she felt she had to keep the time free in case he called her up and wanted to see her. Leona recognised that rushing into a sexual relationship so soon made her feel very vulnerable and put her in the position of feeling close to him but not really knowing enough about him. Was he, for example, away on a business trip or was there another woman in his life?

TOO HOT TO HANDLE – WHEN THE RELATIONSHIP IS GOING REALLY WELL

If a man feels his relationship with you is going really well that is when he most wants it to continue, but for the commitment phobic man it is just the opposite. That is when he starts to have doubts. You are in love, sex is great, you have so much in common. You enjoy doing the same things together, visiting romantic places, dinner for two at your favourite restaurant, long walks on sunny afternoons, dropping into art galleries, or curled up in front of the television watching an old film.

He likes your friends, you like his, he talks about planning a holiday together, it feels as if the relationship has a future. All is looking great and that is the problem. That is the time when a commitment phobic man starts to panic. He too glimpses the future, he sees togetherness raising its head, and what seems lovely to you, feels terrifying to him. He feels trapped and the more he thinks about it, the worse those feelings get. The better you are both getting on the more trapped he feels. He cannot bear it, so he starts to sabotage the relationship or the panic is so intense he takes flight and ends it altogether.

WHEN YOU FALL FROM THEIR PEDESTAL

They have chosen to see you as particularly perfect, they have created out of you an image of how they want you to be. But you are human and like any normal person you have many strengths but also some human frailties. So when you behave in a way that jeopardises their view of you it shakes the pedestal that they have so precariously placed you on. So they start to question their love for you. Could they have been wrong, do you have a fatal flaw that up until now they have failed to notice? It is not you who has changed but their perception of you that has altered. Some commitment phobic men are like fair-weather friends, they are there for the good times, but you don't see them for dust when things get a bit rocky between the two of you. That is because they were in the relationship more for what they could get out of it, rather than what they were prepared to put into it. Once their own needs are not being fully met they are no longer interested. They don't want your low moods, your irritability, your unhappiness. It spoils their fun, it lowers their mood, so why, they say to themselves, should they stick around? These fair-weather lovers are not prepared to put up with the stresses and strains that all relationships encounter from time to time. So if you are upset because you are having a terrible time at work, you have been made redundant, a loved grandparent has died or you are just not very well they are not sympathetic and supportive. Their line of approach is 'snap out of it, don't let your problems spoil our relationship.' You may try to put on a brave face but under such circumstances it is not very easy, so then they blame your behaviour not theirs for the cooling of their ardour and they quit when you needed them most.

WHEN HE IS HAPPY LIVING TOGETHER AND YOU WANT MARRIAGE

Twenty or thirty or more years ago few couples lived together – people just married younger. At the beginning of the sixties only 2% of couples lived together before marriage compared with 70% in the 1990s who choose to co-habit before tying the knot. For many men and for some women as well, there is very often a huge reluctance to move from the more informal arrangement of living together into marriage. That 'rite of passage' seems to send shivers down the spine of men who fear commitment.

The reasons can usually be traced back to the man's childhood. Perhaps he had parents who were unreliable and unloving, or their marriage broke up very painfully and acrimoniously. So he is mistrustful of close intimate relationships, or feels the very act of getting married consigns an otherwise good relationship to the divorce courts. Sometimes it's because previous relationships or marriages have gone badly wrong, so there is a reluctance to try again. Sometimes it's a combination of some or all these possibilities. His ambivalence about marriage makes him reluctant to fully commit himself as deep down he fears rejection or abandonment.

Many couples go into live-in relationships without a clear idea of what they want from the future of that relationship. You meet and fall in love, you become an item. You see a lot of each other, you spend as much time as possible with each other, you develop ideas and interests and lifestyles and friends in common so what could be more natural than to live together? Belinda a journalist on a women's magazine said,

'Ian and I were in love, we wanted to be together, we both had separate flats on either side of the town. I'd spend half my week at his flat, and the rest of the time we would spend hours travelling to see each other. It just seemed stupid to continue to run two homes. I suppose it started when I began to leave some of my things at his flat so that if I did stay the night I had some things there for when I went to work in the morning.

'So one day after a particularly good weekend together I suggested that we should move in together. I think Ian was a little surprised but he agreed and said we could try it, so a week later I moved in. We have been together four years now, and we are very happy. I have started to drop a few hints that I would like us to marry, but so far they have fallen on stony ground. Whenever I mention the subject he quite deliberately, seemingly effortlessly steers the conversation round to some other topic. I don't want to talk him into marriage, or even force his hand. I suppose what I want is for him to want to ask me to marry him, and so far I have seen no sign of that. The problem is the more I think about it, the more I want marriage, and the more insecure I am starting to feel about our relationship. I suppose my bottom line is, that I feel if he really loved me, he would feel like I do but he seems happy with how things are.'

Belinda is very typical of many couples who have decided to live together without any promises about the future. They did not talk about whether it was life-long commitment, but in fact they saw it as something that just felt right for them at the time. The problem for Belinda was that whereas to start with she was happy to live together she eventually changed to wanting marriage.

Many couples who choose to live together both agree that

they are totally committed to each other, saying they do not need marriage, it is after all no more than just a piece of paper, only to find that several years down the line one of them has changed *her* mind. Later on in this book I will be looking further at why it is so difficult for some men to make the transition from a live-in relationship to marriage.

AFTER YOU HAVE ACCEPTED HIS PROPOSAL OF MARRIAGE

This is a classic time for the commitment phobic man to panic. He has been all right up till now. He is in love, the relationship is going well, he has met your family and you his. So he has decided to make it permanent. But that ring on your finger reminds him of the sound of wedding bells, and suddenly it all seems so final, and for him wedding bells turn to alarm bells. It's not so easy for him to end the relationship now that it has been formalised by an engagement.

Because he does not feel able to come out into the open and face you with his fears he starts to sabotage the relationship. It is at this point he starts to find fault with you, the little criticisms creep into your relationship, the arguments begin. You don't know what is happening, or you start to think there is something wrong with you. You speculate maybe he has worries about his work or finances that he is not sharing with you. You are right, he does have a major worry: your forthcoming marriage. His dilemma is he does not know how to tell you, but neither does he know how to continue with the engagement. The panic in him is rising, and he does not know what to do. But what he does know is that he is finding it increasingly difficult to go through with it. So he either breaks of the engagement or behaves in such a difficult and diabolical way, that eventually you have had enough and you finish with him.

Anna's shattered dreams

Anna was the younger of two sisters, lively, bright and very pretty. She had always had lots of boyfriends much to the envy of her older sister. When she was twenty-nine she met and fell in love with Richard, an intelligent, charming and successful businessman ten years older than she. Anna said, 'When I first met Richard I was immediately attracted. He was very confident, outward-going, and amusing. He spoke several languages, he loved travelling just as I did and he had been to amazingly interesting places.

'His mother had died when he was twelve, his father remarried an Italian woman within a year of his mother's death and he went to live in Italy with them. He never really got on with his stepmother; she was a lot younger than his father, and not very interested in him, so a lot of the time he was looked after by his stepmother's older brother and sisters who were married with children of their own. After university in Italy he returned to England, and got a job in the sales force in an international computer company. He now saw little of his father.

'It was a fairly whirlwind romance. We met in the January and six weeks later he had proposed to me. My parents wanted us to wait, but I just knew that Richard was the man I wanted to marry. I had lots of boyfriends, but I had never felt like this before, so what was the point of waiting? We decided on a June wedding, I had always dreamed of being a June bride, because my parents' garden in June is full of the most wonderful roses, tumbling from every wall and arch, it is incredibly romantic.

'It was to be a big affair. My parents had a lovely house in a pretty village near Bath with a little church just across the village green. I had always wanted a country wedding with a marquee in the garden. My sister had a London wedding and I wanted mine to be completely different. At the beginning of May Richard told me that his father had become seriously ill and that he must fly to Italy to see him. He said he was not close to him, but he would feel dreadful if anything happened to him and he had not seen him. I suggested that we should go over together, after all I had not met any of his family. But he said that this time he thought it was better to go alone. After he had been in Italy a few days, he rang me and told me his father was very ill and it was feared he might not last more than a couple of months. He said would I postpone our wedding plans as it would be awful if his father died just as we were getting married. It would spoil the whole thing. I was terribly disappointed, but quite understood how he felt. It was not easy cancelling everything as the plans were well on the way. We had booked the church, the marquee and caterers, but at least the invitations had not gone out. Richard spent a month in Italy and then returned to England because of his work. By mid-June his father much to all the family's surprise was recovering, and it seemed any immediate danger was past. That was great news so I suggested that if everything could be rearranged we could be married at the end of September. Richard agreed and the wedding was arranged for the last Saturday in September.

'So everything was rearranged – the church, the marquee, the caterers, and the flowers. I might not be able to have the garden full of roses but at least the marquee would be there. My mother and I had a fantastic time looking for wedding dresses, the invitations went out, it was all very exciting, Richard was very loving, and seemed happy with all the plans. On the Wednesday before the wedding the men came to put the marquee up. It was a lovely warm, late summer's day, and the forecast was good for that Saturday. The next day all the flowers arrived, cream and white and palest yellow. It looked like the Chelsea Flower Show, flowers everywhere. Some friends from the village had offered to help my mother and sister and me decorate the church and the marquee.

'That evening my mother and sister and her husband and I where sitting exhausted but happy in the marquee talking about the wedding and who was coming. My father who had just arrived home from work came into the garden and said there was a telephone call for me. I asked who it was. He said it was about the wedding but she had not given her name. I walked into the house and picked up the telephone. A voice I did not recognise said, "Is that Anna?" I said, "Yes, Anna speaking. Who is that?" The voice said "I'm Sarah, Sarah H— I'm Richard's wife." At first I did not understand, stupidly I said Richard who? She repeated her name and said, "I'm his wife, the wife of the man you are going to marry on Saturday."' Anna said with tears rolling down her cheeks, 'That was three months ago, I don't think I will ever forget that telephone call, I was absolutely shattered. I couldn't go back out into the marquee, I felt dizzy and sick – I just sat by the telephone shaking. I don't know how long I sat there, but my sister came in looking for me. I told her about the telephone call. I think at that moment I thought it was some awful joke. I could not believe it was true.

'But it was true; somehow I managed to telephone Richard at his flat. When I told him what had happened he was silent. I remember screaming down the phone, is it true, is it true? Then he said, "I'm terribly sorry darling, but yes, it is true. I had wanted to tell you, but everything was going along so fast it never seemed the right time." He said, "I will make it up to you, I really will, please forgive me darling." "But why?" I asked him, "why didn't you tell me that you were still married?" He said he would come down and explain everything.'

When he arrived later that evening Richard faced a hostile reception committee with one furious father, an outraged future brother-in-law and three distraught women. Richard admitted that he had been married briefly but that he was getting a divorce but it had taken longer than he had anticipated. He had thought that by September he would definitely have his decree absolute. He begged Anna to forgive him, he told her he still loved her, and he wanted the relationship to continue.

Anna's father felt so angry with Richard for what he had done to his daughter, that all he wanted to do was kill him. He was also left with a hefty bill to pay for a wedding that had to be cancelled at the eleventh hour. Her mother and sister desperately tried to persuade Anna to have nothing more to do with Richard, but Anna said she still loved him and wanted to give him another chance, which she did.

Anna's father was not prepared to let things rest. What Richard had done to his younger daughter made him suspicious and he discreetly called in a private detective and had him investigated. So it was several weeks later that she realised that Richard had no intention of committing to her and it seemed never had. The detective produced evidence that revealed that for the last six months Richard had also been having an affair with another woman and the affair was still continuing.

To use an old-fashioned expression Richard was an out and out cad and also a liar, and he was certainly not into commitment. He had been separated from his first wife for many years, the divorce had been grinding interminably on and it had suited Richard this way. He was enormously attracted to Anna when they first met and he was aware that Anna had several other men after her, and he had wanted to scare off the competition, so he had asked her to marry him. The visit to his father had been because the divorce was still not finalised and he wanted to delay the wedding. He was also getting cold feet and during his month in Italy with his father's family he had started another affair with the wife of one of his old school friends. He still loved Anna and did not want to lose her, so he had let the plans for the wedding continue. Even after the discovery of his affair he was still begging Anna to give him one more chance. But this time she refused.

Anna had already given him more chances than she should have done, but when you are in love with someone you want to believe in them and what they tell you. Even at the very end Richard was still trying to convince her that he loved her, and that he regretted how he had behaved, and that he would never hurt her again. The chances of a transformed Richard would have been very remote and Anna was right to have the courage to recognise that it was better to end the relationship rather than risk being hurt yet again.

Standing back from that relationship it is perhaps easy to say of course she did the only right and sensible thing, but when you are in the midst of it, things are rarely quite so black and white.

If you are with a man who has frequently hurt you by his cruel or unpredictable behaviour it can be helpful to take a step back and view what is going on as if you are an observer, rather than a participant. If all your antennae say you would have to be mad to continue with this man, that might be the time to take your own good advice.

WHEN HE LEAVES YOU AT THE ALTAR

To the onlooker it seems inexplicable that any prospective bridegroom can allow the wedding day to arrive and to leave the woman he loves standing at the altar. But it is often not as simple as that. Frequently the man involved is gripped by panic or confused about his own feelings. He falls into the commitment phobic's dilemma of feeling pulled in two directions. He feels he loves the woman he is about to marry but another part of him is panicking about the forthcoming commitment of marriage. He is torn between wanting to be with the woman he loves and yet at the same time he is terrified at the thought that marriage means forsaking all others to spend the rest of his life with just one woman. To the man who fears commitment the idea of 'for ever' is indeed a long long time.

As the wedding draws nearer the panic increases and so does the inability to break off the engagement. The day is set, the presents are arriving, the speeches are prepared, you have chosen your dress and your father has paid for the reception. The man who can't tell his bride what is going on inside him will often withdraw emotionally, perhaps seem distant and even unapproachable, but it may just be put down to pre-wedding nerves, that is until the big day dawns and he fails to turn up at the church or register office leaving his bride alone in front of all her family and friends. To be left waiting at the church is perhaps the biggest humiliation of all.

It was 1997 and it was to be one of New York's society weddings of the year and no expense had been spared. Nicole Contos, a beautiful American girl whose wealthy father had splashed out £42,000 on the wedding, was to marry London lawyer Tasos Michael. She wore a cream Victorian designer silk dress and her bouquet was made up of roses and peonies specially flown in from New Zealand. Her guests had come from as far afield as Greece, Israel, Japan, and London. She stood with her four bridesmaids waiting in the church, but there was just one thing missing – the bridegroom.

Eventually the best man showed up to deliver the humiliating news that Tasos Michael was not coming. Nicole's brother George shaking with fury stood in the pulpit and said, 'For reasons I cannot explain, my sister's wedding cannot take place.'

Most brides given these circumstances would have been so distraught that they would have collapsed in tears, or considered sending a member of their family to dispatch the offending bridegroom into another world. But Nicole insisted that the reception should go ahead, as her friends had flown in from all over the world. As she walked into the Grand Salon of the sumptuous hotel where the reception was being held, the band played 'I Will Survive'.

Nicole said, 'I could have sat in my room and cried all day, or I could be with my guests who had come so far to be with us.'

Before the wedding there had been signs of Tasos's nervousness. A few hours earlier he had spoken to Nicole and said, 'I love you, but my feet feel like jelly.' That is how hundreds of bridegrooms feel, particularly if the wedding is a very high-powered affair. But Tasos gave no real indication that he was not going to turn up. And as the picture slowly unfolded it seemed that this reluctant bridegroom was suffering from more than just pre-wedding nerves.

After the wedding reception was over Nicole said, 'I love him and I know he loves me. I just want an explanation. I am supposed to be on a plane right now flying to a honeymoon in Tahiti.'

Her brother's fiancée, who was perhaps seeing things rather more clearly than Nicole, said, 'Frankly, I think Nicole is better off without him. I always had my suspicions about him. He was always very polite, but very sharp. Almost too sharp and a bit shifty. He hasn't bothered to call her.' She also added the interesting piece of information and part of the clue to Michael's failure to show up, that he had twice broken off previous engagements.

Tasos comes from a family who appear to have difficulty talking through problems. Unresolved family rows have meant a rift in his family life, resulting in the fact that Tasos only remains on good terms with his father. His mother found out about the wedding from a friend she met on a bus. So 'taking flight' is an established pattern for him when feelings or situations become difficult or uncomfortable. It seems it is something that Tasos has learnt from his previous experience.

If Tasos had really loved Nicole but was just suffering from pre-wedding nerves, he would have been able to tell her quite how deep these fears were before the big day, or before she left for the church. If he was so panicked that at the last moment he had been unable to go through with it, the first thing he would have wanted to do would have been to talk to her himself. To try and explain why he had backed out so dramatically and so humiliatingly, leaving her at the altar in front of her family and hundreds of friends.

What did Tasos do? He flew to the honeymoon island of Tahiti on his own. The reason he gave was that he had paid for the honeymoon and he saw no reason why he should abandon it. This is not the behaviour of a grief-stricken man, or one weighed down by guilt. It is not the behaviour of a man who regretted what he had done or who had any understanding of how much he had hurt the girl who loved him and who had promised to be his wife.

He said, 'I have no regrets.' Then he said, as if it made it all right, 'I'm not here with anyone else. I am not partying with dolly birds.' Then he added the most revealing comment of all: 'I'm not going to phone Nicole, not yet anyway. I am going to leave it a few days. But she can phone me if she wants. She knows where I am now.'

For a man to behave like that, then humiliate his bride even further, by saying she should be the first one to pick up the telephone, not only shows what an arrogant and insensitive man he is but also that he is really only into his own needs, with those of his bride coming way down the list.

The American papers called him the 'Gutless Groom'. That may be so, but it is possible to have a deep fear of commitment without behaving like a total cad to the woman who just a few hours earlier you had professed to love. The least he could have done was to have telephoned Nicole, or asked to meet her, so he could explain why he had done what he had. He showed that he had little insight into how his behaviour affected others, and was reluctant to admit how badly he had behaved.

The result was that Nicole was left in the air, with no explanation, and uncertain about the future. Her family wanted her to have nothing more to do with him. But she said, 'I really believe that it was last-minute panic. You can't love somebody for so long and then totally turn off your emotions.' Nicola undoubtedly did love Tasos, and she could not just turn off her emotions. Sadly his feelings were rooted in rather thinner soil. Tasos was indeed a man who was afraid to love.

Nicole for her part was perhaps a woman who loved too much and was having difficulty accepting the fact that if she continued her relationship with Tasos she would probably be hurt again and again. She said, displaying all her vulnerability, 'He could have left my ticket, so I could join him in Tahiti.' Her mother's response to this was one of indignation: 'He left you at the altar and you want to be with him in Tahiti. What are you thinking of?' Sensible advice, but she was perhaps ignoring the fact that Nicole was desperately missing the man she loved, and that she was prepared to forgive him and rush into his arms and his bed in Tahiti. I hope time has allowed Nicole to see that if she and Tasos got back together again he would be likely to spend the rest of his life breaking her heart.

Some men never make it to the church because they are no longer in love, and as the plans for the wedding intensify they feel more and more unable to confront their fiancée with the reality of their feelings. Some men do have last-minute nerves, and never make it to the church, but because they love the woman they want to be their wife, they regret what they have done. They know they have behaved cruelly and they want to make amends. They are in touch with the amount of hurt they have inflicted. If you as a woman have been in that position yourself you may be able to forgive the man for abandoning you at the church, if you both love each other, and he is truly sorry. You also both need to understand his reasons for not turning up for the wedding. But it does take time to rebuild trust. It often also means ditching your dreams of a big white wedding for a much smaller and more low-key affair.

I hope Nicole has the sense not to trust Tasos again. Not because Tasos left her waiting at the church, but because he behaved so badly and so hurtfully towards her afterwards. His fear of commitment blinded him to quite how much he had hurt her, and he showed little remorse for what he had done. He was not even prepared to face the music and talk but instead chose to holiday alone in what would have been their honeymoon hotel. His fear of commitment was so acute that the chances are if they did get back together again, he would panic and take flight all over again.

WHEN IT'S THE SECOND TIME AROUND

A man whose marriage has ended extremely painfully frequently finds it difficult to commit to new relationships. This can be because he was so hurt by the break-up of his previous marriage, perhaps because his wife walked out or left him for another man. Sometimes it is because the divorce has been so acrimonious that the thought of another marriage ending in the same way makes him fight shy of the whole idea of taking a chance on love. Perhaps the divorce has been financially disastrous and in his opinion has cost him an arm and a leg, so he does not want to take that risk again. His reasons are at times buried more deeply, for example when he is still in some way emotionally involved with his previous wife. Perhaps because he still loves her, and secretly hopes they may get back together again; or because she uses the children as emotional blackmail, and makes him feel that if he gets involved with someone else she will make it very difficult for him to see his own children. Whatever the reason his trust in women has been so damaged that he has difficulty in committing a second time around.

Jacky was thirty-two when she first met Paul and they both worked for the same large organisation. She said, 'There was an instant sexual attraction but I thought he must be married as he was in his mid-forties, but in fact he was divorced, with four children, from mid-teens to early twenties. I would not have gone out with him if he had been married, I feel very strongly about that sort of thing.

'He seemed really keen on me and asked me out for a drink. Though I agreed, I was very cautious in my response, whereas he made all the running. Even though we were not going out as boyfriend and girlfriend he was constantly suggesting that we meet up and go away for weekends. I thought "sod that". No, I want a proper relationship. I wanted to meet his family, parents, brother and sisters. So we sort of went out with each other for about six months before I finally agreed to go away with him for the weekend.

'Whenever we met he was very flirtatious and he constantly talked about sex and how attractive he found me, but in fact he was rather a disappointment in bed. My previous boyfriends had all been good at sex but with Paul it was all over too quickly. On reflection I think he was rather a selfish lover. But by then I was in love with him so I thought it would get better.

'After that first weekend we saw a lot of each other. He made me feel very attractive and he kept hinting about things like a future together and marriage. He once said "I'd love it if one leap year a woman asked me to marry her." He wanted me to get very involved with his life, he was always inviting me to stay with him and the kids at weekends. He took me shopping when he wanted to buy something for the house, to get my approval. He was always telephoning me and worrying that I would go off with other guys. If we had a row he would be the one to chase me and make it up.

'Then after a few months things started to change, his ex-wife didn't like him seeing so much of me. I thought that was very unreasonable, what was it to do with her? After all, they had been divorced five years. But he did not see it that way, he started to make excuses for her and kept defending her and saying she needed his support, because she was having a difficult time with her current partner. Then he started going round to see her, and was less keen for me to go and stay at weekends.

'Then one day she rang him and asked him to go round urgently; when he got there he discovered she had taken an overdose. Apparently this was not the first time, she had made another attempt two years earlier. There is a history of it in the family: both her brothers had committed suicide. She had left Paul for this other man, and now that relationship was breaking up. He often said to me, "Don't ever leave me without telling me why you're going." Because that is what she did. So I thought he really cared for me.

'Then he told me that he might have his ex-wife back to live with him for a while, as she was so distressed over the breakdown of her five-year relationship. I knew she was only using him, because she was feeling insecure, she knew Paul was going to rescue her, but he couldn't see that.

'I was absolutely devastated. I've got this gut feeling that he wasn't over her. It was frightening for up until then I was so sure he was getting near to asking me to marry him. I panicked. I started really showing him how much I loved him. I kept buying him presents, I gave him cards saying 'I love you'. I wrote him a letter saying I understood that he had to look after his ex-wife, and that I was 50% to blame for being so unreasonable about it. I became a woman who loved too much. He started to think he was James Bond by the time I finished, he really fancied himself.'

What CPMs hate most is a woman who pursues them ardently, that is the role they want to play – if anyone is going to do the chasing they want it to be them. A needy woman or a woman who makes them feel she can't live without them, makes them panic and turn tail and run in the opposite direction. The more Paul did this the more needy and desperate Jacky became, and the more he withdrew. Jacky thought the way to keep Paul was to show him how much she loved him, but to him it felt as if she was smothering him with her love, so he started to reject her.

Jacky said. 'He started to get nasty, always finding fault with me. The more I loved him the more he ran. I would try to telephone him but he had taken the telephone off the hook. He began going to parties on his own. He was constantly telephoning his ex-wife, that really annoyed me; then we stopped making love. I wondered if he was having an affair.

'We had a holiday planned so we went away but things did not improve and when we came back, I told him our relationship was over, I could not take any more. In the end he didn't move his ex-wife into his house, but he blamed me for that.

'I knew what would happen – as soon as I left the scene his wife backed off. He didn't call for two months and then, just as I was getting used to the fact that the relationship was over, we saw each other and it started up again, but it was ripping me apart.

'This time he wouldn't let me go to his house. He kept saying, "We have to be careful, I don't want my ex-wife to find out I'm seeing you." So again the commitment was more to his wife than to me. After we had been back together a few months he told me that he had booked a holiday to go away with his parents and children and I was not included. That was it, that finished it for me. I was so hurt and angry I tore some of the cards advertising the services of prostitutes out of the London phone boxes and sent them to him. I said, "If that's what you want, here it is." I seem to have a history of getting involved with men who can't commit.

'I know what it's like to be rejected. My mother had an affair with a married man. When she got pregnant my father said he did not want me, he said he would leave his marriage and marry my mother if she had me adopted. So two weeks after I was born I was given up for adoption. I was sent to a foster home and then a children's home. I was there until I was fifteen months when I was adopted by my new parents. I have never had any contact with my natural parents. In all my adult relationships I have always been very careful never to get involved with a married man.

'Part of me is scared of commitment. The other part is saying "love me, love me." These two huge emotions are in conflict. I have very low self-esteem. My adoptive parents did love me but couldn't show that much emotion. My mum was brought up in a children's home and there was no cuddling. So second best is what I know best. I think if I'd been their natural child it might have been better.'

What was so devastating for Jacky was that when Paul allowed his first wife to come back on the scene, Jacky once more felt displaced, that she was second best. This was a position she knew all too well. The pain of possibly losing him to another woman was intense, because it mingled with all that unresolved rejection that she had experienced as a child. Her reaction was to shower Paul with love in the hope that he would then love her in return, and that she would not be playing second fiddle to his ex-wife.

If she had been able to stand back a little, and see that even though his ex was probably using emotional blackmail to manipulate Paul, he needed to handle things his way. His wife and mother of his four children had once before attempted suicide, and it was a family pattern as her two brothers had ended their lives that way.

Paul could not cope with how Jacky appeared to him: here was another needy, over-dependent woman. For Jacky her fear of loving and then losing the person she loved was so unresolved that when she experienced this happening in her adult life she was once more the abandoned and rejected baby. A baby whose mother had given her up for adoption because her father did not want her. The price her mother had to pay for the man she loved leaving his wife and marrying her was to give up their child. She had a choice and she chose Jacky's father and sacrificed her baby daughter, so again Jacky was treated as second best.

By chance three years after her affair ended Jacky met Paul again. He invited her for a drink, he said he would like to see her again and suggested that they see each other now and again and go away for the occasional weekend.

Jacky said, 'I loved Paul and I would have married him tomorrow if he had sorted himself out, but I was just not prepared to be someone on the sidelines.'

Jacky realised that the relationship that Paul was offering her was one where she would only get hurt all over again. It is easy when you are not involved, to stand on the outside and see how foolish it would have been for Jacky to continue her relationship with Paul. But when you are in love as she was, it is easy to keep hoping that next time around they will be different. It is possible to change if that is what he wants, but if he shows no sign of this then it is best to do what Jacky did which is to recognise this truth and have the courage to say 'no'.

BREAKING UP IS HARD TO DO

If you're in a relationship that's long past its sell-by date what stops you bringing it to an end?

The fact is that change is never easy and breaking up a relationship, even a not very satisfactory one, is extremely painful. Sometimes love has turned into habit, it might not be a very good habit but it is one you know and are comfortable with. So you let things grind along when it would have been better to recognise the state of the relationship sooner. It is sometimes necessary to admit to yourself you have done your best and that this relationship is clearly going nowhere.

I know from the people I see in counselling and from the many letters I receive that there are great numbers of women who stay in unhappy relationships long after love has died. This is not only because of the potential pain of breaking up and starting again, but because there is a real fear of never meeting a man to spend the rest of your life with. So you cling on to the old and familiar, rather than take chances out there in the big wide world of uncertainty.

THE NON-COMMITMENT ROLLERCOASTER

When an important relationship has just ended, you are particularly vulnerable and that is when you are most likely to make mistakes and jump from the frying pan into the fire. When the initial feelings of shock begin to diminish you are desperate to fill the gap that the loss of the person has left in your life. Someone new appears on the scene who shows an interest in you, and that feels so good that without much hesitation you rush headlong into a new relationship, with little idea if he is the sort of person who would really suit you, because you are not making sensible choices, but trying to ease the pain of a broken romance. So there you are, vulnerable and unprotected to be plucked from your loneliness by someone attractive who is showing an interest in you. So you turn to him emotionally needy and raw from the breakdown of the previous relationship, endlessly talking about the person you have loved. Spilling out all your pent-up frustrations about your broken love affair. Because you are so needy it is all too easy not to see the warning signs of disaster which in other more sober times you would be much more aware of.

HOW THE CPM IS DIFFERENT FROM OTHER MEN

Whereas most men tend to end a relationship because things are going badly, the pattern with a CPM is different from Mr Average. It is the very fact that things are going so well that leads him to sabotage or end the relationship. As you have seen in this chapter that can be after an incredibly wonderful first date, a night of fantastic sex, at the altar or once you have said 'I do'. It is when the CPM sees the relationship has reached a stage where you are expecting more from him than he feels able to give and so he takes flight.

What you need to keep reminding yourself is that it is not something you have done or said that is wrong, it is the fact that the relationship was so right that it has struck fear into the heart of the CPM.

'LET'S CALL THE WHOLE THING OFF'

To be left when the relationship is going so well leaves you feeling 'what has gone wrong, what have I done that he didn't like, have I said something wrong?' and round and round your head these thoughts go trying to make sense of the nonsensical. Many CPMs do not understand their own behaviour because they have never stopped long enough to analyse what they are doing in their relationships with women. He does not want to see why when he moves on to the next relationship that in turn also comes to grief, probably in the same old way.

DON'T LET HIM BLAME YOU

Remember, a man who is afraid to love frequently does not want to look at the real reasons why his relationships are continually breaking down. He needs to justify to himself and to you the reasons why the relationship has broken down. So rather than blame himself he blames you. He may start to find fault with you. If he can convince himself that it is something that you have done wrong, it makes it easier for him to create a distance between the two of you, or get out of a relationship altogether. That way he has rationalised his behaviour at least to himself, if not to you.

Because a man is afraid to love it does not mean he does not want to love, in fact quite the opposite. His problem is that fear is a major element in all his relationships with women. Fear of rejection, fear of being trapped, fear of dependence, fear of having to grow up, fear of being smothered, fear of being abandoned and fear of women having power over him. All these hidden fears make him ambivalent in his feelings towards women. Part of him wanting women to love him and the other part not being able to trust them enough not to hurt him. His defence against this anxiety is to seduce a woman into loving him, and to make you feel that you are loved in return. But underneath all that seduction, the showering of affection, making you feel so special, there is part of him that cannot allow you to get really close to him.

When he sees you responding as a woman in love he panics as he does not know if he can handle how vulnerable this makes him feel. He has got what he wants, the love of the woman he thinks he loves, and now you love him he is no longer sure that is what he wants. The reason is because by continuing to love you in return, he has to move forward into a deeper relationship, one where he is emotionally committed and that is scary.

If he is a worst-case CPM he may find it almost impossible to overcome his fears. But for many CPMs when he really falls in love and he doesn't want to lose you, that is the time when he is the most motivated to try and overcome his fears. That way he too can have a loving and committed relationship.

6

How to handle a CPM

Lady, Lady, should you meet
One whose ways are all discreet,
One who murmurs that his wife
Is the lodestar of his life,
One who keeps assuring you
That he never was untrue,
Never loved another one,
Lady, Lady, better run!

'Social Note', *Dorothy Parker* (1893–1967)

DON'T GO BREAKING MY HEART

If you want to make your man commit, it is essential to know what it is he is afraid of – something which many CPMs don't know themselves. The constant dilemma of wanting to love and yet being afraid to love pervades all a CPM's thinking and behaviour. If he really allows himself to fall deeply in love, how can he be sure that he will be loved equally in return? How can he be sure that the woman he loves won't love him but then leave him? To fall in love only to find that the woman he loves might not continue to feel the same way about him feels so scary and is laden with such potential pain that rather than risk rejection, he feels the only way to protect himself from hurt is to take control and do the rejecting before you have a chance to reject him. Alternatively he never gets too emotionally involved so that he is able to terminate the relationship before he is in too deep. He cannot let himself fall in love as he can't allow himself to trust a woman. Trust is the cornerstone of loving relationships and if he can't trust a woman he can't fully love her either.

What most women are looking for when they fall in love with a man is emotional commitment – the very thing commitment phobic men find so hard to give. The problem is that the majority of these men are very good at disguising this very important fact. The excitement of the chase is an integral part of his relationship with you, whether that chase is very short-lived or takes place over several months or more. When he first has a woman in his sights whom he desires, his passion is running high, and so is his determination to capture you. So it is important that he is good at what he does, otherwise he would not be successful, and failure is not on his agenda. So the phobic man knows what a woman wants to hear, he understands how you want him to behave, and he is good at convincing you that here at last is a man who really does understand you.

A WOLF IN SHEEP'S CLOTHING

It may not be quite as calculating as it seems, because at this stage in the relationship he will be feeling very powerfully attracted to you, so he aims to please. He does think you are special and he wants you to think the same way about him. The confusion is that he is thinking about the way he feels now, and that may mean he is thinking no further than tomorrow morning. He is not really concerned about the long-term effects of his behaviour, just having his needs met now. But because he has come on so strongly or because he has kept up his pursuit so relentlessly, you interpret his behaviour by thinking he has something more permanent in mind.

It is understandable that you think this, because normally if a man behaved in such a way he would want a committed relationship. The difference is he wouldn't behave like this on the first date or two, but only when you knew each other better and when he had a longer-term relationship in mind. But with the phobic type this is not the case at all.

He is a wolf in sheep's clothing and it is easy to be taken in. He is very believable because he wants to win you over so much that he too believes in what he says. He pulls out all the stops in his pursuit, he tries to make everything seem wonderfully romantic. He seems at ease talking about his feelings and seems interested in yours. He knows how to talk to you as a woman, to make you feel relaxed, to make you feel that you are very special to him, because he wants you to see him as special as well.

Such a man will invariably be sexually very seductive because he knows that if you agree to go to bed with him, it is because you really like him and find him very attractive or even irresistible, and that is how he wants you to feel about him at this stage in his relationship with you.

THE DILEMMA OF THE CPM

It is important to keep reminding yourself that the constant dilemma for a CPM is that part of him longs for a loving relationship and the other part is scared stiff of the idea, so the two fears are locked in mortal combat. The reasons why CPMs shy away from commitment, why they run away from love can, I believe, be divided into three different categories.

1. The Tender Trap – The fear of being trapped

This is where the CPM has a fear of the 'forever word'. Instead of the man seeing a committed relationship with a woman he loves as a deeply rewarding experience, he fears that marriage or commitment to one woman will mean the end of his individual freedom, a sacrificing of his personal space. The 'fear of feeling trapped' in a relationship comes very high up the list of reasons why he can't commit; he sees commitment as a dark tunnel from which there is no escape. He is like the opposite to an agoraphobic who fears open spaces. For the CPM the fear is that he will be trapped for ever behind closed doors with one woman from whom there is no escape. Both fears are equally irrational in their way.

Hot on the heels of a man's fear of rejection is the fear

of being hurt a second time around. The once bitten twice shy feeling abounds among CPMs. He may have love and lost and the experience was so painful he does not want to take that risk again. All of these fears are intermingled but they have a very powerful influence on how a man who fears commitment behaves.

2. The Peter Pan Syndrome

This type of CPM is the little boy who never really grows up. The man who lacks maturity, the selfish and narcissistic man who has difficulty in putting the needs of his partner before his own. He frequently has a problem with responsibility, often running away from it altogether or, if he does marry, abdicating almost all of it on to his wife. He panics at the idea of children, for being a father is a responsible task. He also fears that sharing you with a child, or children would mean you have less time for him, so how then would he get his needs met?

3. The Oedipal Complex

This is where the man has so many unresolved issues where his mother is concerned that he is emotionally damaged or restricted when it comes to loving another woman. Maybe because he has been so hurt and undermined by her as a child, that he finds a struggle to trust women in his adult relationships. It could be that he finds it difficult to cut the apron stings and commit himself to another woman. For the married CPM it is often a case of 'and mother came too'. Not physically, though it can feel like it if she is constantly dropping round, or forever on the end of the telephone. It is the emotional hold she still has, where what she says goes, often at the expense of you and the relationship.

Though fear is the central theme in all three of these categories it is uppermost in the first.

A CPM AND HIS FEARS

The fear of being trapped – the fear of getting hurt – the fear of rejection. All are reasons 'why a man is afraid to love'.

FEAR OF FEELING TRAPPED – SEAN'S STORY

Sean came from a family who were dedicated to non-commitment. An attractive man of thirty with a gentle manner, a quick sense of humour and an easy ability to get on with women, his two elder brothers who are in their thirties are also not married, though they too have had plenty of girlfriends. Sean said, 'Once one of my brothers nearly got hitched but my other brother and I managed to rescue him.' He also has two sisters who are about ten years younger than him. When Mary the youngest one, who is eighteen, finished with a first boyfriend Sean said, 'She dumped him, then she telephoned me and said "I am now a paid-up member of the Leonard family."

'Most of my relationships last several months but rarely more. I also occasionally enjoy some one-night stands.

At the beginning of the relationship it's undoubtedly the challenge of the chase that first attracts me. It is important that I find them intellectually stimulating, but they also have to be "well packaged", otherwise I won't be interested. As well as a good sexual relationship I like to be friends. I like a woman I can talk to. That is very important to me. I am still friendly with many of my ex-girlfriends.

'The beginning of a relationship with a girl is wonderful. I usually feel I'm in love, I'm very romantic. I woo her with red roses, flowers, little presents. I take her out, wine her and dine her, and I'm always interested in what she wants to talk about. I like women and I do feel very at ease with them. I particularly like it if to begin with a woman does not respond too easily to my advances. I do tell her I love her because at the time that is how I feel, though perhaps nowadays I use the "L" word a little less frequently.

'If she is happy with the relationship as it is that is fine, but if she starts to respond just a little too much in the love stakes, then I get worried. If I feel the girl starts talking in terms of commitment, or if she is looking for more than I am prepared to give, the warning signs go up. Though I may not say anything, I know that the time has come for me to end the relationship. I think that is why many of them end after about four months.

'I have had a great number of relationships with girls of many nationalities, American, German Swedish and Japanese,' said Sean smiling. 'I find them very interesting and I do speak more than one language but there's the added advantage that after a few months foreign girls are usually returning to their own country because their visa has run out.

'I have recently split up with a girl I had been going out

with for four months. She was very pretty, and I liked her very much. She had been working abroad and we arranged to meet up and go on holiday to Thailand. It was a fantastic holiday, we stayed in a beautiful hotel on the edge of a palm-fringed beach. It was very romantic. We had two lovely weeks together. She was due to return to Japan for a few months, and I was coming back to England. When we came to say goodbye at the airport I told her that the relationship was over.' 'How did she feel about that?' I asked. 'She was very upset, in fact she was crying. I did feel bad about finishing the relationship. I know that is not what she wanted, and it had been such a lovely holiday. But I could see all the signs of her wanting the relationship to move to something more permanent. There was no point in pretending I was going to write and keep in touch when I didn't intend to, so I thought a quick clean break was better.' 'Did you know before you went on holiday that you were going to end the relationship?' I asked Sean. 'Yes,' he said, 'I did, but if I had told her beforehand, it would have completely spoilt the holiday.' 'She may well not have agreed to go, if you had told her,' I suggested. 'I know,' he said, 'which is also why I didn't tell her beforehand.

'If I'm having difficulty finishing a relationship because the girl in question is reluctant to do so, to harden my resolve I will have sex with another girl. Then I have no problem ending my current relationship. It's also a test of how deeply I feel about the girl I'm with. If I have a one-night stand with another girl, and there are no regrets I see that as proof that I am not really committed to the girl I am with.

'I don't believe in running more than one girl at a time. If I met a girl who was with another man, but was prepared to have sex with me I would never have a serious relationship with her. After all, how could I ever trust her? If she was prepared to be unfaithful with me, how would I know that at some time in the future, she would not sleep with someone else?

'Once or twice I have been dumped myself, but when that happens I always try and get the girl back – and then a few weeks later I dump her. It's probably the macho image, but if anyone is going to do the dumping I like it to be me.'

I suspect it is a little deeper than just the macho image. When Sean was twelve, his father left his mother and Sean's four brothers and sisters and ran off with another woman. He never saw his father again and does not want to. The fact that his father walked out when he was a child may have felt to Sean liked being dumped. Someone he trusted was suddenly no longer there. Added to which, loving though his mother was, she was also left coping with two young babies as well as Sean's two older brothers so time and attention must have been in short supply. So understandably for Sean being on the receiving end of someone dumping him would be very painful, it would reopen old wounds from the past for him. So to avoid that pain, he tries to win the girl back again, so that he can do the dumping and stem the pain.

What happens when trust has been broken

If a parent whom you love and trust lets you down badly, it can mean that in your adult intimate relationships it is very difficult for you to be able to really trust someone again. So to avoid experiencing the pain you felt as a child, you keep your emotional distance in your adult relationships. A man who fears commitment starts to panic when he feels himself becoming vulnerable, or if he feels he is seriously falling in love. Loving someone also means that person has the power to hurt you, because they might choose to leave you or end the relationship which would leave you feeling abandoned as you did as a child. So to avoid this happening the man ends the relationship before he becomes too deeply involved.

If you are involved with a man like this it is very confusing, as Sean's girlfriend experienced when she was unceremoniously dumped after a lovely and romantic holiday together. She was getting a lot from the relationship, a man she really got on with, whom she could talk to easily, who seemed to care about her and was a good lover. So the chances are that she had arrived at a point in starting to think of something a little more permanent which for the CPM is a turn-off. So he cools the relationship, and as she does not understand what is going on in his head, his behaviour does not make sense and like so many women who get involved with such men, through no fault of her own, she ends up getting badly hurt.

Time and time again when talking to women who have been involved with men who can't commit they tell me that such men are so easy to get involved with because at the beginning of the relationship they seem to be promising so much. They appear so interested in you, they seem to enjoy talking about all the things that you do, they encourage you to talk about yourself and your life, they empathise with the problems you are struggling with, they find you fun, amusing and very sexually desirable. Their whole approach seems to be saying 'You are beautiful, lovely, wonderful and I find you devastatingly attractive. I want to see more of you, you are so special I want to get to know you better.'

The CPM is the 'grand-master' of the seduction technique which is why when they move into the 'reject stage' it feels so utterly confusing.

Most men who had a really wonderful holiday with their girlfriend would not then dump her when things were going so well. Most could not go on holiday and have a really romantic time knowing all the time that they were going to end the relationship at the airport. The average man would be more likely to end the relationship because the holiday together had not gone well. Not so the CPM. It is just the very fact that it had all been so lovely, that they call a halt. They fear that the relationship has reached a stage where it has to move forward to be more committed than they want to be. So they panic and take flight. Understanding that this is normal behaviour for the CPM can't take away the pain, but it can go some way to explaining what was going on when it has happened to you.

Sean has quite a lot of understanding of his own behaviour and admits he does see himself settling down some time in the future. He said, 'One day I can imagine I might marry and settle down. After all I do want children and a family of my own, but I am certainly not ready to make that commitment yet.' He added, 'If I did marry I would be faithful.'

This is not so for Jake who as far as commitment goes is a worst-case scenario.

JAKE'S STORY

Men who fear commitment frequently invest a huge amount of sexual energy in how they relate to women, but with very little emotional context, which is a classic way of avoiding committed intimate relationships. The 'love them and leave them' type of relationship may be fun and exciting for the men involved but it is rarely so if you are a woman caught up with such a man.

Men who choose to have short-term relationships get a buzz out of their pulling power when it comes to women. This was certainly so for Jake whose approach to women was 'Treat 'em mean, keep 'em keen'. His attitude was born out of the fact that he had been badly hurt by the first woman he fell for and he was not going to let this ever happen again.

He was on a mission of revenge. In his relationships he was punishing all women for the one who had treated him badly.

'Natalie, the first girl I really fell in love with, let me down badly. We were together for three years, it was my first real love and it knocked me for six. What I did was get too deeply involved. I have never let that happen again. She was a year older than me but she wasn't really ready to settle down. I know I was very possessive but she would constantly be looking at other men, sometimes for three or four minutes as if she was hypnotised by them. She knew I didn't like it but she insisted on continuing to do it. We would argue about it all the time. I was always in doubt about her actions and emotions. She said she loved me but I couldn't be sure. Her actions were different from what she was saying. Before I met her I was a player and I always had more than one girlfriend at a time. But with her I shocked myself because I just wanted her and no one else. We had been going out together for some time and things had become a little rocky. I suppose I was beginning to feel that I loved her more than she loved me. We went to a party and halfway through she disappeared. I could not find her anywhere. When she turned up again she made some flimsy excuse about giving a cousin of hers a lift home, but I knew she had been with another man. I was very humiliated and felt really small especially as all my mates knew. In the end I couldn't take any more of her blowing hot and cold so I finished the relationship.

'That experience made me put up a barrier. I didn't really trust women after that. What that relationship did was to open my eyes to women. Some women will try to convince you that you're the love of their life but at the same time they're seeing someone else.

'After I finished with Natalie I met a girl called Sam. After a few months we started to more or less live together. I was with her for about three months. She was lovely. She treated me like a king. I said it was too good to be true. But there was something missing. I just couldn't love her. I couldn't love her because I was still in love with Natalie. It was ridiculous – here was this woman who was really in love with me, but I was still madly in love with my last girlfriend. I just couldn't love Sam. Natalie lived three minutes' walk from Sam's house. In the mornings I'd go and I'd look out to see if Natalie was leaving with someone else. I was still obsessed by her. So I finished my relationship with Sam. She was heartbroken.

'After that I decided there was safety in numbers and I had loads of girls, sometimes as many as five or six on the go at the same time. If I met a girl I fancied I'd take her number, I'd talk to her nicely and keep her interested. I'd suggest going out, maybe I'd buy her flowers or send her a card, I'd make her feel I was keen on her. But my main intention was to get them into bed and I was pretty successful. By having all these girlfriends I thought I was quite macho. I might be with one girl on Monday night, another one on Wednesday and a different girl on Friday. If they gave me the slightest little problem they got their P45. I'd end the relationship and look for more recruits. I was becoming a nasty piece of work.

'If they dared to come to my house, or called me up at an inconvenient moment they were in trouble. I might have someone else there. If they did not like it, my attitude was "too bad". I'd end the relationship and say "Bye-bye, its all over." I never felt any remorse. I would go to night clubs just to pick up girls. I was always quite determined that I was going to score. If I felt I was not getting very far with one girl, I'd move on to another. There was no point in messing around and wasting time. I was very rarely unsuccessful. For a few years I was very wild. I was on a mission to seek and destroy women.

'I've got two four-year-old sons, both by different mothers Sandra and Michelle. I didn't want these girls to get pregnant but they did. Sandra told me, "I can't get pregnant, I've got blocked tubes." Like an idiot I fell for it. I usually always practise protected sex, but we had been going out together for about six months, so I thought it would be all right. I had just finished the relationship with Sandra when a mutual friend told me that she was pregnant but too frightened to tell me. I said "You can tell her I'm not interested and it's not mine" – as men do. Then I started to feel a bit guilty, so I saw her a few times and said I would be at the birth. When the head came out I knew it was my baby. I felt love for him straight away. Nowadays I'm devoted to him and see lots of him.

'By then I was already seeing three other girls. Funnily enough they all had the same name which sometimes got a bit confusing. I was determined to sleep with all three of them. In the end I had two out of three. Michelle 1 told a friend of mine that she was in love with me. I was so intrigued and flattered that I took her phone number. I rang her and we started seeing each other. Within a week she was fascinated and wouldn't leave me alone. I never said "Would you go out with me?" Or "Would you be my girlfriend?" Sometimes we would go out together but sometimes I'd just go round to her house, spend some time together talking and then I would do the business and leave. I suppose the relationships lasted a few months.

'Michelle 2, a friend of Michelle 1, was very attractive, slim and tall and willowy and also very flirtatious. She gave me plenty of signals that she was interested in me. So I thought to myself she's up for it. I thought it would not take long to get her into bed. But she wanted more of a relationship than I was interested in having. She said, "I know the kind of man you are, fly and happy-go-lucky. I can't have a relationship with you." So I did not strike lucky there.

'But by now Michelle 3 was on the scene. She knew my relationship with Michelle 1 wasn't going to last. I'm never single – I always have something on the back burner.

'Michelle 3 couldn't wait for the occasion. She was on my case so to speak. She presented herself on a plate. I didn't even have to do any groundwork. She was ready, waiting and willing. I said to Michelle 3, "I'm not asking for a relationship. I want sex and to have a bit of fun." She seemed happy with this. So I started seeing her. On her twenty-sixth birthday we went out to a restaurant, with a girlfriend of hers and some other girls. After the meal Michelle 3 and a girlfriend of hers and I all went back to Michelle 3's house The two girls said they were tired and went to bed, but then Michelle came over to me and said come on let's do it. I knew her friend was watching us and I thought I wonder if her friend will wake up and be interested as well. I was feeling really greedy at the time. Most men fantasise about having two women. But sadly she did not join in.

'Michelle 3 was on the Pill. She said she had changed the dose of the Pill and that she was having some problems. I imagine she forgot to take the pill or something but the upshot was she got pregnant. I hadn't told her that a previous girlfriend of mine was also pregnant. When my second son was born four months after my first son I couldn't tell either of them about the other. Both women were phoning, driving me mad, they nearly drove me round the bend. As soon as Michelle 3's baby was born she wanted marriage and a committed relationship. She wanted us to buy a house together and settle down but I was not up for that.

'Then she turned from a nice girl into a demon. She would not let me have anything to do with my son, so I have not been able to make a bond with him. Now he doesn't know I'm his dad. He just thinks I'm a strange man. I knock on the door and he says "Who are you?" Michelle says she doesn't want to confuse his head. As I won't commit to her she won't let me have anything to do with him. I'm strict in my principles. All I can do is live for today. I won't tolerate anyone taking advantage of me the way she wants to.

'My success with women is due to good sex. I give them a good time and the word gets around. I have a very high sex drive and I am looking for good sex. One of my ploys for getting a woman into bed is to blank them. I invite a woman around to my house and when they come I sit on the other side of the room. She says to me: "Why are you sitting over there?" And I'll say, "Well I don't want you to think I'm going to get busy." At that point she'll say, "Oh, come and sit next to me." At that stage I know I'm in.

'I always have some women on stand-by. The girlfriend I'm living with now I first met eleven years ago. But we only started going out together eighteen months ago. She's going to be the mother of my child. She's five months pregnant. She would like us to marry, but no way. I could never commit myself to just one girl for ever more.'

Jake has nine brothers and sisters, his father was a womaniser who used to beat his mother up all the time. His parents split up when he was nine and he had little contact with his father after that. He found the whole thing very painful. Life spiralled downhill after the divorce. They had been living reasonably well until then and he had been getting a good education, but all that changed on his parents' divorce. He suddenly had to leave his school, lose his friends and move with his mother and brothers and sister into terrible accommodation. Sharing houses and bathrooms and kitchens. He felt confused and angry. He lost interest in his education and hated the enforced poverty. He left home as soon as he was able to. He said, 'I can show affection but if someone treats me with lack of respect I'm a changed person, I turn the light off just like that. There's no going back. I have to be in charge, I don't suffer any remorse. I know I am hard but that is how I have to be.'

Jake still has a tremendous amount of anger within him. He's angry at what happened when his parents divorced, the way life so dramatically changed, the lost educational opportunities. Having been let down so badly as a child he looked for love and trust when he first fell in love with Natalie, but she too let him down, betrayed his trust, and showed him up in front of his friends. The combination of all these things has meant that he has put up a steel circle of protective armour around him, which no woman is now allowed to penetrate.

Added to which he has the model of a womanising and violent father. Though Jake is not violent towards women, his anger and lack of trust means that his relationship with many of them has been unkind. He frankly uses them, and frequently discards them without much thought for their feelings. He sees it as having a good time, but it is also partly to do with the fact that he is taking his revenge for the hurt that he still feels deep inside.

Men who are afraid of commitment can be extremely attractive, articulate and can appear very self-assured and confident on the surface, but underneath many are harbouring a lot of hurt and anger just like Jake. Many men who have had an unhappy childhood are suffering from low self-esteem or feel very insecure underneath the confident exterior. So to vent their anger, boost their self-esteem and massage their ego they frequently use their pulling power to seduce women. Then once they have achieved this they tend to lose interest in the woman so she finds she is dumped unceremoniously and they are on to the next one. The seduction and rejection pattern is a constant theme among men who can't commit.

* * *

SELF-PROTECTION: LESSON ONE

- *Try first to identify if the man is a worst-case commitment phobic. Jake and Josh in the previous chapter are good examples of this. Check him out – what do his friends say about him? Does he have a bad reputation with girls, if so believe it, don't think he will treat you differently. If you meet in a night club assume he is on the make, however sweet the talk is.*
- *Look after yourself because the chances are he won't look after you, so unless you too just want a good time, don't rush in throwing caution to the wind.*
- *It's easy to be swept along by loving words and romantic gestures, most of us are romantic at heart, but don't be taken in. Words are easy, promises can be easily broken, so what you need to do is keep your feet on the ground. Don't expect too much unless he puts some actions behind the words.*

THE PETER PAN SYNDROME – MEN WHO HAVE NEVER GROWN UP

Immaturity and a refusal to grow up and accept responsibly are high on the agenda of many CPMs. Many of their relationships are very short-term, a one-night stand, just a matter of weeks or a few months. Some avoid commitment by breaking off the relationship before it gets to the living-together stage and others go into marriage or cohabitation but their immaturity, selfishness, and narcissism cause havoc in their relationships with the women they marry or live with.

A man has a lot invested in hanging on to his immaturity. He enjoys being irresponsible and unpredictable, life is for living and life is for having fun. The longer he can prolong that approach to life the longer he can avoid any commitment.

He wants the relationship with you, and provided you play his game he is very happy with being a couple. He adores you, he loves you, he has told you so, hasn't he, surely that is enough, what more do you want, there is plenty of time to think about the future. If you have reached a stage when you want more than he is prepared to give, it scares him and he does not want to think about it. He will either just avoid the issue altogether, or he will go out of his way to make you feel that you are the one who is being stuffy, too conventional, too boringly adult. He will imply why bother about planning for the future when you are both having so much fun the way you are. If he can keep his options open, he feels safe and secure. If you demand more of him than he feels able or willing to give, that is when he may pull up the drawbridge and retreat.

So he starts to justify his attitude or behaviour by asking himself, 'Why settle for a committed relationship with one woman when there are still so many other fanciable woman out there to pursue?' This is a very natural way to feel if you are in your late teens or early to mid-twenties, but if you are still constantly moving from one relationship to the next in your thirties and forties it smacks of immaturity – the little boy who does not want to grow up, the child in the sweet shop who wants a taste of everything.

MILES'S STORY

Miles was good-looking, clever, amusing and outrageous. At forty-five he had never married. His longest relationship had been four years, but many had lasted only a matter of months and the majority were a lot shorter than that.

He had a successful career in television and used this to his full advantage when it came to meeting and seducing attractive and desirable women. He told one woman who knew him well but who had not shared his bed that he had slept with more than a thousand woman. His approach was not very subtle but obviously very successful. He divided women into two categories: ones he just wanted a sexual relationship with, a single night of passion. And ones with whom he planned that the relationship should be a little longer – but not too much longer.

Rosalind, a pretty woman with a figure to die for, was introduced to Miles at a television award party. She was very attracted to him, he seemed to know everyone, he was amusing and witty, and made her laugh. They had both had several drinks when he turned to her and said, 'Do you know, I am extraordinarily good in bed.' She was silently taken aback but replied laughing and much to the delight of the others in their group. 'Well, as a matter of fact, so am I.'

Miles gave her all his attention and those around drifted away leaving just the two of them. Miles would be talking one moment, about books, a television programme, a play they had both seen and then the next moment he would be telling her how desirable she was, what a wonderful body she had, how much he would like to make love to her, how he would like a relationship with her.

Part of her wanted to walk away. He was pretty outrageous, but there was something rather seductive as well. Her head told her that it was probably all part of his chat-up routine, but she was aware that being made to feel so desired was not without its attractions. She had recently come through a rather acrimonious and messy divorce and her self-esteem was not at its best. She said, 'I so easily might have got involved with him, but the person who introduced me had warned me about his reputation, so I refused his offer of dinner and went home on my own. As I was leaving he came up to me and said, "Can I call you?" But I refused. As I turned to go his parting words to me were "I really felt we could have had a good relationship, and you won't give it a chance." I spent most of that night wondering if I had made the wrong decision, but a few days later when I met a mutual friend for lunch, she told me he had got off with someone else that night. "And what's more," she said indignantly, "she is a really nice girl, and in the end he will only dump her like all the others." So I was glad my self-protective instincts had been at work that night,' said Rosalind. 'He must have found out where I worked because he did telephone a couple of times but I did not return his calls.'

Miles's father had died when he was six. He remembers his father playing with him and the excitement of running to meet him when he got off the train from London in the evening. To his mother, Miles and his father were practically perfect. His mother never remarried and she and Miles lived in a large old house that belonged to his grandfather. He was brought up by a mother who adored him, Miles could do no wrong and whatever he wanted he could have. The family were well off and money was plentiful. He in turn idealised his mother and was quite devastated when she died of a heart attack in his late twenties. Shortly after that he ended his only long-term, four-year relationship, inherited a lot of money, and said to himself that he would never settle for just one woman.

Miles is in denial. He completely dismissed the thought that his choice not to commit was influenced by his over-indulged childhood, an idealised mother and losing both parents at fairly crucial times in his life. He said that it was just that life was too short, women were too plentiful, and he got bored too easily. He just did not want to commit to one woman. If you are committed to one woman you don't know what you are missing, you never know what might be waiting for you just around the next corner, your options have to be kept open at all costs, was Miles's belief. Underneath his extrovert exterior there is a darker side, and he is often lonely and at times depressed but then he throws himself into a series of meaningless one-night stands or work at which he is very successful.

THE PETER PAN TRADEMARK

The Peter Pan CPM usually has his life well organised to suit him, he always likes to have a relationship on the go, he may utterly adore you but not want to live with you, he may say he wants you to be together for always, but have no interest in marriage. He likes plenty of time to do his own thing. And what's more he likes you to fit in with his needs and most of the time he pays lip service to meeting yours.

He may be dedicated to watching or playing sport, on Sundays as well as Saturdays and several evenings during the week. His friends feature highly in his life, so he is either involved with them in playing sport or meeting them in the wine bar after work or down at the pub most nights. He may have hobbies that he is very devoted to, which absorb an awful lot of his time, time you feel he could be spending with you. His job may intrude endlessly on your relationship and you often wonder if his devotion to his work is rather more important in his life than his devotion to you.

The Married or Co-Habiting Peter Pan CPM

One of the most common ways that the Peter Pan commitment phobic keeps his distance in relationships is for him to sabotage his relationship with you by getting involved with another woman. He has made the commitment to you, you are perhaps living together, maybe engaged or even married but something deep inside him is scared stiff about what he has done. When his involvement is discovered it is always extremely demoralising and painful to find out that you have been deceived by the man you thought loved you. Which is just what happened to Georgina when she fell in love with Alex.

Georgina loved her job as a teacher. Her first marriage had broken up because of her husband's immaturity and irresponsibility with money. When she met Alex he seemed such a contrast to her first husband. He was kind, sensitive and caring and in a secure job. He worked for a large American company and commuted between the two countries. Georgina said:

'I went to the theatre with a group of friends; most of

them were married couples. In the interval we went to the bar to have a drink. Alex came over because he knew some of the people I was with. He was with a pretty, rather quiet woman who I thought must be his wife. After the theatre we all went out to supper and they joined us. I was very attracted to him, but I did resist his very flirtatious manner as I thought he was married and I did not want to upset his wife. As we left the restaurant he said, "Can I telephone you and perhaps we could meet?" I said, "I don't think so, you are married aren't you?" He said, "No I'm not." And then turning and looking across the room at the woman he was with, he smiled and said, "We are just good friends." I did not know whether he was telling the truth or joking, but I refused to give him my number.

'A few days later he rang after getting my number from a mutual friend. Well it turned out he really was not married so I accepted his invitation. I was quite cool about it all. I had one disastrous marriage and I did not really want to get involved again. But Alex was very persistent. He was very good-looking and I think used to women falling for him. We had been going out together for about three months before I finally went to bed with him. I am not into brief flings. If I go to bed with a man I have to really like him. From then on we saw each other as much as we could. He was always flying back and forth to America, but in some ways that added to the excitement of the affair. As soon as his aeroplane touched down, he would telephone me from the airport to say he was coming to see me. We really painted the town red. He loved to go out for dinner and to the theatre. At weekends we would drive miles out into the countryside to a delightful little country pub. He was so good at choosing romantic places. He was wonderfully attentive, not like some men who look around the restaurant while you are talking. He seemed to have eyes only for me.

'A year after our first meeting we started living together. I think it was then that I first noticed a few changes. He was still flying back and forth to America. Before, everything I did seemed to please him, now he started to criticise me, to complain if the house was untidy or if I was preparing for a class the next day or correcting homework when he wanted to go out together.

'I loved my job but if he was around it irritated him if I got back late from work, or if I had to attend a parent/teacher evening. I did not think much of it at the time, just putting it down to the fact that he was probably jet-lagged, or taking time to adjusting to living together.

'We had been living together about a year when he said he had the opportunity of working in America for a couple of years and he wanted us to move over there to live. I was very reluctant to leave my friends to go and live in a country I did not know, and particularly to give up my job. But he was so persuasive and so lovely to me it was just like how we were at the beginning of the relationship and I loved him very much, so I agreed.

'He went on ahead as he had to start his new job and find somewhere for us to live. I could not join him until the term had finished and I had sorted out my visa and let our house.

'While we were apart he wrote me the most wonderful letters. They were so romantic I read them over and over again. He kept saying how much he loved me, how he was missing me and counting every minute until we could be together again. He wrote about all the things we did when we made love and how perfect our life together would be.

They were really beautiful letters. I was missing him terribly and though I was very sad to leave Scotland and my job I longed to be with him.

'He met me at Kennedy Airport. I remember he was late and he blamed it on his work. I felt let down for he had been so romantic until then. It seemed very unromantic not to be there when all I could think of was seeing him after several months apart and running into his arms. I don't know quite what it was but somehow he was not the same as his letters. I just sensed that almost immediately. I could not put my finger on it. Then that night we made love and it was so fantastic I thought I was imagining it, and that everything was fine.

'To start with life was rather lonely as Alex was working long hours, but I liked where we were living and I soon made friends and started to see if I could get a job teaching. Then one morning after I had been there a couple of months the telephone rang and a woman's voice I did not recognise said "Do you know your husband is having an affair?" and put the phone down. I was so stunned I just sat down in the kitchen in a complete state of shock. I tried to trace the call but the caller, as they say, had withheld her number. When Alex came home I did not tell him about the call but I said I felt there was something wrong and I asked him if he was having an affair. He became very irritated and told me not to be so stupid, and of course he wasn't. I thought of all the things he had said in those beautiful letters, so again I thought maybe I was imagining it. I told myself that perhaps it was someone trying to cause trouble, but something was still niggling me, so I guess I started to look for evidence.

'I did not want to tell him about the telephone call because that would look as if I did not trust him and I knew he could just deny it again.

‘Several weeks later I discovered the truth. I found a letter in his briefcase but this one was not addressed to me, but some woman I had never heard of. I am ashamed to say I opened the letter, as I read it tears started pouring down my cheeks. It was very clear for all to see that he was indeed having an affair. But perhaps the worst of it was that what he had written to me he had written to her, about loving her, missing her and wanting to see her, even writing about making love. That made everything completely meaningless.

‘That evening when he came home I dressed up. I had cooked a nice meal with a bottle of wine. He said: “What is all this about?” I said, “It’s a surprise.” Now looking back I don’t know how I was able to do it, I think it was my anger that kept me going. When I went out to get the pudding I picked up the letter which I had hidden in the kitchen and put it on a large plate and carried it in and put it down in front of him. He froze and then just looked at me incredulously. This time he could not deny it, the evidence was literally staring him in the face.

‘I said icily, “The surprise is – I’m leaving you. I am flying back to Scotland as soon as I can arrange it.” Inside, I wanted to die. I felt my life was in ruins. There I was, far away in another country, having given up so much to join him. I felt so alone. He had begun the affair just weeks before we starting living together.

‘He cried, he said he was sorry, he begged me to forgive him but, he said he did not understand why he had behaved the way he had. He said he did not want to lose me. But for me there was no going back. I had been in one unhappy and unreliable relationship and I certainly was not going to stay around in another.'

Safety in numbers?

It is frequently the change to a more permanent relationship that makes a man cheat on his girlfriend or wife. Rather like the old adage 'there is safety in numbers'. When Georgina first met Alex he was with another woman. He brushed aside the fact that he had any real commitment to her. The reality was that his previous relationship had got to the stage where the woman was wanting more from him than he was prepared to give, so he finished it. But not before he had embarked on a new relationship with Georgina. When his relationship with her got too close for comfort, he began an affair.

THE INTERMINABLE ENGAGEMENT

The same was true for Amy. She had been in a relationship with Jim for ten years and got engaged after seven, ever since when Amy had tried to get him to agree on a wedding date. But Jim always came up with an excuse. First he wanted to sell the flat they were living in and start married life in a little house. Or the market was slow and time went by and the flat did not sell. Amy felt he was insisting on an unrealistic price for the flat and would find fault with every house they inspected, discovering something he was sure he could not live with. Then just as they thought they had sold the flat and found a house that they liked Jim said he was uncertain about his job, and maybe he needed to make a change, he wanted to be on a more secure footing before they got married. This went on for three years and Amy was getting very fed up. She was thirty-one and wanted to settle down and start a family. Their sex life had taken a downward turn since they became engaged, with Jim wanting to make love less and less.

Amy said, 'The other thing that was worrying me was that Jim seemed close to a girl at work but he always denied that there was anything going on. He said that she was just having a hard time and he was just providing a listening ear. He told me that this girl had a boyfriend and had become pregnant but he had left her shortly before the birth of her baby daughter.

'Then about three months after the baby was born she tragically died. It was a cot death. Jim was terribly upset. I felt sorry for the girl but didn't understand why he was quite so upset and we rowed about it endlessly. I felt he was too involved, but Jim said it was reasonable to feel sad over the baby's death as he felt very sorry for its mother.

'One night we were having a terrible row and he suddenly broke down and told me that the baby was his. He said he had only slept with this girl a couple of times and she had told him she was on the Pill.

'I felt totally devastated. I had wanted marriage and a baby and Jim had one by another woman.'

Jim insisted that he loved Amy and wanted them to be together and get married. Amy told him she needed time to think about what she wanted to do. This time it was Jim who pushed for the wedding date to be set and Amy who held back. She went back to live with her parents but Jim telephoned and called round to see her all the time and after they had been apart for six months she finally agreed to marry him and they set a wedding date for later that year. It was then that he told Amy that he didn't know if he really wanted children any more. He said he was afraid of committing himself to having children as the death of his baby had been so awful that he did not know if he could risk putting himself through that again. But Amy could not take any more. She was shattered and exhausted. She returned her engagement ring and ended the relationship.

If you are in love with a man who fears commitment this behaviour of seduction and rejection appears inexplicable. This was certainly so for Amy. What makes a man propose marriage then pull out all the stops to avoid walking up the aisle? Why does he tell her he loves her one moment and betray her the next? It does not seem to make sense. It is confusing unless you understand that you are involved with a man who is afraid to commit himself. It's not that he does not like you, enjoy your company, or want to be with you. His running away or rejection is because he has committed to a relationship as far as he is able to. He realises that the relationship has reached a stage when more commitment than he has already given is expected of him, and that is something he is unable to do. Amy's expectations were totally reasonable, which was that the engagement would lead to marriage, but the problem was that Jim was too scared.

MEN WHO CAN'T TRUST WOMEN

One of the reasons why many CPMs find it difficult to trust women is because they feel they have been let down by or rejected by the person who should have been their carer and protector. A man who has had a cold rejecting mother grows up feeling intense frustration because his mother was constantly withholding her love. So as an adult he sees women as hostile, cold, and withholding, at the same time he has this idealised vision of a woman, as all giving, nurturing, and unconditionally loving. So when you do not totally cater to his needs, it puts him in touch with the deprivation and desperate need for love and attention that he felt as a child and did not get. He is a man on the outside, but inside is this desperately needy little boy craving love. He is so needy he finds it almost impossible not to have his own needs met or to tolerate or understand yours. So when you choose to fulfil some of your own needs rather than his, he creates merry hell. He insists that you meet his needs rather than your own. For example: Your mother has not been very well and you say you want to go and see her next week. He raises every objection in the book, he says, 'How can you go when you know I'm having such a difficult time at work? That is really selfish of you. You never think of me; you always do everything to suit yourself. Your mother is perfectly all right, you are over-reacting.' He has many ways of manipulating you and making you feel guilty. Maybe your mother is fine, but what he is failing to see is you have a need of your own which is to check that your mother is OK, and if she isn't, to be with her.

So as adults men who have had cold rejecting mothers are very needy people longing for the woman they are with to make up for all that they missed out on as a child. The reality is that no one woman can continually fill that empty yearning hole and make up for all the rejection of the past. But if the man does not recognise that his demands for your time, attention and love are almost insatiable, he will go on demanding the impossible. Rather than see it as his problem he sees you as yet another woman who has failed him. So he either creates a huge fuss when his needs are not being met, or he finishes the relationship and heads off in search of a new woman whom he hopes will not let him down.

No one wants to admit that they are selfish or immature or behaving unkindly or insensitively and especially so the commitment phobic man. But if he is willing to look at his own behaviour, and if he is prepared to stop and look at the part he plays in his relationships with women, he has the potential to work things out.

SELF-PROTECTION: LESSON TWO

- *Be aware – Try to identify early warning signs: Like Miles who is in his 40s and never married – why should he change the habit of a lifetime when he is having so much fun? Jim who though engaged to Amy kept finding excuses not to fix the day. Alex who cooled on the relationship as soon as they started living together.*
- *Don't let him walk all over your needs. The Peter Pan CPM is very likely to try and do this, as part of his problem is that his needs are rather more important to him than yours. So don't be 'so much in love' that you make excuses for him, or turn a blind eye to what he is doing, he will only do it all the more. He needs to learn you too have needs.*
- *If he boasts about past conquests be wary. If he insists that you clear your diary just for him, don't. See your friends, visit your parents, go to the gym, keep up your social life, carry on with your life. If you drop everything for him and the relationship does not last, you will feel empty, abandoned and completely at a loss.*

OEDIPAL COMPLEX

The Oedipal complex or conflict is the battle which happens according to Freud around the age of four or five. This is where the child struggles for the exclusive affection of the parent of the opposite sex. It is based, as I am sure you know, on the well-known story from Greek mythology – King Oedipus was the royal offspring who did not recognise his own parents and mistakenly killed his father and fell in love with his mother.

Every child has to be helped to lose the battle for the exclusive affection of the opposite sex parent. This is especially so for boys who in order to establish their own male identify (at around the age of four or five) must move away from the female and begin to identify with the male.

If at this stage the mother is overprotective to her son, or excludes the father and sets up so-called cosy twosomes with her son at the father's expense, the little boy might have trouble losing the oedipal battle. In adult life he then may be too dominated by his mother, or fear that if you allow a woman to get too close to you you risk getting pushed around. Alternatively because he has experienced the central woman in his childhood as manipulating, he may well have a problem trusting women enough to form close intimate relationships with them, which is why he avoids commitment.

A child needs to see that his parents have a loving and secure bond, and that they jointly and individually love their child and provide a secure base. If the parents are at war, remote and distant from each other, not giving each other love and support, or sexually not interested in each other it is more difficult for the child to work through these powerful feelings. If a couple are disillusioned with each other then they may divert their need to be loved to their child. Women in unsatisfactory marriages frequently try to resolve their problems through their children. They do this in many ways: by being extremely demanding, coldly rejecting, smothering and controlling, or giving the child so much time and attention that a special bond is created between them and the other parent is excluded. If the father is too uninterested, too passive or too weak to intervene, the child becomes too dependent on its mother.

Children soon realise that they can divide and manipulate their parents to their own advantage. So you might get a situation where the father tells his son that it is now time for bed, and the boy who naturally wants to stay up later runs to his mother and begs to be allowed to stay up longer. Instead of encouraging the child to go upstairs to bed she undermines her husband and says, 'You don't have to go to bed yet, let's play a nice game, I'll read you a story, or we can watch this programme together.' Thus creating a cosy bond with the child, taking control and undermining her partner's relationship with his son in one fell swoop. If this sort of thing continually happens the child holds much too much power in his young hands, and he carries this lesson in manipulation into his adult relationships with women.

Smothering Mothers and Passive Fathers

A little boy whose mother smothers him with love and excludes the father can prevent him separating from the mother figure and establishing himself as the young male of the household. She is overprotective, her life revolves around being in control of everything that is happening in her son's life. Instead of encouraging him to learn to fight some of his own battles and take decisions for himself she tries to do all that for him. She cannot let her children become independent and she will do her utmost to continue to be over-involved in their adult lives. So the man grows up with the feeling that all women are manipulating, powerful and controlling. If that is the case he feels he has two options, one to become passive and withdrawn in his relationships with women, or he is continually struggling to dominate and control them. His fear is that all women are like his smothering and over-controlling mother and he does not want to risk that happening again.

She Who Must Be Obeyed

Many commitment phobic men have ambivalent feelings about women because they perceive them as controlling and powerful. They fear that once they allow themselves to get into a woman's hands she will take them over, devour, or emotionally castrate them. The slightest sign of feminism in a woman has them running for cover.

In John Mortimer's *Rumpole of the Bailey*, Rumpole, a successful and independent-minded barrister refers to his wife, an equally independent-minded spirit, as 'She Who Must Be Obeyed'. This is more in terms of affection than really meaning it, as he in fact behaves much as he wants to, despite her best endeavours.

A man who grows up in a family where his mother definitely wears the trousers frequently chooses to avoid close and intimate relationships because of his fear of domination and control by women. So the moment he perceives this as happening in his adult relationships with women he panics and distances himself from the woman he loves. He associates commitment to a woman with giving her the upper hand. Once a woman has the control, his experience tells him, she will use it against him. She will become critical and diminish him, hurt and undermine him. So he tells himself that she is not to be trusted.

William, a highly intelligent and successful litigation lawyer, said, 'My wife's father was totally downtrodden by his beautiful and arrogant wife, who when she finished with him dumped him unceremoniously for another man and then proceeded to do exactly the same thing to her second husband.' William, who is married to the daughter of this first marriage, is terrified that his wife is going to turn out like her mother. William continued, 'There is no way I am going to let her daughter do that to me.

'My own mother is similar, she can eat several men at once for breakfast. My mother's third husband who is a lovely man but weak, has totally given up and lets my mother get away with murder.' One of William's greatest fears is that he will be taken over by his wife and become a replica of his submissive father and his weak and inadequate father-in-law.

The pattern he has seen is that his mother ruled his father.

His experience of women is that given half a chance they take over, they run the show, they are the ones who hold the power and control. Men who allow women to take on this controlling role he sees as weak, insubstantial, non-macho, in fact a walkover. If these fears are not recognised or unresolved the man sees all women as potentially out to control him, just as his father was controlled by his mother.

If a boy has a strong role model as a father who stands up to his controlling wife, he can also learn to be strong and confident and to break away from his over-dominating mother, but all too often strong dominating women choose to marry weak, passive men.

A small boy who does not have a strong role model as a father can do very little to counteract his mother's behaviour so he feels powerless. He feels subjugated to her, with little chance of being allowed to openly express his anger and resentment. So his particular panic button in the commitment stakes can be pushed whenever he feels a woman is moving into control mode. He takes flight and refuses to engage in any real conversation about the problem. He sulks or he loses his temper. His way of gaining control is to stonewall. He seems impenetrable. The more he does this, the more you protest, and the more he likens you to his dominating and controlling mother or to yours.

The trouble is that as the woman in his life you may just be making a reasonable request, or expressing your own views which are at odds with his. But what he experiences happening is you trying to take over. His response seems over the top, because he is not reacting to something you have done, rather that something you said or did triggered past unresolved fears of being dominated or controlled.

Because that is how he expects all women in close intimate relationships to behave. It is only by understanding this and seeing you as you really are, that he is able to work at those fears.

Edward's mother was left reasonably well off when his father died while Edward was at university. His mother had always spent money very freely, which Edward remembers had caused rows between his parents. Two years after his father's death she remarried a man who had a careless disregard for money. If he had none he did not worry and when he did he spent freely, or gave it away to worthy and not so worthy causes. Edward married and had two children. Fifteen years on he was struggling to make ends meet with a house in London and both children at fee-paying schools.

His mother spent money as if there was no tomorrow. Edward's father's side of the family believed in inherited wealth and that one generation was the custodian of the family money for the next generation, but his frivolous and irresponsible mother had no such beliefs. Edward tried to talk to her about her spending, and his concerns that she would have a penniless old age the way she was going. But she shouted and remonstrated with him and said that he was mean and greedy and only thinking of his own selfish needs.

Edward and his wife also argued about money. He felt his wife was not as careful with money as she should be. She had to account for everything she spent. Edward hit the roof if she spent any money without telling him, or if she paid any household bills without referring to him first. His way of trying to control his mother's spendthrift ways was to see the very same faults in his wife and condemn them.

But his wife was not his mother and she was averagely careful about her spending and resented Edward's control and constant criticism.

It was only when they were both able to explore through counselling what was happening in their relationship that they were able to sort it out. Edward was able to let go his obsessive need to stay in control and his wife agreed that joint discussions about money matters were essential. In counselling Edward was able to work at his terror of overpowering and controlling women. He was able to see that was not where his wife was coming from, and he acknowledged how his behaviour was nearly wrecking their relationship.

Controlling Mothers

Many men who have a controlling mother do enter into committed relationships but then sabotage the relationship by becoming abusive, cruel and over-controlling. They try and get the upper hand because they fear that if they don't you will. At the beginning of the relationship the man is charming, attentive, and seems very much in love with you. But once married or living together, a change takes place. He starts to undermine you, finds fault and criticises everything you do. He may try to gain even more control over you by cutting you off from family and friends. So he may start to object to your family and friends, always finding fault with them, or complaining bitterly when you want to spend time with them.

It is always you who is in the wrong. He complains that you telephone them too much, are too influenced by what they say, you spend too much time with them. He insists that you see less and less of them. If you don't there are arguments and rows until you eventually give in, in the vain hope that it is worth it for a quiet life. It does not end there because his insecurities and low self-esteem are such that he needs to continually keep control, so the more you give in the more he will demand that you do. Very controlling men are frequently battling with low self-esteem, and their way of dealing with this is to diminish the woman they are with so that they can feel better about themselves.

Strong independent women feel particularly undermining to a man who is struggling with a low self-esteem or poor self-image. Some commitment phobic men have been so dominated by their mothers, reinforced by the absence of any father figure, or a very weak and ineffectual father that they find it virtually impossible to trust women enough to form loving relationships with them.

Idealised Mothers: In search of the perfect woman

Many men are caught in the Oedipal conflict with an idealised mother which drives them in search of the perfect woman. But perfection does not exist so when they discover any imperfections they abandon the woman they were once so in love with and set out on their search once more.

If a small boy loses his mother in his early years either through death, divorce or a prolonged separation he is left with intense feelings of grief for the lost, loved, idealised mother. As an adult he is searching for the perfect loving relationship he experienced as a small child, so unconsciously he is comparing every woman he falls in love with to his imagined perfect mother. Each time he falls in love he experiences very intense feelings. He often describes the woman as his soul mate, the only woman in the world who totally understands him, someone who is just perfect for him. The problem is once her human frailties appear, as indeed they will, because the perfect woman does not exist, except in his projected image of her, he will become disillusioned and start to notice her imperfections. Once this process has begun he becomes ambivalent about his relationship with the woman he once so idolised. He will either start to move out of the relationship bit by bit or suddenly draw the relationship to an abrupt end, leaving you reeling and wondering what has suddenly gone so wrong. The reason is that only by ending the relationship is he free to continue his search for the perfect woman. Having found her the same old story will be repeated again and again. It is only when he draws breath and starts to look at why all his relationships fail in the end that he can begin to make changes in himself rather than expecting perfection in his mate.

MEN WHO HATE WOMEN

To describe men as hating women sounds very harsh but perhaps it is more understandable if you realise that their hatred is usually motivated by fear of women. A woman-hater is torn between his desire to be loved by a woman and his deeply buried fear of her. Men who hate women are frequently found among commitment phobic men. This is particularly so when a man has difficult, negative and unresolved feelings about his mother. Or when he has been brought up in a misogynist and authoritarian household where his father was overbearing and bullying towards his wife and children.

Martin, like many men, was reluctant to come for counselling. He saw it as an admission of failure, a sign of weakness. As a man he believed he should be able to sort out his own problems. He did it at work very successfully so why did he need to involve a third person in sorting out his marriage? But Maggie his wife was insisting that things had got so bad that she was threatening to leave him. When Martin started to describe his own childhood it seemed lonely and bleak. His father had been in the army and he treated his two sons like army recruits in their very first week of square bashing. He shouted and yelled at them for the tiniest misdemeanour, and lashed out at them or his wife if he was not obeyed instantly. Every weekend Martin and his elder brother were given a list of jobs to do. One of Martin's was sweeping the lawn, if even one leaf was left, his father would insist that he had not done the job properly, and would scatter the leaves over the lawn again and insist that he sweep them up again. His mother never stood up for him, as she seemed terrified of her husband's rages. Martin remembers feeling sorry for her, she was frequently in tears and obviously unhappy, but then as he grew older he started to resent the fact that she never tried to protect her two sons from her tyrannical husband, and he began to despise her. His elder brother was very cowed by his father and became a silent and withdrawn child, like his mother. In his teens with no safe outlet for Martin to express his thoughts and feelings, as nearly everything he did and said was jumped on by his father, Martin became deeply angry inside. As he could not express this to his father, he became rebellious at school and bullied other children in the playground. The seeds of his father's bullying behaviour were firmly established by the time he left school and like his father he had learned to tyrannise and abuse.

Men who emotionally batter women

Many violent or emotionally battering men are repeating a pattern set by their fathers who see themselves as a number one subscriber to 'macho man' culture. Any exposure of their more vulnerable side is to be avoided at all costs. As a child Martin experienced his father as a man who believed women needed to know who was boss, and who was prepared to drive his point home by resorting to physical violence or emotional bullying. He had to have the upper hand at all costs.

So the message Martin received from his father was that it's OK to treat women badly; women are weak and passive and they deserve it. As Martin grew older he was also increasingly angry with his mother for being so passive and failing to protect her two sons from their bullying father. So with the combination of all these negative experiences his contempt for women was born. A man who is brought up by a misogynist father learns these lessons at his father's knee. Martin never hit his wife, but throughout much of his marriage, he had put Maggie down, undermined her and shouted and screamed at her whenever she challenged his opinions. She was the receptacle for all his pent-up anger that he could never dare to express to his father and the frustration that he felt towards his mother for never supporting him and failing to protect him from his abusive father.

The emotionally battering man is just as dominating and

destructive as the man who uses violence to gain control. The only difference is that there are no bruises to show for it, no broken ribs, or black eyes. You may not end up in casualty, but you will certainly feel emotionally battered and bruised, only it is more difficult to prove it to yourself and to the outside world.

When the man who loves you treats you badly

Many CPMs with an unresolved Oedipal conflict have very ambivalent feelings about women, usually because of his unsatisfactory relationship with his mother. As an adult he transfers these unresolved feelings on to the women he becomes involved with. So alongside needing the love of a woman he also fears being as dependent on her as he was on his mother because of all the pain that involved. He is so terrified of being abandoned, of you leaving him, that he looks for ways to ensure that you don't. So he tries to undermine you, to destroy your confidence, to make you so weak and downtrodden that you are unable to leave him. If you threaten to leave he will then turn on the charm to persuade you to stay and once he has reeled you back in, his controlling tactics are once more back in place. Alternatively he projects all the parts of himself that he does not like on to you, then blames you for being quite impossible which enables him to leave the relationship in search for pastures new in the vain hope that a new woman will provide all of his needs. But the reality is that in the end every woman will fail to come up to his expectations and so history will go on repeating itself.

*   *   *

SELF-PROTECTION: LESSON THREE

- *Don't make excuses if he behaves badly towards you. He may well have had a rotten childhood, a cold and distant or manipulating mother, an uninterested or bullying father but that does not give him a licence to treat you unkindly.*
- *If he is thirty-something and still living at home, he probably won't move out until his mother dies, and do you really want to take over where she left off? Avoid endlessly waiting around for him to leave for that matter also. He may be promising to leave, but unless he follows that through with action, don't wait around endlessly, cut your losses and move on.*
- *The CPM who gains an understanding of his behaviour is able to make changes if he wants to, he can learn how to handle emotionally committed and intimate relationships. So it really is worth trying to persuade him to go for counselling. It can make a real difference.*

Edward like many other married CPMs feared emotional commitment, but he loved his wife and adored his children, and eventually he did agree to go for counselling and they now have a closer and more fulfilling marriage.

A CPM who treats you badly or finds fault with every woman he falls for is sometimes running away from something he fears even more: his own imperfections. His fear is that if you get too close to him you may not like what you see. To protect himself from this he gets in first and finds fault with you. The problem for a man like this is that deep down he does not really believe he is lovable or good enough for you, so he plays on your insecurities to prevent you seeing his failings and then rejecting him.

A man who as a child had a very rejecting or critical mother may be very choosy about the woman he falls in love with because he wants someone who is flawless enough to come up to his mother's expectations – a task he has been failing to do all his life. He spent his childhood trying to be the perfect son, but whatever he did, however hard he tried he never quite managed it in his mother's eyes. Whatever he achieved, it was never good enough for her. She would always find some unforgivable failing and point it out. This left him very torn and ambivalent about intimate relationships. On the one hand he is afraid to let you share his life because like his mother you will find his flaws, his mistakes and dump him, but on the other hand he wants a wife who is just as perfect as his mother wanted him to be.

A child who is brought up in an atmosphere of criticism often becomes a critical adult who in his turn criticises the person he loves the most.

EXPLORATION – UNDERSTANDING – ACTION

Three steps in understanding the behaviour of a CPM

1. Exploration

Remember a CPM is a man in conflict

Half of him wants a relationship with you and the other half is afraid of what you might expect of him. Because of this he is torn in two directions. At the beginning of a relationship he feels safe, because of the very fact that you are not committed to him. So he can give full rein to his desire to have you, and to have a relationship with you. He may even indicate that he is looking for a meaningful relationship not just a passing affair. He is not trying to deceive you, he is expressing how he is feeling at that time.

Sometimes very intense initial passion does last a lifetime. Two people meet and fall in love, they just know that this is the person they want to spend the rest of their life with. But the majority of men take their time before they express such intensity of feelings. They take the trouble to get to know you, to find out what you are really like. Remember, a man who is really interested in commitment will be much more likely to take his time when it comes to the courtship game of love.

2. Understanding

Recognise that he does not think the way you do

The confusing thing is that the sort of behaviour many a CPM displays at the beginning of the relationship is that of a man you have known for some time, who has thought about the future, and is seriously thinking about a long-term committed relationship. For your part, if you were expressing such a high level of desire and longing, that would be because you were seeing this relationship as having a future together. So it is perhaps natural to assume that this is how he is feeling. Wrong – that is a fatal mistake with a commitment phobic man. It's easy to assume that the CPM thinks the same way as you do. But what you need to understand is – that he doesn't. The future may not be part of his thinking, but it needs to be part of yours. By this I am not suggesting that you should be manipulating and calculating or drag him yelling and protesting into marriage. He sees you as very desirable so he will go all out to get you. He is not concerned with the long-term effects of what he might be doing or saying. That does not mean he necessarily does not want a long-term relationship with you, it's that he has not really thought about it in any great depth.

So it is up to you to set the pace and not make the mistake of thinking that at this stage in the relationship he has his sights set on any long-term goal. He is not really thinking about what the future might hold, what he is concentrating on is a much shorter-term goal – that is a relationship with you.

3. Action

If he is promising the moon, a little scepticism is a wise response

So don't be taken in by his high-octane assault on your emotions. Give yourself time to see if you want to take your chances on love, or should you take note of the warning bells ringing in your head and make the decision that he is a worst-case commitment phobic and that it's better to bail out before you are too deeply involved? The questions you should be asking yourself are:

- Is this man right for me? Someone you feel that you could love and trust and who would be able to feel the same way about you. If you have many doubts at this stage, don't just ignore them, don't let your heart rule your head. It is still early days, you need time to see if these fears are unfounded or if your initial instincts were spot on.
- Am I allowing myself to be swept along by all these romantic feelings, because if so I need to get a grip on reality. If a relationship is going to last it has to be built on solid foundations not fantasy, and a relationship like that takes time, so don't get sweet-talked into taking any short cuts.
- Am I turning a blind eye to all his faults because he seems to want me so much? It feels so fantastic to be so utterly desired that you convince yourself that this would make up for the shortcomings in the rest of the relationship, or indeed the things about him that bug you.

It is very important at the beginning of the relationship that you stay in control of yourself and your feelings. The more he seems like your knight in shining armour, the more you need to keep your feet on the ground and refuse to join him in that land of make believe.

Instead take time getting to know each other, explore what his attitudes are to long-term relationships, look at what his previous relationships have been like. If he has a bad track record, don't assume he will be different with you, he might be, but not if he is a 'worst-case CPM'. Make sure that he as well as you recognise that a lasting relationship needs to be built on solid foundations. If you pile up the bricks without the cement in between they will all come tumbling down.

WHAT YOU CAN DO TO HELP REDUCE HIS SENSE OF PANIC

At the beginning of the relationship the commitment phobic man will go all out to woo you, but once he feels he has wooed and won you might start to see signs of change in him. This is not because he doesn't want you now that you have fallen in love with him, it is more to do with the fact that he is uncertain about where the relationship is going. He is afraid, because he has not thought of this before. Up until now all his efforts where focused on his pursuit of you. Now he has you and he knows that his feelings are reciprocated or he realises that you have started to fall in love with him, he frequently starts to panic.

This may be after just a short time together or after you have been together for some time. It is at a point when he realises that you are expecting more of him than he perhaps knows how to give. It dawns on him that you see this as a fully paid-up committed relationship, or when he thinks that you have expectations that the relationship will move forward and become more permanent.

THE CPM'S PANIC ATTACK

The most typical response when a CPM feels fear and sees that you are expecting more from him than he feels able to give is that he has a 'Panic Attack'. That means that his behaviour towards you changes and that usually involves either fight or flight. That way he is then able to put either emotional or physical distance between you; it is only when he has established that, that the rising panic inside him is able to subside.

- Where he once made you feel so good, he now begins to criticise you. He finds fault with everything you do. He comments unfavourably on your appearance, weight, clothes you wear. It is so much easier to 'fault-find' with you than to admit that there is anything about him that has changed.
- He 'sets limits' around the relationship – telling you he loves you a little less often, making love less or losing interest altogether, failing to telephone you as he used to, cancelling dates, turning up hours later than he promised. If you are living together he reduces the amount of time you have together. He works late at the office, or brings work home, he is always busy with something else, like sport, hobbies or meeting his friends.
- He may even end the relationship altogether. It may be some or all of these things and more. But one thing is certain, it will make you feel totally confused. Why, you ask yourself, is the man who up until now you thought loved you, expressing such doubt about you or the relationship?
- Don't blame yourself. It is unlikely that there is anything wrong with you, it's much more likely to be his fear of commitment that is causing the problem. But because you think it's you the chances are that you will bend over backwards to try to please him. You think that if you show him how intensely you love him he will be reassured and show you love in return. But this is the very thing that increases his panic, because he either feels overwhelmed by your love or more trapped than ever.

Rules to reduce his panic attacks

- Don't drop everything that you are doing so that you can be available for him when he calls.
- Don't cancel previous arrangements with friends if he calls to invite you out.
- Don't sit around waiting for the telephone to ring.
- Don't call him and suggest a date.
- Don't tell him that two can live as cheaply as one and suggest that you move in with him.
- Don't tell his friends that you can't live without him.
- Do fill your life with things you want to do, people you want to see.
- Do be pleased to see him when you are together, don't nag him to see more of each other.
- Do show him that you have an independent life away from him.
- Do make it clear that you have commitments and you are not prepared to drop everything and dance to his tune.
- Do accept invitations from friends to parties, events, the theatre and even a date or two if you keep them at a purely friendship level.

In a relationship with a CPM it is important that you look after yourself so don't drop everything else that is important to you and let your life revolve around him; if he becomes the only important part of your life, and it does not work out you will feel totally empty and bereft because you have allowed your life to get out of balance.

HOW TO MOVE THE RELATIONSHIP FORWARD

This is a very crucial stage in the relationship. It is not the time to shower him with love or tell him he is the most important person in the world. If he is having second thoughts about this relationship, it won't help if you bend over backwards to please him, and you won't be doing yourself any favours either. There is no point in having a relationship where the price you pay is subjugating all your needs to the man in your life. That won't make him stay, or if he does stay it will only allow him to walk all over you, before he eventually leaves you.

Establish your independence

So when you feel there is a change in his behaviour towards you, don't go all out to show him how much you love him. Don't drop everything else so that all your life revolves around him. Don't be available any time of the day or night. That will only increase his sense of panic. What you need to do is to withdraw from him a little, not in an angry, hurt sort of way, but more subtly. Perhaps by being a little less available to him, going out more and doing things with other people, spending a weekend away with friends, avoiding long telephone calls or ending them first. Try not to see it as game-playing, but more as creating some space between you both, so that his feelings of panic can subside a little. That then may enable him to view the relationship more rationally, and assess quite how much he is missing you, and what it might feel like to lose you altogether. As

G.K. Chesterton said, 'The way to love anything is to realise it might be lost.'

It is only by retaining your independence, by being reasonably self-sufficient and by not allowing everything to revolve around him that he will be okay about his relationship with you. Recognise that if he thinks that you are a woman who loves too much he will feel like taking large steps in the opposite direction.

If he is going to learn to overcome his fear of commitment, like any person who is fearful he can only take small steps at a time. It is confusing to be involved with such a man, because for many CPM it is not that he does not want a committed relationship it is that he is afraid of having one.

Get to know his family and friends

No man is an island and if he tries to keep himself as such, you will not have anything like a complete picture of him. By meeting his parents and his brothers and sisters, you will get to know him better. You will see if he is loving and close, whether it is a family where everyone talks openly and easily, or do they talk too much and no one really ever listens. It is a time when you learn a little about the family culture, what their expectations are of each other, how caring or uncaring they are. But you will also learn about him. Do they refer to a long list of broken hearts in his wake, does he have the reputation of loving and leaving, are his brothers and sisters in stable relationships or do they avoid them, or are they involved in ones that are constantly breaking down? Does he have a problematical or unloving relationship with his mother? Is she smothering and domineering, is she over-indulgent and spoiling, or cold and rejecting? Did he have a very acrimonious or expensive divorce, so that he is terrified of committing himself again? I am not suggesting that you find excuses for his behaviour, or that you try and become his therapist (though it might help if he found one for himself), but what I am recommending is that by knowing something about his family of origin you will have more idea why he behaves in the way he does. Nor am I saying that all men who have these sorts of experiences turn out to be afraid of commitment, but some undoubtedly do.

Make sure you are speaking the same language

You need to steady the pace, to slow it down to bring a bit of reality into the relationship if you want it to have a future. Then stand back a bit and take a good hard look at this relationship. Are you speaking the same language? Is his idea of commitment where he wants to take you next weekend, whereas you think as he seems so mad about you he must be thinking in the long term.

With a commitment phobic it is easy to misread the signals, so now is the time to check them out. You see, because he is so good at sweeping you off your feet with his enthusiasm, it is easy to feel that his idea of a committed relationship is the same as yours. You know what you mean by a commitment, what you need to establish is does it have the same meaning for him.

For example when he talks about all the things he wants to do with you, running along the shore at midnight, taking you to the most romantic city in the world, shopping together in Portobello Market, he is thinking about all those romantic moments, the high spots in the relationship. It all sounds wonderful but he is not necessarily thinking about all the in-between times and he may not be thinking about any long-term future plans together. So it's important that you don't assume he is. Keep your feet on the ground and give yourself a chance to see if the way he talks is the same way that you are seeing the relationship going.

And finally

For many CPMs it is only once they are married that the panic sets in. It is then that their fears break through to the surface, causing hurt and confusion, in their wake.

After the honeymoon is over

Sometimes the panic can surface as soon as you wave goodbye to your family and friends and set off on your honeymoon. For others it takes a little longer for the warning signs to appear. It can be totally confusing if it happens once you are married. Here after all is a man who has made a commitment to you in his marriage vows and now he seems to be acting in a way that makes you feel he wished he hadn't. It can be the very act of marriage that triggers fears of being trapped, put into a cage from which there is no escape. He looks at the woman he has married and his love turns to panic as it suddenly hits him that he has promised to spend the rest of his life with this person and 'for ever' seems a terrifyingly long time. For other married CPMs it is more of a slow burn approach, as he finds the emotional intimacy and togetherness of married life difficult to cope with. So he perhaps throws himself into work, hobbies, or affairs as a way of maintaining his independence and/or emotional distance from you. But I will be dealing with that later in this book.

7

Learning to understand each other

Mary: It was hard to communicate with you.
You were always communicating with yourself.
The line was busy.

Act II, *Mary, Mary,* Jean Kerr, 1960

HOW TO COMMUNICATE BETTER

All loving, satisfying, intimate relationships are based on good communication. Where you love and respect each other, where you feel safe to express your needs, where you can admit to your strengths and weaknesses and where you feel you understand each other's needs. The need for good communication is important in all relationships and this is particularly so with a CPM. It is so easy to get your wires crossed and not be clear about what he is thinking and feeling, because his is a world of mixed messages, loving you and being scared what loving you implies. Deborah Tannen, a professor of linguistics and author, highlights the differences in her book *That's Not What I Mean*. She says that men and women differ in their conversational style and therefore can often misunderstand each other; and that this is particularly so when they move into deep more loving long-term relationships where women feel 'After all this time he should know what I want without my telling him', whereas men feel 'We should be able to tell each other what we want.'

Communication is always about balancing opposing needs for involvement and independence. Though all human beings need both intimacy and independence, intimacy in relationships tends to be more important to women and independence to men. And the reality is that a CPM frequently has a greater need for independence than other men.

A married man who fears commitment because of these conflicting emotions can so easily sabotage or undermine the central relationship, by being over-committed to work, by having an affair, or by being more committed to his mother, father, brothers and sisters than he is to you. He can also keep his commitment fears at bay by being emotionally unavailable to you.

So it is particularly important to be able to recognise what the problem is that you are dealing with, and equally important that you are both able to communicate with each other. You can't begin to alter your view of things or the way you behave or your actions without being aware of what you are doing, Simply put, if as a man or a woman you understand you have a problem with commitment then you have a choice about doing something about it. If you don't understand, then you are likely to flounder around in the dark relentlessly repeating the same old behaviour.

So I felt it was important in this book not only to explore and try and understand why some men have problems with commitment, but having gained that knowledge it was also essential to show how to open up the lines of communication. That way the issues that threaten to drive you apart can be understood and tackled together.

TECHNIQUES OF COMMUNICATION

It's all too easy to go about it in the wrong way, because negative emotions such as anger, fear, frustration, disappointment all take their toll. But it does not have to be like that if both of you are prepared to listen to each other and make changes.

If you want to achieve an emotionally satisfying relationship as a couple you have to find the right balance between you, in your search for intimacy, closeness and distance within that relationship. It is quite usual for men and women in relationships to seek different levels of emotional intimacy. The most common reason why relationships run into difficulties is because of a breakdown in communication. It is also the most frequently presented problem when it comes to why couples come for counselling.

Rebecca, a very lively and outgoing woman in her late thirties, had come with her husband Sam to counselling because she felt that they no longer communicated about things that were important to them as a couple. Their level of talking rarely strayed beyond which child needed to be collected from their music lesson or Brownies, why they had run out of bread yet again, or who was not pulling their weight when it came to household chores, or the fact that the grass needed cutting.

Rebecca felt she was second best to Sam's job and his many other work-related commitments. The person she felt he was least committed to was her, his wife. The job she felt was increasingly getting more and more of his time and attention. Rebecca sat quietly listening to her husband who was sitting opposite her, leaning back in his chair with his arms folded and not looking at her. He was explaining very coolly and analytically that for one third of the time he thought that his wife might leave him, but that the other two thirds of the time he thought that she was probably not likely to, as she was committed to the marriage and their three children. When he had finished talking she looked at her emotionally buttoned-up husband with tears streaming down her face and said, 'Don't you understand, I don't want you to coldly work out in percentages my dissatisfaction with the marriage. I want you to say to me, I love you. I don't want you just to speculate whether I would leave you for another man. I want you to show some feelings about how you don't want me to do that. I want you to tell me – it is me you really want. I want you to tell me that you love me like I love you. I want to be special to you, don't you understand?' she pleaded.

Sam looked at her and smiled nervously, and shifted a little uncomfortably in his chair. Then after a long silence and a little prompting he said, 'I do have feelings, I know I do feel these things inside me, it's just that I don't know how to express them.'

Part of the problem also was Sam did not feel the same need as Rebecca to talk about feelings and emotional issues. He said: 'My way of dealing with much of my life is to sort these things out for myself in my head. Also if it is something that really concerns me, I know I don't share it with Rebecca as I don't want to add to her burdens.' It was only by looking at this further that Sam was able to see how much he was cutting Rebecca out of his life. How can you really feel close to someone if so much of you is withheld from the person you love and who loves you? But Rebecca also had to try and accept that though Sam could learn to share more, it might always fall short of how much she would like. But what she needed most from him was to feel he was really committed to her. That he made her feel that she was special, as he had done in the early days of their marriage, and as he learnt to do again.

It is important that both of you are able to understand your different individual levels of need in emotional closeness and intimacy and work out a situation where both of you have many of your needs met, but it won't be all of them. Because if one person's needs are continually sacrificed on the altar of their partner's needs, the dissatisfactions will grow and grow in the person whose needs are being ignored, and as sure as night follows day the love they felt for that person will eventually die.

Avoid the broad brush approach – Aim to be more specific

Let us take as an example the spouse like Matt who spends all his time at work and you never know when to expect him home. You have been working hard all day, looking after three small children, or trying to juggle work and a young family. Six o'clock – seven o'clock eight o'clock slips by. You keep expecting to hear his key in the door, the children want to see him before they go to bed, one needs help with their homework, the other wants you to read them a bedtime story. Time goes on: you don't know whether to cook the supper, to eat your own supper or wait for him. So the frustration and anger mounts. At last you hear his key in the latch.

As he comes through the door, the following dialogue takes place:

Him: Hello darling, I'm home. (He calls out happily)
You: What time do you call this then, I have been expecting you for the last couple of hours.
Him: (His mood changing.) Quit nagging, what is the point of coming home at all if all you can do is criticise me, I've had a bloody awful day; I don't want more of the same at home.
You: (Your anger rising.) Well don't bother then, stay at the office. You spend enough time there already, so it won't make any difference.
Him: (now also furious) Don't worry, I will in future.
Result: Bang goes your evening, and there have probably been many more evenings that have also ended up that way.

You will undoubtedly both be too angry to sort it out there and then, but don't make the mistake of avoiding tackling the subject. When things are calmer say to your partner, 'Can we please make some time when we can talk things through together? Perhaps when the children are asleep, or out.' Having arranged a time don't go in on the attack or blaming mode like: 'You are quite impossible, you never let me know when you are going to be home.' But start with talking about how you feel. For example: 'I want to talk to you about something I get very hurt by. I never know when to expect you home.' Then explain how it is for you, not knowing whether to let the children stay up a little longer so they can see him, or put them to bed. What it is like coping with their disappointment if they are expecting him and he does not arrive. How you don't know whether to cook a meal or wait for him. How if he is going to be late back you might like to arrange to get a babysitter so you can go out to the cinema or for a drink with a girlfriend. Remember to tell him how it feels to be you, but don't go into a full frontal attack, and really listen to what he has to say in response.

Then it's time to get practical. Ask about the practicalities of the situation from his point of view, discuss with him what ideas you have that would work for you. Can he tell you what time he will be back when he leaves for work in the morning? If that is not possible can he ring you at around five o'clock or when he is leaving the office to tell you when he will be back? Find something that goes a reasonable way to suiting both your needs. The important thing is both of you need to feel you have benefited from the arrangement. So you know where you are and can plan things to suit you around that. Then when he does get home there is a welcoming reception committee, or you have been free to go out for a couple of hours and you are both pleased to see each other when you are together again.

When you need to dig deeper

In many discussions and arguments there are two or more levels on which we operate. One is a more surface level and the others are far deeper. But you need to tackle the more obvious issue before digging deeper. So let's take this typical scenario a little further. Of course you mind about him having no understanding about how frustrating it is for you if you never know when to expect him, you need to be explicit about that and together arrive at a solution, so you don't feel he takes you for granted and he feels you are glad to see him when he returns home.

But let's say that the deeper issue is that you feel that he is getting more and more involved with his job and this is at the expense of his commitment to you. If this is happening in your relationship what you are talking about may not be what you really want to say.

You say: How on earth do you expect us to have any sort of marriage when you spend all your time at work?

But the real issue is: I feel he would rather be at work than at home with me and the children (if there are any). I feel unloved and neglected. I fear that he finds work more interesting than me.

What *he* hears is: 'I have a demanding, nagging wife who doesn't understand the work situation. Damn it all, I am after all working my socks off to provide for her and the kids, what more does she want?'

Again, find a time when you can talk, and explain to him what you are really feeling, and listen to his situation at work. Then look at options. He may have a demanding job, long working hours may be part of his workplace culture. But if he does not schedule time for you and the family, then at the end of the day he will not have a family there to work for.

So you may need to recognise that you are not married to a nine to five man. But he needs to appreciate that if he is working late most evenings then he has to reassess his priorities. Maybe he agrees that for a couple of evenings a week he is home at a reasonable hour. That if work is taking him over during the week then weekends and holidays should be sacrosanct. Maybe he could pay for a babysitter so that the two of you could have a night out together once a week.

What is important is that you reach an agreement that suits you both. That means that you settle for an arrangement where both of you are getting an equal proportion of your needs met, where neither of you feels that you are always sacrificing your needs to those of your partner.

Let's take another example. **Your gripe is that he spends most of his free time playing sport or with his friends.** **You.** You are more interested in playing football than being with me and, what's more, I can't stand your friends.

What he hears is – **Him.** You are a selfish man, and what's more so are all your friends.

The real issue is. **You.** I am stuck at home looking after the kids all week and weekends as well. I would like to have some time when I can go out and do something I enjoy. It's not that I don't like your friends – they are all right really, but because you see so much of them it leaves very little time for us to do things together.

So discuss how you feel, but also come up with some suggestions that would result in a fairer distribution of leisure time and work out a solution together. Which could be that he sees his friends a couple of nights a week and plays football on Saturday afternoons, but not four nights a week and all weekend.

Don't go in on the attack – you will only get a defensive response

If you go in on the attack he will only feel criticised and that you think it's all his fault. If you want him to listen to you then don't start the conversation in blaming mode. How you say it is important. I am sure you know yourself that if you feel you are being criticised you are unlikely to be receptive to his needs or request.

Use 'I' messages rather than 'You' messages

So use the 'I feel' message, not the 'You are' message. For example, 'I feel – hurt, lonely, upset, insecure.' Don't start by saying: 'You are – selfish, inconsiderate, a complete bastard.'

It's important to make it clear it's his behaviour that you don't like, is annoying you, upsetting you or making you angry. It's not that you don't like him as a person. If you erode his self-esteem and say he is a complete bastard, he won't feel good about himself or you. So then he is likely to set up a counter attack, to deny your accusations, lapse into silence, walk away from you altogether by leaving the room, going to the pub, or rushing back to work as soon as he can.

Choose your time with care

When are you most likely to have an argument? When he or you have just returned from work. When you have been sitting in a traffic jam, when he has been fighting for space on a hot stuffy overcrowded and late commuter train. When you are tired and it's late at night. When his boss has been giving him hell. When the children have been driving you up the wall. When he has been drinking a little to much. When you are trying to avoid sex.

These are all classic times when arguments are most likely to happen. So they are the times to be avoided as it's unlikely that anything much will be discussed rationally and that anything will be resolved.

So if you want to really talk things through and hopefully get his undivided attention, it needs to be at a time when both of you are feeling calm. When you can have some time on your own without the children interrupting you. Don't make the mistake of thinking that because things are calm you must not broach the subject; it's just when things are calm that you will have the best opportunity to sort things out between you. If things are not talked through resentments build up and if you don't talk about them they won't just go away.

It's good to talk

As a woman you and I may agree with this statement, but many men do not necessarily feel the same way. In my experience more men than women seem to have difficulty talking about their feelings. In counselling the biggest complaint I hear from women about the men in their lives is that the men can't really talk about their feelings and don't want to hear about hers either. If your man falls into this category you may need to set up your stall and embark on a sensitive yet effective sales pitch. In other words if you can help him to see what is in it for him he will be much more motivated to talk more openly about himself and his needs, and in turn to listen to your needs and how you feel.

When you are trying to communicate with each other it's important that you both understand the rules of good communication. So to avoid it being one-sided explain to him what you are doing and suggest that he tries this approach as well as you. That way when he has an issue, a problem or grievance that is troubling him you are more likely to understand and respond to his needs, as, hopefully he will to yours.

Remember the Golden Rules of Good Communication are:

- Be specific – Avoid the broad brush approach.
- Say what you mean – avoid two-level discussions.
- Don't go in on the attack use; 'I feel' messages, not 'You are' ones.
- Choose the right time.

How to encourage a man to talk

Show him: Appreciation, Acceptance and Trust.

If a man is reluctant to talk, you can help him by encouragement and particularly by acceptance and appreciation. As women we talk to share our thoughts and feelings, for us that creates closeness and intimacy. Men tend to need a reason to talk, they don't just talk for the sake of sharing.

Men may talk to express their views on politics, the work or job they do, their interest in sport or women. When men talk together they are much more likely to give information to each other, to express their views, their thoughts on a wide range of subjects. What they are far less likely to do is share how they feel with the other men. This is not part of themselves that they generally feel safe enough to expose. So it is not really surprising that men often feel ill at ease when it comes to their intimate relationships with women; when the woman in their lives wants them to talk about how they feel rather than what they think.

For most women talking about feelings is not so difficult because that is how we relate to each other, to our families and friends a lot of the time. This different level of experience and practice is one of the reasons for women's dissatisfaction about many men's reluctance to talk, and the frustration of men who do not understand why all this talk is so important to women. It is often not so much a case that men won't talk, but that they don't know how to express how they feel or that doing so makes them feel too vulnerable.

Many men find a sense of panic setting in when they think a woman wants to talk about issues involving their relationship. So more often than not they back away. They are not sure what is expected of them and so they feel they don't know what to say. Alternatively they feel if they open up to the woman she will either see him as weak and unmacho, or she will take advantage of him by drawing him out and then going for the jugular. The result is that they withdraw even more from the woman as they see her request to talk as a demand or too threatening. The man's refusal or inability to talk then feels like a further rejection to the woman, and she ends up feeling that they don't care about her or worse that they don't really love her enough to try and meet her needs.

Because as women our needs are to talk and be listened to, we therefore assume that this is what men also want. Of course some do, but many more shy away from too much talk. If a man has a problem he is more likely to want to withdraw from us and think it through quietly. They often do not want to share how they are feeling but prefer to try to sort it out on their own. Alternatively they push uncomfortable or difficult thoughts well into the background so they don't have to deal with them at all. They believe that these thoughts will go away, and maybe for them they do. The problem is that this is rarely how the woman sees it.

So if you want your man to talk, then in the main don't expect him to initiate the talk. But you can help him to talk by sharing some of your thoughts and feelings with him in the hope that he will at least listen to you, which is a good beginning.

You could talk about what sort of day you have had at work; if he sees you doing this then he might join in and talk about his day. Maybe you have concerns about the children and so by initiating the conversation about them he then may be able to respond about how he feels about them. As long as he can trust you and he does not feel blamed or criticised there is every chance he may follow your example and respond to your need to talk and be listened to. Remember men will rarely initiate 'relationship talk' without being prompted.

Relationship Talk

When a man starts to open up he needs to feel accepted, he needs to see that you understand his point of view. You may not necessarily share it, though it helps if you genuinely do, but you do need to show you value it. You need to show him you can accept him even though you may or may not agree with what he is saying. You need to show that it may be different from how you think or see things but that is all right. To begin with talking is likely to be much more about fulfilling your needs than his. It is important that you make it clear to him how much you appreciate him listening and talking to you. Just saying something as simple as 'It means so much to know you are really listening to me' or 'It makes such a difference to be able to share my feelings with you.' Most men underestimate how much it does mean to a woman to be really listened to, so tell him. As he gains more understanding of how good it feels to you to be listened to he might try it out for himself.

Learning to listen

If a man starts to open up, it is terribly important that you really listen to what he is saying. However good we think we are at listening most of us are not quite as good as we think we are in that department. It is vital that we do really listen to what our partner is trying to tell us and that, as I have said, goes for men too.

It is all too easy to listen with one ear while the other ear is listening to what we are planning to say when our partner has stopped talking. We are particularly prone to do this if we feel strongly about something, or if we have been waiting too long for an opportunity to talk about what is troubling us, or when we are very angry. It's easy convincing ourselves we are listening when really we are concentrating on our own thoughts rather than what our partner is saying to us.

Think back to the early days of a relationship: You are in love, you are walking on air, you adore each other, you can hardly keep your hands off each other. At the beginning of a relationship you spend time learning about how the other person thinks and feels. You listen to what the other one has to say, you make time to be together, you show you value them as a person, you try to understand each other's needs, you tell them how much you care, and you make them feel loved and appreciated. These things should not stop because you are living together or married.

Admittedly you can't live at those dizzy, heady, heightened 'in love' times for ever, but you can continue to love each other in a deeper more enduring way. But so often these very things that made it possible for you to communicate in the first place fall by the wayside. The listening and talking you did in the early days of your relationship should not just be happening in the courtship stage but should be the solid foundations that you build your marriage or relationship on; once established they should continue throughout that relationship.

In a good marriage or a good relationship you should be good friends as well as lovers. If a friendship between two people is to last you have to care enough about the other person to listen to them and to support them. To be there in the difficult times, not just in the good times. To respect them as a person, to enjoy the similarities and respect their differences and it is just the same with a marriage or committed relationship.

How to make your partner feel that you are really listening to them

The secret of making someone really feel that they are being listened to is to give them your undivided attention so they are not competing with the children, the telephone, the television or any other outside intrusion.

Active listening

Active listening is almost the number one lesson in counsellor training and it is a very valuable lesson in relationships. All too often when listening to another person we don't give them our full attention. The essential element in active listening is to concentrate on your partner's feelings rather than your own. And secondly to show them you are doing this.

- Don't jump in and interrupt them with your own thoughts and feelings when they are in full flow.
- The technique in active listening is to check out with them that you fully understand what they are saying. You do this by reflecting back to them in your own words what you understand they are saying. 'So you feel that I spend too long on the telephone in the evening talking to my sister, and there is no time left for us to be together', or 'you hate the fact that I wear the same old clothes around the house while my pretty clothes just hang there in the

wardrobe', or 'it really annoys you that my Mum and Dad always come here for lunch on Sundays but we hardly ever see your parents.'

- This checking system or reflecting back what you think someone has said to you is invaluable because it makes the person talking really feel they have been heard. If they feel that you have understood what they have been saying, then they are more able to listen to you in return.
- It also gives you a chance to check out that you have really understood what they were saying, rather than thinking or assuming that you know.
- If you have not got it quite right it gives your partner the chance to say what they mean more precisely so that further misunderstandings can be avoided.
- For the person talking, to hear what they were saying repeated back to them sometimes may make them realise that actually what they have said is a little unfair, or rather too harsh.

The import thing about listening to what your partner has to say is that though you may not agree with them, you are acknowledging that they have a right to express their views. That way you are not just dismissing them, or implying that what they are saying counts for nothing.

How a man thinks he is helping

If you are trying to talk to the man in your life about something that is worrying you or you are concerned about, then the worst response a man can give is one of anger or aggression. The second worst when you want to share your concerns or worries with him is for the man to say, 'Don't worry yourself so much about it' or 'It will be all right, don't blow it up out of proportion.' He thinks he is calming you down and reassuring you, but the effect of his remarks is that as a woman you feel dismissed. You feel as if he does not understand what you are feeling and – worse still perhaps – that he does not care.

What you are asking for is time to talk your worries through with him, to look at why you are feeling the way you do, and what you might do about it. You do want his contribution but you are not after a brief reassurance or instant solutions. One of Sam's complaints about Rebecca was she was over emotional and hysterical, and Rebecca said that she felt so frustrated with Sam as he rarely expressed what he was feeling, that it made her respond like a two-year-old, desperately screaming and yelling because she never felt she was getting through to him. But when Sam learnt to be much more open with her Rebecca learnt that she did not have to scream and shout to get a response. They also agreed to schedule time to spend together each week; with four demanding children and a very busy and absorbing job this was not easy, but they both saw it as a priority. That meant they could enjoy being just the two of them and they were really able to talk about what mattered to them both. Six months later when they returned for an agreed counselling appointment to see how the relationship was progressing, they both said they felt they were equally committed to each other and the marriage was stronger than it had ever been. They also said smiling at each other that the children seemed happier and more secure. They left to have lunch together before Sam dashed back to work and Rebecca set off to collect her youngest daughter from school.

Both Rebecca and Sam worked hard to negotiate and compromise over their different needs of intimacy and independence and they were able to achieve a loving and supportive relationship. As Sigmund Freud said, 'The ability to love and the capacity to work are the hallmarks of full maturity.'

Show him you appreciate him

One of the most important things you can do for the man you love is to show him how much you appreciate him. When he has taken time to talk with you, tell him how lovely that was, or how much better that made you feel. If he tells you he loves you, tell him how you love to hear him say that. If he makes love to you wonderfully tell him so. When he shows care and tenderness towards his children, reinforce how good that is. When he cooks a meal, paints the bedroom, or cuts the lawn, tell him how delicious it tastes or looks. Appreciation does need to be a two-way thing, so hopefully he will also learn how to make you feel good too.

8

Getting to 'I do'

It has been since time began,
And ever will, till time lose breath,
That love is a mood – no more – to man,
And love to a woman is life or death.

Ella Wheeler Wilcox, 1850–1919

WHEN HE IS RELUCTANT TO POP THE QUESTION

Many men nowadays are afraid to make the commitment of marriage. They see marriage as a trap, as a hole they want to avoid falling into, as a state of affairs they want to run away from, a noose around their necks, a dead-end relationship from which they must escape. Many CPMs will settle into live-in or cohabiting relationships but their particular stumbling block comes when the question of marriage rears its ugly head.

WHEN YOU ARE BOTH HAPPY TO HAVE A LIVE-IN RELATIONSHIP

For a small proportion of men a cohabiting relationship where they are fully committed to their partner in a life-long union is thc samc as marriage. They are genuinely just as committed to the woman they love as any married man is to his wife. If the woman feels that for her the man she is with is a hundred per cent committed to her and she is genuinely happy with a live-in relationship then there is no problem. But life has an irritating habit of not being quite as simple as that as men and woman often settle into living-together relationships with quite different agendas. You may see cohabitation as a life-long committed relationship or as a prelude to marriage, when what he is actually saying is 'I'm committed to you, darling, in my fashion.' And he is not talking about that forever ingredient.

DOES HE HAVE A POSITIVE VIEW OF MARRIAGE?

Men who hold these lacklustre views of marriage see it as something that turns relationships sour, or that marriage spoils a perfectly good relationship. Marriage, they believe, is what all women are secretly trying to lure the unsuspecting male into. It has that 'For ever' sign hanging over it so must at all costs be avoided.

These negative views of marriage are deeply entrenched and go back a long way. Such a man frequently has had first-hand experience of marriage ending in divorce, either his own or from previous generations, perhaps his parents' marriage, or that of uncles and aunts to whom he was close. This may even extend to marriage breakdown in his grandparents' generation as well. So his view of marriage is that it is a problematical relationship which only causes pain and unhappiness. His experience tells him that people who are married quarrel and fight or indulge in long and protracted silences where no one talks to each other or they only communicate through the children.

Some men who have experienced marriage breakdown as a child go into marriage determined that theirs will be different. They see it as a chance to recreate the happiness that they feel was missing in their own family of origin. But for many other men the effect is that they end up feeling so anti-marriage they are determined they are not going to touch it with a barge pole. They are not going to risk ending up as a victim of an unhappy marriage, they are not going to allow marriage to contaminate what they feel is a good relationship.

Many men who fear marriage are less fearful of live-in and cohabiting relationships so they enter into these more freely and it is only when the question of marriage appears on the horizon that they start to panic. The parameters of living-together relationships are not clearly defined as is marriage and the bonds seem looser. So very often when two people embark on such a relationship they hold very different views about what they mean by commitment, and often make the mistake of assuming that they hold a joint and complementary view. Similarly you may start off with both of you happy just to live together but people and relationships are not static and what happens is that whereas one of you is happy to continue to live together the other one now wants marriage.

SETTING LIMITS WITH MR FOREVER ON HOLD

Men often accuse woman of trying to tie them down before they are ready. If you are only months into a relationship and are already starting to suggest how he should redecorate his home, hinting that two can live as cheaply as one, so why not move in with each other, or you are lingering in front of jewellery shops or flipping through the pages of *Bride* magazine – then they have a point.

On the other hand if it's perhaps two years into the relationship and those heady romantic dizzy days of being newly in love have moved on to a cosy routine, you are entitled to look for more commitment, if that is what you want. If your relationship is at a stage where you are spending most of your time together, taking joint holidays, his friends are your friends and your friends are his, you are reminding him when it's his mother's birthday, or you are living together, then the likelihood is that you will be thinking about the future. This does not need to be a solo experience, you need to know how he is thinking. Two or three years into a relationship is frequently crunch time because often he is happy with how things are and you are wanting the relationship to move forward. You need to know what your limits are and so does he. If he is going to be 'Mr Forever on Hold' and you are wanting to share your life with him now and in the future, he needs to know. If you want marriage, and maybe also children, and he seems happy with the status quo, don't pretend to yourself and to him that it is not important to you. Don't think that if you secretly wait and hope that your needs will suddenly dawn on him, they won't. I am not suggesting that you propose marriage to him, though you could do. What I am suggesting is that you can engage in 'future talk'. That is, what *you* want from this relationship – and how does that compare with what *he* wants?

If all his promises are jam tomorrow but never jam today, if his sentences are littered with perhaps, maybe, possibly, conceivably, someday, then you need to let him know that this is not good enough for you. It may seem like a big risk, and indeed it is, in so much as he may then start to make moves to end the relationship. But in the end if he really is not into commitment that is what would have happened anyway; all you will have done is brought forward the sell-by date. Catherine Zeta Jones, the arresting actress from *The Darling Buds of May* made it clear to former *Blue Peter* presenter John Leslie, after they had been together two years, that she wanted marriage. He backed off. She said: 'I was fed up waiting for him to propose.' He said he felt he was 'being browbeaten into marriage'.

HIGH PROFILE ALTAR-DODGERS

The aversion of CPMs to tying the knot is to be found across all classes and backgrounds, the unknown and the well-known. Sophie Rhys Jones played the waiting game for six years with Prince Edward. The actor George Clooney is still not walking up the aisle with his delectable girlfriend actress Celine Balitran. When it comes to Hugh Grant and Liz Hurley it's difficult to know which of them is dragging their feet when it comes to matrimony. When the beautiful model Elle Macpherson told Green Shield heir Tim Jefferies that she wanted marriage and children, he told her he didn't, so their three-year relationship broke up. The chances are that if he was not prepared to marry her after three years, it is almost inevitable that the same thing would have happened if she had waited another three years before confronting him.

Elle is now in a new relationship with French banker Arki Besson and they have a baby son. So if your relationship is not going in the direction you want the point to remember is that ending a relationship may be painful but it does free you up to meet a man who is happy to commit.

If you really want marriage and possibly children and you have been together a year or two it's important that you express what your needs are if your relationship is going to have the sort of future you want. The point about being open with your thoughts is that the man then understands what you want from him if the relationship is going to continue. It is not about ultimatums, but it is about the fact that you have needs, and that one of your basic needs is for a committed relationship. If the man loves you and does not want to lose you, it gives him the opportunity to focus his ideas and to see if his desire for you is greater than his fear of commitment.

CHECK OUT THAT YOU HAVE THE SAME AGENDA FOR THE FUTURE OF YOUR RELATIONSHIP

Many men who enter into live-in relationships do so on the understanding that this is something they are happy with for now. Theirs is a 'here and now relationship', they are not seeing it as a promise for the 'happily ever after'. A fact they may well not have shared with you. Their internal script goes something like this:

The Commitment Phobic's Living-together Agenda

1. I'm not ready for marriage.
2. I want to keep my options open.
3. I don't believe that any two people can promise to love each other and be together for ever. It is unrealistic.
4. It's fun playing Mr and Mrs and coming home to each other at the end of the day. It's great and it suits me for now. But please don't think this is a forerunner to the real thing.
5. Marriage is just a piece of paper. I'm happy living together. What difference would marriage make?
6. Marriage spoils relationships – look at my parents' marriage. Half my friends are unhappily married. Just look at the divorce rate in this country – I don't want to become another divorce statistic.

The Woman's Living-together Agenda

1. I'm happy with a live-in relationship for now. I don't know what I want for the future.
2. Living with a man makes me feel better about myself, because if I don't have a man who wants me I don't feel valued enough. If I don't have a man I don't have a life.
3. I'm not ready for marriage yet, but when I am this is the man I want to marry.
4. He wants us to live together. What I really want is marriage but if I hold out for marriage I might lose him.
5. To me, living together means that one day we will get married.
6. What I really want is marriage, but he hasn't asked me yet. If we live together perhaps he will.

HOLD OUT FOR THE COMMITMENT YOU WANT

If marriage is what you want don't be fobbed off with a live-in relationship. There is no point in betting on the chance that he might change his mind and pop the question. That sort of living arrangement is unlikely to lead to marriage. Don't suggest that a live-in arrangement would be rather fun while keeping your fingers crossed behind your back that once you are installed his thoughts will turn to marriage. It's a bad idea and the chances are they won't.

So if you are considering the prospect think very hard before you go down this bumpy road. So many couples have come to me at a crossroads in their relationship where the woman wants marriage and the man is happy to continue in the live-in relationship, that I know what a common experience this is. When I asked them how they first got together they seemed to have just slipped into living together without any real sharing about their commitment to each other or any real understanding of the future of that relationship.

Never assume that because you feel and think the way you do that is also how your partner thinks and feels. The only way you can ever begin to find out how you both feel is to talk about it. If you have made the assumption that when a man suggests living together this is going to be followed at some later date by a proposal of marriage you are likely to end up broken-hearted.

Think once, Think twice – Don't compromise

If you are engaged to be married, the wedding date has been set and it's only a matter of weeks or a couple of months away, then living together is likely to be a forerunner to marriage. But if not I believe many more women should think twice before embarking on a live-in relationship. Why are we as women so keen to play wife and homemaker for the man we love when he is not prepared to make the commitment we may want.

As a woman you may come out relatively unscathed if living together is something you choose to do because you are not interested in any long-term commitment from that particular man. If you just want to live with a man because you enjoy his company, or he is great in bed, fine. If you want to live with a variety of men before you finally settle for marriage, then fine. If you hate the idea of marriage and never want a ring on your finger, fine. If you think marriage is demeaning and a subjugation of women, then living together may suit both of you – fine. The danger is if you move in with a man you are madly in love with but you are less certain how he feels about you. You may be hearing wedding bells ringing in your ears, but he may be hearing alarm bells in his. So don't deny to yourself the risks you are taking.

If you think that living together without a real commitment is going to influence him to marry you, you are probably seriously deluding yourself and stand a very good chance of getting badly hurt. If he suggests that you live together because he is not sure about you and wants to see what it's like, think twice.

Living together should not be your audition for the part of his wife. He either loves you or he doesn't. If he doesn't know how he feels about you, then frankly he does not deserve to have a live-in relationship with you.

If you move in under those circumstances the chances are that you will spend a lot of time, and a huge amount of emotional investment in finding out several months, or in the worst-case scenario, several years later, what you feared in the first place, that he is not committed enough or not enough in love with you to want to marry you. By then your self-esteem will have been ripped to pieces as the years have passed and oceans of tears have been shed in the hope that he will one day eventually ask you to marry him.

Imagine the scene:

You and your boyfriend Michael have been going out together for two years, you are very much in love, happy with each other and your parents like Michael. You are both going to visit your parents for the weekend. You have been working hard all week, you get into the car on Friday evening and drive though the busy traffic to your parents' house. They welcome you both warmly, you all go into the house together. A delicious smell of cooking comes from the kitchen. You rush upstairs, have a quick shower and change and come down to join your parents. You and Michael are both feeling excited, your parents sense something is going on and look expectantly across the room at you both. Michael glances at them nervously and smiles; you say, bubbling over with happiness, we have something to tell you and, looking at Michael, 'Michael and I are going to get married.'

'Darling – That's marvellous news,' your mother says. Your father hugs you, your mother kisses you both. The air is filled with joy and excitement: a wedding in the family, a daughter who is in love with a man who wants to make her his wife. Your father laughing says, 'This calls for a celebration, we must have some champagne, we must celebrate this wonderful news.' Your mother is spilling over with questions: 'When did all this happen, how did he propose, when are you going to get married? Oh how lovely, darling, I'm so happy for you both.'

Imagine the same scene:

You arrive to stay with your parents, the same delicious cooking smells, you come down the same stairs to your parents, only this time you say, 'Michael and I have decided to live together.' However much they like Michael, their reaction will almost certainly not be the same. There will not be lots of joy and excitement expressed, your father will not rush out to buy champagne or insist on a celebration, they will not ask you how he proposed this idea to you. They will not be rushing out excitedly to tell the family and friends the wonderful news. This is not because they disapprove of you living together, though some do, they may be quite accepting about the news. After all, many couples choose to live together rather than marry. The fact is for the majority of people living together is just not as committed as marriage.

DON'T FOOL YOURSELF

Are you in a live-in relationship and if so are you possibly trying to convince yourself that if you hang in there long enough your partner will ask you to marry him? Are you pulling the wool over your own eyes and failing to see the signs that your partner has no real intention of making a deeper commitment? The problem is if you are into denial about what is really happening in the relationship you could be setting yourself up for a fall. So try the following quiz.

HOW TO RECOGNISE THE TELL-TALES SIGNS OF A CPM WHO FEARS THE 'M' WORD

1. **When the word 'Marriage' has been mentioned has he said:** a. I love the idea of marriage, b. Marriage is just a bit of paper, c. I don't feel ready for marriage yet, d. he said nothing at all.
2. **You have dropped hints about how one day you would like marriage and children – has he said:** a. Marriage always spoils a good relationship, b. My parents' marriage was nothing but arguments and rows, c. I think if two people really love each other then I'm all for marriage, d. I don't think it's possible to love someone for ever.
3. **You are having dinner with friends and the subject of marriage comes up.** a. Does he leave the room, b. try to change the topic of conversation, c. drag up all his favourite mother-in-law jokes, d. listen with interest.
4. **You are invited to a party together.** a. He flirts with every pretty women in the room. b. He spends virtually all the evening talking intimately and animatedly to just one woman, c. He circulates but also spends time with you, d. he says you go on your own, your friends are so boring.
5. **It's a year of weddings, and many of your friends are getting married.** a. He gets sentimental and serious-looking during the service, b. He is much more interested in attending the stag party than going to the wedding, c. He looks scared when the bride throws her bouquet in your direction, d. He really enjoys the whole event, even some of the girl talk about the big day.
6. **You say if we were to marry I would like to buy somewhere together, he says:** a He does not want to be

tied down to a mortgage, b. He is saving up to travel around the world, c. He loves the idea of creating a home for the two of you, d. He would love to but you will have to save for a down payment first.

7. **Does he exclude you from other important relationships?** a. No he always includes me, b. His children if he has any, c. When he visits his parents, d. His firm's Christmas party to which partners and spouses are invited.

Question one a-4. b-1. c-3. d-2. Question two a-3. b-2. c-4. d-1. Question three. a-1. b-2. c-3. d-4. Question four. a-3. b-1. c-4. d-2. Question five. a-4. b-2. c-1. d-3. Question six. a-2. b-1. c-4. d-3. Question seven a-4. b-1. c-2. d-3.

Points score.

1–10. This man has a serious problem, he is in the worst-case category of commitment phobia. Therefore he would be unlikely to be anywhere near ready to make any long-term commitment.

11–21. He has a problem with commitment, but he is not so entrenched that he cannot change. If your score is at the top end of the range he is more likely to be able to change.

22–28. If he had a commitment problem, he is either over it, or well on the road to recovery and if he is really in love, would be able to make a fully committed relationship.

DON'T BURY YOUR HEAD IN THE SAND IF YOU THINK HE HAS A PROBLEM WITH COMMITMENT

It was four years before Danielle saw the writing on the wall. Danielle, a PA to a company director, had at thirty-five been living with John, a man she adored, for four years. Much of their time together had been incredibly happy. But time was passing and she wanted more commitment from him. She said, 'One day it suddenly dawned on me that I was basically being "kept in the closet". He was a wonderful friend and lover but I began to get more and more fed up with the fact that he was excluding me from a large part of his life. To begin with I thought it was because we were so in love that he wanted me all to himself, then I realised there was more to it than that.' She said bitterly, 'I was never introduced to anyone, neither his family or friends. When we went out together he was always very careful that we did not go to places where we might see anyone who knew him. When he saw his children he always did so on his own. The reason he gave was that if his ex-wife found out about us she might stop him seeing the children.' Over the last couple of years Danielle remonstrated with John about these things, but to no avail. After four years together she made the decision to leave him.

'I could not take any more so one day when he was at work, I packed all my things and left. I secretly hoped that as he was always telling me how much he loved me, and how he wanted us to be together that he would ask me to come back and promise more commitment. Nothing of the sort happened. He simply got on with his life, with his job, with his children, without even a backward glance. My life was in ruins but he seemed unscathed. I feel so bitter that sometimes I lie awake at night plotting how I would like to kill him, he has hurt me so much, and seems to care so little.'

It took four years out of Danielle's life before she finally realised her man was never going to fully commit to her, let alone marry her. He was so convincing that she believed him when he told her that they had a very special relationship.

There is no point in not confronting him because you are afraid that if you do he will end the relationship. He might do, but unless you are happy with things the way they are, your feelings of hurt and frustration will increase. Be realistic, the chances are if he is not prepared to give you the commitment you want, that is because one day he is going to end the relationship anyway. What you have done by confronting him is to bring that date forward and saved yourself possibly months or even years of further pain and shattered dreams.

On the other hand if you explain how strongly you feel about the commitment of marriage and possibly children, and he loves you and does not want to lose you, then he might be able to make the commitment that you long for.

Sometimes love is not enough

So you love him, but if he is not willing to give you the commitment that you want, there comes a time when it is wiser to end the relationship, rather than wait around hoping that he will change. Confrontation can move the relationship forward as you will see later in this chapter, with Olivia and Katie: they were able to get the outcome that they desired. It could end the relationship, but if that is what is going to happen anyway, you are probably only bringing that date forward, and in that case it could save you many years of pain and frustration.

Danielle had stayed in the relationship far too long not only because she loved John, but she realised as she started to explore her feelings that she was afraid to cut loose from the relationship that was very good at times because she was scared of being on her own. Danielle realised during those four years together that she increasingly wanted marriage and children and she was not going to get it from this relationship. It was not an easy decision to make because the loss was heartbreaking and long-term gain was unpredictable. But if a man can't offer you the future you want, to stay around for years hoping he will change his mind is going to hurt you even more in the long run.

Why am I still in this relationship?

If you are not getting what you want from the relationship, four vital questions to ask yourself are:

- *He will come round to marriage and children in the end.*
- *I am afraid of being on my own.*
- *I might not meet anyone else.*
- *Financially I fear I can't manage on my own.*

These are not good enough reasons to stay in a relationship that is not meeting your fundamental needs.

It takes courage to leave the man you love

But if you want marriage, children, a life-long commitment and he is not willing to give you that there are some very difficult choices to be made. The tendency is to stay there and hope that because he loves you it will be all right in the end. You hope that by showing him how much you love him that he will feel secure and respond to your needs. He talks about the future and being together, but he goes quiet if the word marriage is mentioned. So you feel that if you wait a little longer, try a little harder, give him a little more time, in fact if you don't put him under any pressure, then he will come round to the idea of marriage in the end. But the reality is that if you want marriage you need to make your needs clear.

The importance of confrontation – ask yourself this question:

If you really want marriage, is he being fair to expect you to continue to be his partner, to love him, to cherish him, to have great sex with him, to have his children? To clean, cook, shop, wash-up, share the bills, the mortgage, the holidays, when he is not prepared to marry you? Your needs are very valid, so if he has no intention of meeting them you need to know.

OLIVIA'S STORY

Olivia, an arresting and startlingly clever girl, was in her early thirties when she met and fell in love with Luke, an extremely attractive university lecturer of forty-four. Olivia left university with an easily acquired first, spoke several languages and was addicted to travel. Her parents got used to getting calls from all over the world and rarely knew where she was going to call from next. She was independent and resourceful and also seemed to find jobs wherever she went. She had a very wild and promiscuous time throughout most of her twenties. When she was twenty-eight she became pregnant. She was not in love with the father of her child and had no desire to marry him, though he pursued her in the hope that she might change her mind. Shortly before her daughter's birth she accepted that for the moment her travelling days were over and, very pregnant, she returned home to her parents' home and announced to her unsuspecting mother that she was soon to become a grandmother.

When Olivia's daughter Rosie was four years old, Olivia met Luke who at forty-four was twelve years older than her. Luke had never married but had a series of relationships, the longest of which had never lasted more than two years. He adored Olivia and within months of meeting each other he and Olivia bought a house together in the university town where Luke lived. He was a fantastic honorary stepfather to Rosie.

In many ways they were intellectually and emotionally close, they loved each other's company, they both held strong political views, they loved the house they were living in and had a large circle of friends.

But there was also another side to Luke; Olivia noticed that even from the beginning of the relationship Luke never really shared himself and his things totally with Olivia. In the early days of their relationship he did not interact with her and in many ways they functioned totally separately. He earned more than her yet expected all finances to be shared equally. He would say to her, 'I bought all the food this week, so next week it's your turn' or if they went out for a meal he would sometimes says 'It's your turn to pay.'

But domestic tasks were no problem to him, and he was happy to share those equally, the ironing, the cleaning, the shopping. He was a great cook, and would prepare the evening meal if he was home first from work. In fact he was meticulous about the kitchen which always looked as if nothing was ever actually cooked in it. It always had to look spotless with not a thing lying around, which was rather difficult for Olivia who had her mother's rather more happy-go-lucky approach to tidiness. Luke travelled abroad a lot in his work, and sometimes Olivia was able to go with him leaving Rosie with her adoring grandmother.

Sometimes they would talk about marriage, or to be more accurate Olivia would bring the subject up. One day Luke asked her outright if she wanted to be married. Olivia admitted that she did and said to Luke, 'I want a partner for life. In fact I want to get married and have another baby.'

After that conversation Olivia started to notice subtle changes in Luke. He stopped complimenting her on how she looked. He knew she loved clothes and dressing up to go out, and where he once used to always notice what she wore, and take a delight in that, he now no longer commented. If he said something nice about her, this was now quickly followed by a cutting or putting-down remark. One night when she had gone to a lot of trouble to prepare a special meal of roast lamb Luke said as he took the first mouthful, 'The lamb is delicious but it is rather spoilt by the fact that you overcooked the vegetables.'

His obsessional tidiness demands that were once limited to the kitchen began to extend to all areas of the house. They began to argue more, and Olivia felt she could never get anything right. Luke became more controlling than usual over the money and this led to more rows.

Luke went to America to work for a couple of weeks, and in his absence Olivia thought a lot about the relationship and where it was going. She knew she loved him very much, but she was also deeply hurt by the fact that he did not want to marry her or for her to have his child.

When he was due to return from America Olivia said she could not meet him at the airport, something she normally always did. When Luke returned home he found Olivia less warm; he complained that she seemed wrapped up in herself and her life and indifferent to him.

He started to panic, he became aware he was in real danger of losing her. Olivia explained, 'Luke suggested that we went out to dinner, so that we could talk, as with the demands of jobs and children that is often not easy at home. He booked a table at our favourite French restaurant. I remember thinking, I'm going to let him start the talking, its usually me who introduces the subject of our relationship. He told me that he hated the arguments we were having, and that he had been thinking about the subject of children. He said, looking rather pleased, "I have been thinking about it, and I have decided that if you want a child then have one." Olivia looked at him and said, "Luke, that is not good enough, you see, if we have a child I don't want it to be just because I want one. I want you to want me to be the mother of your child."' Luke looked away across the restaurant and said nothing. The next day Olivia asked him to move out.

Luke went round to see Olivia's mother, begging her to talk to her daughter as he did not want to lose her. But neither could he commit himself to marriage. Her mother said to Luke, 'If you had committed yourself to Olivia you could have had her. That was what she was looking for. I know my daughter, she is very proud and you have hurt her desperately. She wanted you and the whole bit about marriage and children. For her that is true commitment whereas what you were offering her fell far short of that. She knows that if she settled for less the resentment and sense of rejection would eventually erode her feelings for you, so there is no point in you asking me to intercede for you.' Olivia's mother continued, 'Olivia told me that many years ago you were totally in love with a woman who then left you. It seems to me that you have not really allowed that love affair to pass into history and it is a shrine you constantly revisit.'

Like so many men who are afraid of commitment Luke was torn between longing for a close and intimate relationship and a fear of fully committing himself. He had grown up with a father he increasingly disliked and whom he now hated and a mother who was distant, rejecting and uninterested in him. He had to learn to suppress his longing for his parents' love. As a little boy in order to survive he had to be emotionally self-sufficient and now as an adult he was finding it difficult to let down those barriers enough to form a loving and trusting life-long relationship. Olivia's mother who in many ways was very fond of Luke described him as a 'tormented soul'. But she also knew how painful it was for Olivia to have asked Luke to move out.

Luke went abroad for a month, and Olivia felt a sense of freedom as she knew Luke was not just around the corner, and even if she wanted to she could not contact him. But at the same time she was missing him dreadfully, and would find that the tiniest thing would bring her to tears. When Luke returned from his month's travelling he looked dreadful, thin, pale, and unhappy. He went back to work, his friends at work who knew them both started to take sides, some blaming Luke for being so unfair to Olivia, and others saying that why should Luke at the age of forty-four want to marry and have children. But mainly they were saddened for they were a much-loved couple, intellectual, beautiful and fun, their house was always full of friends, and they gave marvellous parties.

Despite saying he did not want children of his own, Luke was very devoted to Olivia's daughter, Rosie. So Olivia and Luke would often meet, as Luke came to the house to babysit, while Olivia went out or to work. It became obvious to both of them that they seemed not to be able to live together or to exist apart, and they decided to go for counselling.

Luke learnt over the weeks that for him his very worst fear was to lose Olivia. As he talked he realised he could not bear it, he had never loved anyone as he loved her. Slowly as he talked about how he felt, first with his counsellor, and then together with Olivia his fears of marriage and a child of his own gradually slipped away. It was just before Christmas when they decided that Luke should move back in with Olivia. Then in February on a cold and frosty morning, Olivia appeared at her mother's house. As her mother open the door Olivia stood there smiling, and looking radiantly happy, she said simply, 'Luke has asked me to marry him.'

They had a summer wedding, it was Luke who wanted to marry without delay, Luke who threw himself into discussions of all the wedding plans, not because he was afraid he would change his mind, but because he adored Olivia and Rosie, and could not believe how he had so nearly lost them both.

Olivia wanted a dress all in gold, she and her mother

searched high and low from Knightsbridge shops to the tiniest second-hand shops. They found a wonderful 1930s golden dress, that floated and swirled around Olivia, just as she had imagined it would.

The garden and the marquee were a mass of flowers. On the wedding morning Olivia hid little bags of pretty coloured sweets in the garden around the marquee, for the children to search for during the reception. Her daughter Rosie ran to her grandmother to show her the sweets she had found, and looking up at her grandmother she said, 'Mummy and Luke are going to have a baby one day, I do hope it's going to be a girl like me.' 'I know,' said her grandmother smiling and gathering Rosie into her arms, 'that's just what Luke has told me too.'

You have to take responsibility for your own needs

Olivia loved Luke deeply, but she also knew what she needed as a woman which was marriage and a child with the man she loved. She also felt that if a man really loved her, and wanted to be with her for the rest of his life, then why not marriage, that was after all she felt the deepest commitment of all, it was the way she needed to be loved. By making this very clear to Luke it enabled him to really look at what he wanted, and ask himself why he found commitment such a big step. He was also willing to go for counselling to explore his feelings, and Olivia, for her part, was prepared to go with him. She knew this was taking a risk, that she could have her hopes raised, only to find that he could not give her the commitment she wanted.

If you are in love with a man who appears to want to be

with you but is somehow reluctant to make the commitment you want, it is very important that you take the responsibility for what effect this is having on you into your own hands. If making your needs clear to him means he might finish the relationship, it is probably 90% certain that the relationship would have ended eventually; what you have done is bought the date forward, and avoided perhaps many more years of waiting for him to give you the commitment you want. But it could also have the effect that he would be prepared to talk about his fears, to really look at why he objects to marriage, and if he loves you enough, and really does not want to lose you, go for counselling, if you can't sort it out between you, and he still wants to be with you.

CHLOE'S STORY

Chloe fell in love with Tim, a worst-case CPM, when she was twenty-four. By reading her story I hope it will help you to identify the very typical behaviour pattern of a worst-case CPM. I hope that if you find yourself in a similar situation, it will set alarm bells ringing and you will run like mad in the opposite direction before you get too deeply involved.

If you are already in too deep, I hope it will help you to identify the problem and get out before it becomes even more destructive. It does take courage to do the healthy thing and get out; it is painful but you will recover and go on to make new and hopefully loving and committed relationships that you want.

Chloe, an exotically pretty woman with lovely long blonde hair, warm and funny and vulnerable with an intelligent and lively mind, was only twenty-four when she met and fell in love with Tim, an extremely good-looking PR consultant. If she had been older and with more experience she may have been able to spot the signs of a worst-case commitment phobic man.

Many commitment phobic men move into cohabiting relationships and that is when the panic sets in, others don't reach for the panic button until marriage becomes an issue, then all hell breaks loose. For whereas once he seemed to love you and want you, suddenly he seems hell bent on destroying the relationship. Then when he has pushed you to the very edge of despair, and you have steeled yourself to end the relationship, he transforms once more into his old romantic and irresistible self again, begging you to forgive him for how unkind he has been and promising that if you give him a second, or third or fourth chance this time it really will be all right. So you capitulate, you love him and you want to believe what he is telling you. This pattern was to be part of Chloe and Tim's life for eight years.

Chloe said, 'I first met Tim at a party and there was a sparkle between us immediately, we were just so relaxed together and talked so easily. He gave me his full and total attention as if there was no one else in the room, it was lovely. We had been talking together for ages when suddenly he bent over and kissed me very passionately. I could taste the wine on his lips and tongue: it was very exciting. To start with I thought of it as a light-hearted relationship but for me within weeks it very quickly grew into something much deeper and I thought he felt the same.

'I realised I was in love with him, the feeling was so strong it felt like a physical sensation of falling. We began a physical relationship almost straight away and it was very intense. But after our third date, there was a slight change.

That was the first time he put me down, and though I did not recognise it at the time it was to become a pattern throughout our life together. If anyone did that to me now I wouldn't stand for it, but then I made excuses and told myself that there is a really good side to him, maybe he is using this as a bit of a defence mechanism because he does not want to become too involved too quickly. After all, we had only known each other a few weeks and he was only a couple of years older than me.

'But I remember the incident very clearly. It was his birthday and I gave him a present that I just knew was absolutely perfect for him. It was a book with wonderful pictures by the artist we had both been talking about at the party where we first met. As he was in the middle of opening it he said: "I hope this isn't . . ." and he described exactly what I'd given him. The book, the title everything. I think he knew what he was doing as he was doing it. I was so disappointed because I had chosen well. Yet he made me feel as if I had done something wrong. I felt a failure. I said: "OK, I think I'd better go." But he stopped me from going and suddenly was delightful, and said he was really pleased with the present.

'After we had been going out together for a few months he was spending so much time at my flat, which was tiny, that he suggested that we rented somewhere together. Things were going really well between us, I adored him, he was always telling me he loved me and so I agreed. We found a lovely little flat and we moved in together. We became really devoted to each other. It was summer and we would sit on a roof terrace drinking wine and watching the sun go down. It was very romantic.

'But after we had been together a few months he started

to be critical again. He was critical of my appearance and the way I dressed. He said my clothes were too revealing, which they weren't. He said if he was sitting opposite me on the tube he'd be able to see up my skirt. If we were going out he would say aren't you going to put some make-up on? Bit by bit he eroded my confidence about my appearance. Then he would withdraw from me and become very cold, I couldn't understand it. If I asked him why he was hardly talking he would reply, "I just want to have a night off." Once he said, "I don't want to get involved with you." I said "But you already are." I thought perhaps he was seeing somebody else. I couldn't work out what was going on.

'He didn't want me to meet his parents. When they came round to our flat I had to leave. When we went out with friends he wouldn't sit with me, it was as if he wanted to deny that we were a couple. I felt very hurt. Once a man at the next table thought I wasn't with anyone and started paying me attention. Then Tim was furious, totally overreacting and blamed me for it in a very over-the-top aggressive way. He was very suddenly very jealous and possessive.

'After a few months of this I went through a personal crisis. I thought it must be something I was doing wrong. I was so in love I hadn't experienced such intensity of emotion before. Then just as I was at my lowest ebb he started to be very sweet and thoughtful again. He was full of little surprises, like on my birthday when he turned up at work with a dozen red roses which he presented to me in front of everyone. He seemed to mature a bit and once again became more definite about wanting a relationship. We had some very good times together and did lots of interesting things at weekends.

'After we had been together for about four years lots of our friends were busy getting married. We'd have dinner parties and they'd say "When are you two going to get married?" Tim would visibly go pale and leave the room and go to the kitchen and start the washing up.

'In the beginning I thought it was funny, but then I started to think why is he reacting like that instead of saying, yes, I'd love to marry her. I did challenge him and he said, "I'm not ready for marriage yet."

'Time went on and I started to think if he's not going to marry me, then we shouldn't be together any more. I tried to break it off; by then we had been together six years. If I'm honest most of that time I had wanted him to ask me to marry him. Then, because I had waited so long I started to fall out of love with him. I wondered should I try and find someone who would love me and who wanted marriage as much I did.

'He could tell something was wrong. I suggested that we should find separate places to live. He said, "Don't be silly." He didn't believe I meant it. I started looking surreptitiously. The physical relationship had deteriorated badly because I didn't want to sleep with him any more. I think it was because he wasn't giving me the other things I wanted. Then as I tried to break loose he started to make me feel he did love me and I fell back in love with him all over again. I'd actually given up thoughts of marriage and thought I'm happy as we are, why do I need marriage? Just as I thought that, he asked me to marry him.

'He'd booked a holiday in Sicily. We had been there about a week and we went out to a delightfully romantic little restaurant on the edge of the sea. Suddenly he got up from the table and went down on one knee and said

"Will you marry me?" I was shocked. I nearly choked on my wine. I said "What?" He said again, "Will you marry me" and I said smiling, "I'll let you know in the morning." He ordered champagne and we had a lovely evening.

'In the morning I accepted him. I said, "You've kept me waiting for seven years, I am entitled to keep you waiting for just a day." He had of course known I was just playing with him. I think I also kept him waiting because he was such a vain man and I knew all the restaurant was watching.

'When we returned from our the holiday we told everyone we were going to marry. Our friends and families were delighted. I wanted a traditional wedding with all the trimmings. He threw himself into planning everything with me including the honeymoon. Then about three months before the wedding he went back to how he had been soon after I first met him. Cold and withdrawn. Criticising my taste and my appearance again and saying I needed to lose some weight. Appearance has always been very important to him, his and mine. He suddenly started taking part in lots of sports, rugby, rowing. Just before Christmas there was his department's office party and he told me that this year partners were not invited – so I did not go.

'We had to fill in some forms for the vicar and he kept stalling. One moment he was very distant and the next all right again. I never knew where I was. I kept asking him if there was anyone else, but he said there wasn't.

'On St Valentine's Day I decided to bring matters to a head. I said, "You don't want to get married, do you?" He went silent and then said, "No I don't."'

'Then he admitted he had been seeing someone else at work. He had actually taken her to his office Christmas party.

'We had a dreadful emotional scene, I was devastated. He told me it was all my fault, and that it would have been all right if we had married as soon as we had returned from Sicily. He said about her, "When I go to work and I see this girl she's looking lovely and I know that I've just left you at home and you're looking a mess." That was incredibly hurtful, I know I didn't look a mess. But when you are at work you have pretty clothes on and your make-up and hair done so it's different. He made me feel that I wasn't good-looking enough and that it was my fault that he had gone off me. I took it deeply personally. I started thinking no man will ever want me. If he'd said he didn't mean it, it might have been all right but he didn't.

'He was amazed when I told him to leave. He was standing in the bedroom staring out of the window. He reminded me of a little boy. The next morning he left, he went to work and I couldn't go out, I felt dreadful all day. I kept looking out of the window expecting him to come walking across the garden to see me, but he didn't. Because we'd been together for eight years suddenly I was alone and it was awful.

'A few days later my mother and my sister came up and we went shopping. I bought lots of pretty clothes, shoes, make-up, the lot. It made me feel good for a bit. I thought, I'm, thirty-two and that's it, it's all over, I'm damaged, I won't be able to trust anyone again. I went through a very bleak patch in my life. He had destroyed my confidence completely. After we split up he ended his affair and went out every night with friends and got drunk.

'I saw him a couple of months later. We'd arranged to meet and talk about what to do about practical things. I felt very nervous. I asked him if he had missed me, and he said 'No'. It felt very cruel.

'Then six months after we had spilt up we met up again. This time he hugged me and kissed me and then he asked me if we could get together again. He thought we could just carry on where we'd left off. I said, "I'm sorry, I don't feel the same for you any more. I've gone through it once and I can't go through it again." I can remember saying to him when we broke up, "You'll really regret this, there'll come a time when you'll want to come back and I won't want you." And that's actually what happened. People had said to me there'll come a time when you'll be glad you didn't go through with it and they're right.

'He really is like Peter Pan. He doesn't want to grow up. He doesn't want to commit to anyone. He still hasn't. So I just think he wants to go through life having relationships but not really settling with anyone. He said he saw the whole concept of marriage as stifling and ageing.'

There were early-warning signs in the early days of Chloe's relationship with Tim. The sudden mood swings from being loving and attentive to becoming cold and critical were undermining her and putting her in the wrong. Then there was not wanting to be seen as part of a couple when they went out, and particularly interestingly why he insisted on her leaving their flat when his parents came around. I suspect it was his mother's arrival on the scene that contributed to this behaviour.

Men who have mothers who smother or suffocate them, who are overprotective, can make them very fearful or contemptuous of women. Chloe said that once she accepted that she was part of Tim's life they would sometimes go and stay with his parents. His mother was really over the top in how she treated Tim and his elder brother; it was just like they were still children. She would rush around doing everything for them, encouraging Chloe to do the same. The trouble with this type of woman who is overprotective or controlling is she wants to invade every part of her children's lives. She wants to be there for them, fighting all their battles for them, protecting them from ever experiencing the ups and downs of growing up, never allowing them to make their own mistakes. Even when they are adult and involved in their own relationships she tends to want to have her say in how they should run their lives and she always wants to know just what is going on so that she can see whether she approves of it.

When Chloe and Tim first started living together he did not tell his mother, as he felt that she would not approve and so each time she visited he asked Chloe to leave. In his relationship with Chloe, Tim was constantly torn between wanting her love, and interpreting the love of a woman as taking him over, interfering in his life. His experience of love was being suffocating and he imagined that if he got too close to Chloe this would happen to him all over again. Chloe said, 'I was with Tim for eight years. I was thirty-two when we finally split. It took me eight long years to realise that he never was going to make the commitment I longed for.'

DON'T IGNORE THE EARLY-WARNING SIGNS

Throughout Tim's relationship with Chloe he sabotaged the relationship every time it was going well. But what was to become a pattern in their relationship had in fact begun on their third date. He put her down about the birthday present she had so carefully chosen for him. Each time the relationship was going well, Tim started to criticise her, thus hurting her and distancing himself from her. When they were out together with other people, he ignored her, as if to say we are not part of a couple, and it was ages before he could actually acknowledge his relationship with Chloe to his mother. Such early-warning signs indicate that the conflict within this type of man is enormous. If you are a woman involved with a man like this, there seems no rhyme or reason for why he switches from hot to cold, from loving you one moment to becoming the cold critical lover the next. The tendency is to look for what you have done to cause such mood swings. But the reality is that his exterior behaviour is rarely rational, from loving you he switches to seeing you as the enemy, and then tries to destroy you. It is this very irrational behaviour that indicates this is a man with a commitment problem. The more extreme it is as in Tim's case the worse the problem, and the less the chances are of the man overcoming it.

Letting him off the hook

The truth is that the problem is within him, but it suits him very nicely if you are willing to soul search and examine what is wrong with you. His criticism of you is his way of softening you up, undermining you and making you feel insecure. You are doing him an enormous favour if you accept what he is saying. It is commonly known as 'letting him off the hook'. If he can put the blame on you, then he is let off having to look at his own shortcomings. It's so much easier if he can ignore his own bizarre behaviour and blame it all on you. The fundamental reason why Tim and other men like him are unlikely to change is just *that* – they rarely if at all take responsibility for their own behaviour, so rather than try to change themselves they move on to new relationships, where they keep repeating the same old pattern.

Will Carling the English rugby captain is a prime example of worst-case CPM. He seems addicted to beautiful blondes, and has moved from one to another leaving a stream of broken relationships in his wake. His particular way of ending a relationship it appears is to embark on an affair, so that by the time one relationship ends he has another woman waiting in the wings.

He famously fell in love, he claims, with Princess Diana, when he had only been married to Julia Carling for less than two years. Julia certainly felt the breakdown of their marriage was to a large degree due to his involvement with the Princess. She said when she discovered their friendship 'It came like a bolt out of the blue.'

Carling first hit the headlines in the late eighties when his stormy relationship with Nikki Turner, the pop-group publicist, ended and he became involved with another blonde, economics graduate Victoria Jackson. But within two years, Julia Smith later to become the first Mrs Will Carling was on the scene. Victoria later described Carling in a Sunday paper, as 'A sex-mad womaniser', revealing that he always signed his love letters 'Big Willy'! She said, 'Will was always a ladies' man, who couldn't resist powerful women. He's sex-mad and has an obsession for blondes.'

After the end of his marriage to Julia, Carling met and fell in love with Ali Cockayne. She claims that they were planning to marry when he left her and his eleven month old son Henry, in September 1998, for Lisa Cook. Lisa is a mother of two and blonde wife of David Cook who was England's rugby vice captain with Carling in the mid-1980s.

When Carling left Ali Cockayne he said, 'I still love her, but not enough, I'm not passionately in love with her. I've been unhappy for a long time [they had only been together two years] and that wasn't making her happy. It wasn't creating a healthy environment for Henry. So I felt it was best to leave.' Then he continues with perhaps the most revealing remark of all: 'I want passionate love. I want a soul mate – a partner that I can travel to the Grand Canyon with, tell everything to – what hurts me, what I love, what frightens me. Perhaps I'm being idealistic or naïve, but I believe that person is out there somewhere.'

This probably sounds wonderful to Lisa Cook if this is the seduction tactic he is using. It is powerful stuff to be told you are his perfect 'soul mate'. But Lisa and the blondes that come after her, as they undoubtedly will, should look at Carling's track record, and realise that none of his relationships have lasted more than two years. Carling is showing all the signs of the CPM in his hot pursuit. He is obviously very seductive, and the women get swept along in his desire for them, but the problem is like a lot of CPMs he can't sustain it.

But even more importantly a man who is looking for his perfect soul mate, who believes there is some woman out there who will meet his every need, will soon become disillusioned when he discovers you are only human. When he realises that you have needs of your own which may be at variance with his needs, that is when you will topple from the pedestal he has put you on. Love for him is only about that highly passionate, slightly mad, in-love stage of a relationship. It is not about the more enduring love that survives the ups and down of married life. Which is why when that stage starts to subside he will move on in search of yet another 'soul mate', leaving a trail of broken hearts in his wake. This is what Melissa experienced.

MELISSA'S STORY

Melissa is an extremely attractive and vivacious woman in her early forties. She was totally devastated when her relationship with Jack came to an abrupt, unexpected and extremely painful end.

When Melissa was in her late teens she fell madly in love with a man who treated her very badly. The relationship ended bitterly when he left her because she became pregnant. As a student with no money and no family support she felt that she had no alternative but to have an abortion. Melissa said: 'He destroyed my trust in men. I was shattered and I was determined that no other man was going to hurt me again. I built up a wall against men.'

For the next seventeen years she had a series of disastrous relationships. To avoid getting hurt again, she chose men whom she did not like very much, and would not have wanted to marry. If she met a man she thought she might fall in love with, she crushed that relationship before it even got off the ground. She said 'I've not allowed myself to fall in love, because of my fear of being let down again, but then when I did fall in love that is just what did happen all over again.'

In her late thirties Melissa felt she wanted to fall in love, to marry and settle down. She was no longer interested in her party-going, high-living lifestyle. About a year later she met a man and fell head over heels in love and all her barriers came tumbling down. He was very keen for them to live together, and soon after they met he moved in with her. But she soon started to notice changes in him. He was lovely to her one moment and ignored her the next. After several months of this and much heartache on her part, he suddenly left her and went off with another woman. To make matters worse he also owed her a substantial amount of money.

It was several months later that through mutual friends she met Jack. She said: 'I was not really interested in him at first, I was still hurting from the break-up of the last relationship. He was ten years older than me, and not particularly attractive. I've really always been out with really good-looking men. Jack was successful and rich and ran his own company, and he pursued me relentlessly, always telephoning, sending me flowers and asking me out. I had only known him two months when he asked me to marry him. I just laughed it off, but it was very flattering.

'After about three months of this I started to enjoy his company. He was clever and amusing and I liked all the attention. He made me feel very special and in the end I fell in love again. We then had a wonderful six months during which he spent lots of money taking me on some wonderful holidays, we saw each other all the time and spent every weekend together. He had an acrimonious divorce and his children were not speaking to him, but I was instrumental in getting them back together again. They were all fond of me and I adored them, even his relationship with his ex-wife improved. Everybody told me Jack was absolutely potty about me. Then suddenly he became very moody and made every excuse for an argument. I did not see him for about two weeks – his choice not mine. Then by chance I found out he had been with another woman, this was within weeks of everyone telling me, including him, that he was absolutely mad about me.

'After about ten days he telephoned me and said he had made a terrible mistake. He said that she was only after his money and would I have him back because he realised what we had together was very special. I thought about it and decided to allow him one mistake and took him back.

'Within weeks we were engaged and we had a wonderful engagement party with both of our families there. It was July, I moved into his house, and everything in the garden was rosy, he was his loving self again. A month before Christmas he told me he had never been so happy and he wanted me to set a date for the wedding. I was over the moon.

'Then a week later he suddenly announced that he wanted a two-week break. I was very upset and did not understand this sudden change. We had so many things planned, Christmas parties and family things, and we were planning to spend New Year together in Madeira. At his request I moved back to my house. Every time I rang him he was cold and distant. He made it clear that I was not to come to his company's office party and then he told me we would not be spending Christmas together.

'Christmas was a nightmare, I sobbed from morning until night; I couldn't eat, I just smoked and drank and lost a lot of weight. After Christmas as most of my clothes and belongings were in his house I telephoned him to ask if I could collect some of them. He said he would arrange something in the next couple of days. Then I got a call from one of his daughters to arrange for me to go over and get them. I asked her why her father couldn't speak to me and she told me he was in Madeira with another woman.

'I thought I was going to faint. I could not believe it. I had to go and collect my things from his house with his children there. They were very embarrassed, it was so humiliating. I couldn't believe that he'd left it to his children to do his dirty work for him.

'When he returned from Madeira he telephoned me and told me that he would never be as happy with her as he was with me. If he tried to come back now I wouldn't have him back unless he was prepared to do a lot of work on himself.

'At the end of January I saw him with this other woman coming out of a restaurant. I went bananas and hit him in front of everyone. It is not like me to make a scene but I was so hurt and angry. I now can't get the image of them together out of my mind. She had long blonde hair, a really short black skirt, very pretty. She was a bimbo type and he was looking so pleased with himself. He obviously loved having her on his arm. I haven't heard from him since.'

Melissa had got so used to getting involved with hurtful men and emotionally abusive men that she was perhaps no longer able to distinguish a man who was going to give her the commitment and love she craved, from the man who was likely to treat her badly.

This pattern of behaviour was reinforced by her childhood experiences. She kept nice men at arm's length because she thought that once they really got to know her they would not love the person she really was. This feeling started in childhood where she was one of five children and she always felt her parents preferred her brothers and sisters to her. She said, 'I was the least favourite child, my sisters particularly were loved much more than I was. I knew I could never came up to their standard in my parents' eyes.' Which is what she continued to feel all those years later when she met men whom she really liked and with whom she felt she could have fallen in love. She was terrified that once again the pattern established with her parents would be re-enacted and that she might be found wanting by someone she really cared about. It had become a habit – a pattern that she found hard to break.

THE ROAD TO RECOVERY FROM A SUPER DANGEROUS CPM

What enables a worst-case CPM to continue on his destructive path is the very fact that he does not see it as his behaviour that needs changing. So he blames it on the women in his life, or he claims that somehow the relationship has gone wrong and so he feels entitled to move on.

Chloe and Melissa where engaged to the men who walked out on them, and Will Carling's girlfriend was the mother of his child. So such men really do owe it to you to talk about why they are ending the relationship. Sometimes, like Melissa, it is not possible, which makes the ending particularly hard, because he is not there for you to listen to your feelings of hurt and anger. Which is why all those pent-up feelings exploded in Melissa when she saw him with his new woman in tow.

Talking at this stage is not about trying to get him to change his mind, but it is trying to make sense of what has happened. As you talk look particularly at his behaviour, and how his feelings have changed. Don't be pulled into continually questioning what it was that you did wrong, what was it about you that made this man whom you thought was in love with you, suddenly leave. Your self-esteem and confidence may have been so eroded that you even find yourself making long lists of all the reasons he had for leaving you – well, don't. Remind yourself it is not that you did something wrong, it is what you represent – a committed relationship that he can't cope with.

Chloe and Melissa were intelligent and successful career women and both extremely pretty, yet they both were made to feel worthless, that there was something wrong with them; they were continually questioning what it was. Chloe wondered if another man would ever fall in love with her, and Melissa if Jack's reason for leaving was that she was not really pretty enough or good enough.

What is important to hang on to is that if you have been loved and left by a CPM it is not that there is anything deeply, fundamentally wrong with you. It is that the man you have been involved with has a deep and unresolved problem about committed relationships.

What I have been describing with Chloe and Melissa is men whose fear of commitment is in the category of 'worst-case scenarios'. But the majority of CPMs do not fall into that category. But what they do need is space in their relationship with you. Although all of us need this in a healthy relationship, if we want to avoid it being claustrophobic and smothering, a CPM will probably need rather more space and independence than you. If you are in love with a man, and want to marry him, as a women you will want that relationship to grow in closeness and intimacy. But for the CPM though he wants a loving relationship, he will also need space and distance within it. Once you are committed to him, in many ways it's your independence that is attractive to him, the women he is least attracted to are those who are over-dependent or clinging.

Katie is a very lively, attractive and intelligent woman. She is independent and emotionally fairly strong and she successfully combines her career and two small children.

HOW KATIE WAS ABLE TO GET WHAT SHE WANTED

Katie is in her late thirties and when it came to the subject of marriage she had quite a tough time. But she and her husband Philip have now been happily married for the last eight years.

Katie and Philip first met when they were both nineteen. Their relationship has not been without its dramatic moments: perhaps the worst was when Philip panicked and called off the wedding just five weeks before the big day.

Katie said: 'There is an assumption that if a marriage is cancelled at a very late stage, then, of course, you have to split up; you can't possibly hold your head up with dignity and still stay together. It doesn't have to be the end of the relationship but it is very traumatic and it completely shattered me when it happened. At first I thought that he didn't want me, but then as I slowly got over the shock, it became quite apparent that he did.

'I met Philip just before my nineteenth birthday. I had always said that when I fell in love it would be with someone who is really really tall, I'm five foot eight. I've always had this thing about men over six foot with blond hair. Philip is five foot nine with sandy hair. I think the first thing that attracted me to him was his sense of humour. We met at a party and we started going out together and then we sort of just slipped into a relationship and it carried on from there. He was working somewhere in the North of England and I was doing a secretarial course so we were apart a lot of the time over the next year or two. After college he got a job near where we were both brought up. When we were about twenty-two we started living together. I had been spending a lot of time at his flat and it went on from there. I thought it was a good idea and Philip agreed. We have slipped into most things in our life, which is probably why the big planned wedding never materialised.

'When we first met I was against marriage. I was a feminist and happy just to live together and that was fine with Philip. Marriage was never mentioned. My mother did not approve of living together and throughout my teens it had always been something we'd rowed about. I still think it's the sensible thing to do. I'd encourage my children to do it.

'It was in my late twenties that I changed. I decided I wanted to get married. God knows why. Quite a few of our friends were getting married. I thought if it was good enough for them it was good enough for me. Philip and I had been to some weddings and ever since I was a little girl I'd had this dream of "the dress". I remember when I was young my mum and I would walk past the windows that were full of these beautiful brides' dresses. I used to love looking at them. My mother got married after the war, but with the clothes rationing she could not buy a lovely dress and my father wore his demob suit. So I think she always had this dream of me in a fantastically beautiful dress.

'At the time Philip and I were happy living together and

marriage was probably the last thing on his mind. We had a mortgage and jobs and were a couple. But I think I was changing: we had been living together for about seven years by then, and suddenly I wanted to know that he would be prepared to marry me.

'I thought if other people took it up as a life option then why couldn't we? It became absolutely the bee's knees. I'd started seeing weddings as good fun and a nice time to gather your family together and your friends. I actually said to Philip: "Would you marry me if I wanted you to marry me?" And he would give me a very non-committal sort of answer and I would say "Why, why?" And then I just wouldn't leave it alone.

'Once it had come into my head, it would not go away. I did push him quite a lot but then that had always been my role in the relationship. I am the decision-maker. I remember saying: "I want you to go down on one knee and propose to me. I want you to want to marry me." Looking back on it it's crazy really I suppose. But I wanted that commitment.

'In the end he did propose though he didn't go down on one knee. It was in our flat and we were sitting on our floral sofa with a cat on my knee, and that was fine. We chose an engagement ring together and we told my mum and dad, who were really pleased. They liked Philip and were pleased he was going to look after me.

'We started to plan the wedding. We decided against church as I felt very uncomfortable with that idea, as I'm not a committed Christian. So we decided on a register office with about eighty people, a marquee in the garden and a jazz band. I never went for the big Christmas Tree dress but I was in love with the idea of something wonderfully simple in pale cream.

'The weeks went by and I tried to consult Philip about arrangements, but he got more and more peculiar, distant, troubled. He started to sleep badly and was quite nasty to me in lots of little ways.

'It was five weeks before the wedding. I remember saying to him, as I was about to take the wedding invitations to the letter box: "Are you sure you want to get married?" So I must have known really. He said he did and I went out and posted the invitations.

'That weekend Philip couldn't sleep and he was up all night and in the morning I said we had better sit down and talk about this, so we did. We talked for ages and ages. It took him a long time to say what he actually felt, then eventually he said: "I'm sorry, I just can't go through with it." I felt dreadful when he told me. I cried and cried, I was really hurt and angry and totally unable to understand how he was feeling. Then he left and went to stay with a friend.

'I had to tell my mother and that was awful. She rushed off and was sick. I felt I had to console her, when what I wanted was for her to comfort me, but that is not the role she plays. She's been there for me a lot since but that day she couldn't see inside and she did not really know what was going on.

'The worst part was having to ring up all the people we'd sent all the invitations to, to explain to them that the wedding was off. I had to keep going through it all with them, it was terrible. Then we had planned the really lovely honeymoon in Kenya. I had been looking forward to it so much but it had to be cancelled. I did an awful lot of crying.

'After he had been with his friend for a few days Philip came round to see me. He told me that he wanted me, it was the marriage he could not go through with. I know he didn't feel very good about what he had done.

'It was a very difficult few months. I was angry and hurt. I do get very upset when people let me down. To begin with I was in such pain myself I didn't understand how he was feeling. But I know now it was a terrible time for him too.

'I think he was also scared that I would show him the door. He didn't want that. So we muddled on. To begin with I couldn't let go of it. I was like a terrier with a rat and kept picking it up and shaking it. Every time I felt shaky, I would bring up the fact that he had called the wedding off. I felt very insecure and it probably made me very clinging. For a time it affected our sexual relationship. It did go into a decline.

'Philip didn't really want to talk about it; he has always been like that, reluctant to talk about his real feelings. But for me, I had to talk about it, I needed to understand why, and in time he also needed to know why. It seemed he couldn't accept that he could make a success of being a married man because no one in his family had. His parents divorced when he was ten and his father went off with his secretary with whom he had been having an affair. His grandparents were divorced and so were most of his family. Whereas my parents have been married forty years, they do everything together and have never spent a night apart – they don't even socialise separately. The problem was Philip could not believe that he could be the exception in his family and had no trust in his ability to make his marriage work. He thought his marriage would be cursed and so he just kind of flipped.

'Understanding this did make a difference, and over the next year or two the damage was repaired because I guess he was able to convince me that he wanted us to be together.

'Then we both hit thirty, he is six months older than me. We were discussing the big three-O one day and Philip said: "I would like to get married now, but I can't do it the way we were going to do it." I thought I can't risk him letting me down again and having to go through ringing round telling everyone it was cancelled again, so I agreed to forego the sort of wedding I really wanted. I now wish we'd done it the way we were going to do it with the family pictures and all that. But Philip just couldn't see himself having that sort of wedding. So in the end, as far as he was concerned, it was a case of getting it over and done with, I think. When my brother got married a year later my sister-in-law said, 'We thought we'd give your parents a proper wedding seeing as you couldn't do it." That was incredibly cruel.

'So having agreed to get married we invited a few close friends and just went off to a register office very quietly. I bought a knee-length, straight strapless dress with a bolero jacket and Philip said he thought it looked like anaglypta wallpaper.

'After the marriage we had a really lovely lunch with our friends. We did not have a honeymoon as there really was no time to organise anything like that. We spent the night in a beautiful hotel in the Cotswolds, with a four-poster bed, and lackeys piling wood on to huge open fires everywhere.

'The next day we sat up in our four-poster bed, drinking and telephoning our parents and lots of our friends to tell them we were married. Mum was very good about it, I think she understood after the first time and I had warned her that this might happen.

'We rang Philip's dad and when we went to pay the hotel bill he'd paid it, which was really nice of him. Specially since we'd ordered a bottle of Scotch on room service. We had a holiday planned in Tuscany for later that year so we called that "our honeymoon". We met another couple there who'd been through the same aborted wedding plans, and they were having their delayed honeymoon. We don't see much of them now as it looks like divorce is on the cards.

'I used to find it painful to go to other people's weddings but I think I have got over that now. Philip's not the kind to express his feelings, he takes after his father. But somehow I knew he was the sort of guy who would come up with the goods one day. I still think he could have gone through with the big wedding and been happy.

'In the end we probably did get married at the right time. The issue of him deciding against the marriage doesn't come up very often now. If we have a bad time over something, and I really want to go for the jugular then I bring it up. He says, "Don't keep bringing that subject up, it's all over and done with." He has never really said he'd made a mistake agreeing to get married and then backing out. I would have liked him to have done that.'

PHILIP'S STORY

'I met Katie at nineteen. We were introduced by a mutual friend at a party, we were matchmade I suppose you could say. I remember holding hands with her and thinking how nice she was. I remember her hair, which was longer than it is now with a central parting and she was wearing a shirt and jeans. I asked her out and it seemed to go from there. We were apart quite a lot as I was away working in the north of England, and she was living at home and working locally. This went on for a couple of years, then I moved back to the south of England and found a job. I had my own flat and Katie would come and stay a lot. She was spending so much time there that a year later she suggested that we got a flat together so I agreed. I was still very much a bachelor, enjoying the nights out with male company. So it was quite a hurdle to find myself living with someone at only twenty-two.

'I suppose I thought it seemed quite a good idea, but also I'm a bit of a coward and not good at confrontation, I tend to go with the flow. I think she saw it as taking charge. I saw her as wanting to assert common sense into the relationship. I don't have great self-discipline. She'll win an argument and get things done whereas I will slob around and let life pass me by. Except as far as work is concerned – work has always been important to me, I'm dedicated to that and I've made a great success of that so far.

'Katie takes more responsibility to make the relationship work than I do. She has always been the driver in terms of arranging things for us to do, like why don't we live together, rent a flat, get a mortgage and it was the same about getting married. I would say she did start dropping hints. She is definitely the driver. After we had lived together for several years, she started saying things like "One day we'll get married." She probably told me to ask her to get married. It was the thing people our age seemed to be doing. I couldn't understand the significance she lent to it at the time. But as it seemed very important to her I suppose I eventually thought why not?

'But as the plans went ahead so the doubts set in. I think for the first time in my life I realised things were being taken out of my control, arrangements being made that I didn't like and I didn't really feel I wanted the public show. I've always been someone who doesn't want to be the subject of an audience. I'm quite happy to be centre of attention of a small group of people, I don't have a problem with that but no more than that. I was made to play piano recitals at twelve or thirteen which completely freaked me out – and ever since I've rarely been able to play the piano for someone else. So for me there was an element of not wanting the spectacle of a wedding and here was a wedding being arranged, out of my control; it seemed that her family jumped on to everything.

'Then I started to think that at twenty-seven I was far too young to get married. As each day went by I'd say to myself, "I'll tell Katie tomorrow." But I didn't. I was only able to say no when the invitations had gone out. I thought, Oh shit, I really am going to get married if I'm not careful. In retrospect it was the first time in my life that I had actually put my foot down.

'It wasn't about I don't want to marry Katie, it was that I was scared of marriage. If we had got married then I just wonder whether we would still be married now. I might have resented it too much.

'I know she had to force things out of me. I get imperceptible moods but Katie knows when there's something bubbling underneath. She put me on the spot and said "You don't want to get married, do you?" It was then that I told her that I didn't. I don't remember what she said. But I know she cried a lot and was very miserable. God knows what her parents thought but I didn't become a social leper overnight.

'My parents' marriage broke up when I was nine or ten. I was told their marriage became rocky as a result of my birth, because my mother went off sex then. I don't know if that's the real reason. But divorce runs in the family. My father's parents were also divorced. His parents' marriage broke up when he was in his teens. There are an awful lot of divorces in my family – three generations at least. My parents' parents were trailblazers in that particular fashion parade,' Philip said mockingly, 'so I had a fairly blighted view of the concept of marriage.'

What made you change your mind? I asked Philip. 'I was bludgeoned into submission. I was clubbed to death,' he said laughing. 'No, seriously, I think when I reached thirty I grew up a bit. I realised marriage wasn't the huge threatening thing I thought it was. We were also able to bypass some of my fears by doing it on the quiet with just a few friends present, which suited me. Katie didn't ask me to go through a big ceremony again and I probably wouldn't have if she had asked.

'I think Katie didn't actually want it, with hindsight. As you get older you don't want the big do. It's a young person's thing. We were more settled and she'd become less dogmatic about things. Marriage is important to her; I think that ultimately it was what she needed rather than what I needed. The commitment of marriage I think is always less for a man than for a woman. Marriage is much more important and exciting for a woman because of nest-building feelings I suppose.

'Our marriage was a very low-key affair. We had a few friends at the ceremony in a public convenience that doubled as a register office and a registrar with a withered hand and a speech impediment and it pissed down with rain and we had a very good time.

'It wasn't deadly romantic. After having known Katie for that period of time it was an affirmation rather than a celebration. We did not have a honeymoon. I didn't miss it. I don't have any regrets – well, I do regret hurting Katie.

'I think now Katie realises she was a victim of her over-zealousness and she misread the situation. Not that I wasn't wrong in saying, Yes, let's do it, because I shouldn't have done that the way I was feeling. I think she realises she probably overcooked it at the time in terms of thinking she could deliver a fait accompli as she had about the flat and the mortgage. I think for the first time in my life I realised things were being taken out of my control, arrangements being made that I didn't want. But I didn't really realise that until the invitations had gone out.

'So we got married at the right time as far as I'm concerned. We have two lovely children now and I would not have wanted children outside marriage.'

Philip was a chip off the old block and like his father before him he had great difficulty in talking about his feelings. Throughout most of the engagement, despite his increasing fear, he had put off talking to Katie about how he was feeling. Even after he had backed out of the wedding, getting him to talk about why was like drawing blood from a stone. It would have been easy for Katie to assume that it was all over, that Philip did not really love her enough, and that that was why he called the whole thing off, but she didn't. She was hurt and angry and miserable but over the weeks that followed she was able to help Philip talk about his fears that had caused his panic attack.

Philip's father was a typical product of his upbringing. Philip said, 'My father didn't show his emotions. Instead of wearing his heart on his sleeve he wore it firmly tucked inside his blazer. I think he loved me as much as he could but really he was a cold, hard man.'

Philip's grandfather was a hopeless alcoholic, and for much of his life Philip's father had to father his own father. He had battened down his own needs and feelings and just got on with it. And Philip had done much the same when his own parents divorced when he was a little boy of ten.

He chose to stay with his mother. He thought it only seemed fair as his father had left her for someone else. It would mean he could stay in the same house and go to the same school, he also thought life would be easier with his mother and he could get away with more.

He was an only child and he remembers his mother crying a lot. Philip felt he was quite hard in terms of not being able to comfort her, or put his arms around her. If Katie cries he can't bear it either. Because he finds Katie's tears hard to cope with he becomes irritated or leaves the room. If there is something worrying him he becomes withdrawn or moody, which Katie finds equally hard to bear.

Philip denies that his parents' divorce has affected him. He said, 'Maybe it did, but I've always taken the stance that it didn't change my life.'

But of course everything that happens to us as children does affect the way we are. It also influences how we behave in our adult relationships. Philip's mother was rather wild, scatty and slightly mad, very absent-minded but could also be great fun. She worked full time and he had a series of au pairs. When she was not at work she was out having a good time. Philip was packed off to boarding school at the age of seven. Motherhood did not have much appeal for her. Like his mother he finds responsibility and decision-making difficult, this also goes back to having too much responsibility too young when his father left home for another woman and Philip stayed with his mother because he felt responsible for her now that his father was not around. Even as a young child he did not really feel she was terribly well-equipped to cope with day-to-day life. But it was a family where feelings were never talked about so there was never any opportunity for him to express what he felt. He learned at an early age to bottle up his emotions and just get on with his life.

It was Katie who was the driving force. It was she who decided that they should live together, that they should rent a flat together, and get a mortgage and buy a house. And Katie who then wanted to change from the living-together arrangement into marriage.

By choosing Katie, Philip could transfer his responsibility and reluctance to make decisions on to Katie. So she made the decisions for both of them. But where marriage was concerned that was one decision Philip eventually realised he had to make. He hated confrontation, so he delayed it and delayed it.

The experience of all those failed marriages in his family of origin made him think that marriage spoiled things, or worse, was likely to end in divorce. So why change the status quo? These fears, plus his fear of being the centre of attention made him panic so much that he cancelled the wedding with only five weeks to go. It was only two or three years later when he had gained an understanding of why he had behaved as he did that he was able to conquer those fears and ask Katie to marry him, and mean it.

What Katie and Philip's story shows very clearly is that there are ways that can be found to help a man overcome his fear of committing himself to marriage. Philip's panic attack forced Katie into having to cancel the wedding. She was devastated and tremendously hurt but Katie was strong enough to withstand the indignity of the wedding being called off at the last minute. Even though she was hurt, unhappy and miserable she was able to talk to Philip and understand that it was not that he didn't love her, but he was ambivalent about marriage and phobic to boot as well as shy of being centre stage on the day itself. Now when she hears about men pulling out of the wedding at the last moment she believes very strongly that does not necessarily mean it is all over and that the man does not love you. Philip like many men caught up in the commitment phobic's dilemma loved Katie but his fear of that final commitment of marriage, and perhaps of the 'for ever' tag overtook that love.

Philip wanted Katie but because he had an underlying fear of commitment, each step down that road of their relationship had to come from Katie from the living together to the mortgage and buying a house together. When she had pushed him a step too far, he rebelled. But he too was able to distinguish that it was not that he no longer wanted Katie, it was that he could not cope with the whole idea of marriage. Added to which his fear of being centre stage at his own wedding made him feel like that twelve-year-old little boy who was forced to play the piano in front of hundreds of people. A wedding in front of an audience of eighty strong of both family and friends raised in him all those unresolved childhood fears.

But, for love of Katie he was prepared to explore his fears, and with the greater understanding he was then able to propose marriage to Katie. He loved her and he did not want to lose her. He also realised how important marriage was for her.

Philip is wrong about one thing. Katie really did want a traditional wedding, with a dress she had always dreamed about, a marquee in the garden full of family and friends and photographs to remember the occasion. But she had to let those dreams go, because in the end being married to Philip was more important than a traditional white wedding. Maybe one day Philip will realise quite how hard it was for Katie to let go of that dream. If he could acknowledge how much of a sacrifice Katie made for love of him, if he could really tell her how much he regretted the hurt he had caused, she might really be able to put the past finally to rest.

HOW TO MOVE THIS RELATIONSHIP FORWARD

If like Katie and Philip you have been together for some time and he has been dragging his feet and if you are rather more keen on the idea of marriage than him, talk things through very thoroughly. If it's fear of the big day itself, it is a good idea to make quite sure that you plan the sort of wedding day that does not totally overwhelm him.

Is the man in your life displaying all the signs of a CPM?

- Don't be drawn into colluding with him in his belief that his behaviour is acceptable.
- Don't deny the truth if it's staring you in face, it's always jam tomorrow never jam today.
- Don't settle for a relationship that is on his terms, meeting his needs, and you are the one having to do all the compromising. If your needs are constantly being ignored, the effect is so undermining that you often roll over and take more of the same – don't.
- Do talk to him about how you are feeling, if you want

more commitment tell him. If you just assume that he knows this, you are giving him the perfect opportunity to ignore your needs.

- Do take an honest look at the relationship. Is it a relationship of broken promises? Does he promise marriage, but only in a jokey way? Are you engaged and it looks as if you are about to make the *Guinness Book of Records*, for how often he has delayed naming the day.

If any of this applies to your relationship and it is at a stage where you are wanting more from it than you are getting, it is probably crunch time. Avoid getting into aggression or shrinking-violet mode, what you need to be is assertive, and to be open and honest about what you want.

Happy Endings

Firstly, if he has expressed a fear about the 'M word it is important to understand why. If it's because he is not deeply in love with you and he wants to keep his options open, then there is no point in holding out for marriage. Marriage to a man who does not love you enough would be soul-destroying.

Secondly, if he does love you, but is battling with his fear of commitment, it is time to make it clear to him what you want from him in this relationship. That is, a fully committed relationship, which means marriage and possibly children. If that is what is really important to you don't accept a lesser commitment.

Thirdly, if he wants this relationship it's a question of moving on to really exploring and understanding what his fears of committed relationships are based on. This is the key to unlocking his fear of commitment. If you are not able to do this together this might be the time to consider some counselling to really explore this in greater depth.

Hold out for the relationship you want

If you both love each other it is important to hold out for the relationship you want. If you have been together for some time, or are living together and you have reached a stage where you want the relationship to move on to marriage, then, as I have said, make this clear. I am not suggesting that you propose to him, though in these times of equality there is no reason why you shouldn't. But he does need to know how you feel, and you need to understand what he is feeling and thinking as well.

He then has a choice, he can accept that if he wants this relationship then it is up to him to ask you to marry him. If he does not want marriage, he knows that comes with a price tag, and that means losing you.

You too have choice, to accept his proposal, or if he does not want marriage, you can continue with the relationship you have (but can you be sure that will not be at too high a cost?) or you can end it. Painful though that will be.

It is important to value yourself enough not to sacrifice your need for marriage, and possibly children. You can't make him marry you, and that would not be a satisfactory option anyway, but what you can do is be specific about what you want from the future of this relationship. If he can respond to this by loving you enough to conquer his fears the story could have a happy ending.

9

Are you addicted to commitment phobic Men?

I won't telephone him. I'll never telephone him again as long as I live. He'll rot in hell before I'll call him up. You don't have to give me strength, God; I have it myself. If he wanted me he could get me. He knows where I am. He knows I'm waiting here. He's so sure of me. So sure. I wonder why they hate you as soon as they are sure of you. I should think it would be so sweet to be sure ... Oh God keep me from that telephone. Keep me away. Let me still have just a little bit of pride. I think I'm going to need it, God. I think it will be all I'll have.

A Telephone Call, *Dorothy Parker*

THE LURE OF THE UNAVAILABLE MAN

So, you are a strong independent woman looking for a man to fall in love with, but the problem is you keep falling for the wrong sort of man, that is a man who won't commit – right? No! Wrong, or at least partly wrong. If you are constantly falling for the wrong sort of man, it could be because you too fear commitment. You may be rationalising your fear of commitment by telling yourself that you are unlucky in love, that you are a lousy picker, that the really great guys are always married to someone else, or they are gay or the problem is that they live 2,000 miles away.

Have you ever thought that the reason why you seem to always end up with a man who seems reluctant to commit is because you may be commitment shy? By choosing such a man either consciously or unconsciously you may be masking this truth from yourself. His real attraction for you is that he seems to be fleeing from committed long-term relationships. This may be more reassuring to you than you realise if deep down you too are afraid of close and intimate relationships. Chasing a man who runs in the opposite direction allows you to continue to complain about his lack of commitment without having to confront your own fears. You project hidden fears within yourself that you do not wish to own, and that you are frightened to confront, on to the man and then you can safely blame him for the very thing you can't deal with or don't like in yourself.

TORN IN TWO DIRECTIONS

Like the man who can't commit, part of you longs for a committed relationship, but the other part fears it. Sometimes it is so much easier for us to choose not to own our own problem or fear, but to dump it in the lap of the other person and then blame them for what we don't want to accept about ourselves. So the appeal of the unavailable man may say as much about your fear of commitment as it does about his.

Some women openly admit that they don't want a committed relationship and are happy with their single lives. Others genuinely want a committed relationship and the closeness and intimacy, the love and the pain that entails. But many other women blame men for lack of commitment, without having the slightest idea that the fear of commitment lies within themselves, which is often why they subconsciously choose to fall in love with unavailable men.

DANGLING THE CARROT OF LOVE AND NEVER QUITE DELIVERING

The attraction for many women of risky, arrogant, unpredictable men is the very fact that they are unpredictable. You don't know what is going to happen next: it's fun and exciting one moment and agony the next. The fear of the unknown and the challenge they present makes your pulse race. According to Chrissy Iley, the writer and journalist who claims to be addicted to bad guys, 'They are cathedrals of unreliability and experts at emotional abuse, unequalled at blowing hot and cold and masters in the art of dangling the carrot of love but never quite delivering.'

A CPM will take you to the top of the world and then spin you around till, like in the children's game of Blind Man's Buff, you don't know which direction you're going as you try desperately to catch that elusive person darting around you in all directions. You are in heaven one moment and in hell the next, but one thing that you will never be when involved with such a man is bored. Because a relationship with a bad guy means that when the relationship is good it's very good but when it's bad it's horrid.

ARE YOU ATTRACTED TO THE BAD GUYS?

Chrissy Iley, writing in *The Sunday Times*, about her own relationships with men, says: 'I have always thought that bad boys are more fun. That is if you think cruelty, neglect, emotional terrorism, disempowerment and betrayal make a fun place. And obviously I do. I don't mean men who are going to be physically abusive or boringly super-macho; it's just that they know how to play at it in a way that appears charming. And let's face it, all the most interesting human beings are demanding, high maintenance, elusive, ridiculous and maybe clever enough to destroy you but probably not. And there's the challenge, which is part of the addiction. I have had the same relationship with men over and over again. The relationship involves an elusive person, who is extremely funny or a genius in some way, and is extremely attentive to me. There is a huge connection; but then I am forsaken, which I mistake for total abandonment. Then we fight; then if he is nice to me at all, I am supremely grateful, because everything is so distorted. Then he is cruel and nasty, and I think this is an illusion of how he wants to affect me, therefore he cares.'

She says of one man who dumped her after she had been seeing him for six months: 'I had been speaking to his secretary virtually every day when one morning I rang and asked to speak to him. She told me she could not put my call through. When I asked why, his secretary replied, "It's like this, Chrissy – Mr Hetherington doesn't know anyone of that name."'

RECOGNISE YOUR OWN ADDICTION

The lure of the elusive mate is particularly powerful if you are acting out some unresolved relationship from your childhood. If you had a remote elusive father and spent much of your time as a small girl desperately trying to make him take an interest in you, you may be repeating this pattern in your adult intimate relationships. You might be playing out the same old routine by falling for a man who won't commit. Here is your second chance to heal old wounds and this time the stakes are even higher. If you can succeed in attracting his love and attention your inner needy child tells you that these old hurts will cease to matter quite so much. Where before you have failed you now hope you will succeed. The challenge which the elusive lover presents is that of fighting for his love, the love your father failed to give you. But the other side of that particular coin is that part of you has damaged self-esteem, because of never feeling that you were lovable enough to attract you father's attention. Therefore, you fear any man getting really close to you because he might not like what he sees. So if you are repeatedly drawn to a man where genuine closeness is impossible or even extremely difficult you can continue to hide behind your screen. You don't have to reveal all of yourself. You can keep up all the romantic illusions without having to follow through, sustain long-term feelings for another person, or allow them to see your less attractive side – whether that be your erratic moods, untidy tendencies or obsessions with your calorie consumption.

An American study on couples who were reasonably committed to each other showed that even twenty-one months into a relationship around 20% of couples will still be hiding things from each other that they believe spoil their image.

Doctor Catherine Surra, of the University of Texas, is a veteran researcher into the process of commitment. Of her recent research she says, 'I wanted to know how people get close to marriage – how they decide to go ahead or not.' She monitored fifty-four couples and asked them to record their attitudes, interests and relationship histories; then she asked them to provide monthly up-dates on how likely they were to marry, and why they were more or less sure that their partner was 'the one'.

Her research identified two types of relationships. She calls the first 'relationship-driven commitment' that goes along in an orderly fashion with each partner reporting a regular increase in commitment. The second type – 'event-driven' – is a rollercoaster ride, with commitment soaring one month and plummeting the next. (Research Paper, 1997.)

In event-driven relationships, according to Surra, the couples react strongly to what has happened recently, like attending a friend's wedding, or having a serious argument. With event-driven couples there is often a pattern of big fights, splitting up, talking it over and getting back together two weeks or so later. Surra says in her research paper, 'Women in event-driven commitments reported significantly higher amounts of conflict and negativity than those in relationship-driven commitments. Having a turbulent event-driven relationship does not necessarily mean the couple is any less in love than a more relationship-driven pair, but Surra says: 'I would predict lower marital satisfaction in this kind of relationship. I think in the long run, event-driven couples are more likely to run into trouble.'

Much research shows that it takes a couple of years at least to have a reasonable idea of what the other person is like, and whether or not you suit each other. You may fall in love quite quickly, but it takes a little longer to be sure. Perhaps that is part of the problem of someone who fears commitment. It's not that they have a problem over falling in love, the problems occur when they are not really sure whether what they are feeling is the real thing. Maybe there is someone just around the corner who is going to be their one and only soul mate. One study showed that a courtship of two years makes a couple more likely to stay together, and of course for many commitment phobics they are not around long enough to really get to know each other. Their fear of commitment has meant that they have long since decided that they need to move on.

THE BATTLE FOR ANOTHER WOMAN'S MAN

Tiffany, at thirty-one, had had three long-term affairs with married men. The first one began when she was nineteen. He did eventually leave his wife only to marry someone else, which devastated her. When I first met her she was very determined that the man she was now in love with loved her, and it was only a matter of time and acquiring the necessary courage for him to leave his wife and four children for her. She angrily rejected any suggestion that there was any pattern or underlying reason for falling in love with married men. Of course she wanted these men to commit to her, she said. Did I think that she enjoyed the agony they inflicted on her? She brushed aside any questioning about why she got involved with them in the first place, or why having become involved she then expected them to leave their wives and children for her. Their relationship fluctuated between marvellous love-making and intense afternoons or evenings together and then Jim telephoning her and saying that he could not see her that evening as arranged as he had to go home as he had promised to be with the children as his wife was going out. She would scream at him, why couldn't he get a babysitter and he would shout at her that they were his children and he wanted to spend some time with them.

The argument would escalate even further and he would end up by saying that he could not go on like this, it was all too stressful and he was going to end their relationship. A marriage in difficulties and an hysterical mistress. She would spend the night weeping into her pillow and the next day ring him and say she was sorry for being so unreasonable, it was just that she loved him so much, and was disappointed at not seeing him. He would then tell her he also loved her and wanted to be with her, but he could not just walk out on his wife and children, and ask her to give him more time, they would be together one day. This pattern had been going on for four years. It took time but eventually Tiffany was able to look at what childhood patterns she was repeating. She loved her father and he adored her. She was the apple of his eye. Tiffany said: 'He made me feel extraordinary, special and different, I was rather a plain little girl but he called me "my little princess". I wasn't liked very much at school by the other girls and the teachers. I think as a teenager I was rather precocious.'

But he had a secret, in that he was an alcoholic, and totally inconsistent. So one moment she was the centre of her father's attention and the next he was not really interested in her. He had long dark moods, where her mother would encourage her to go and try and cheer him up, but it rarely worked. He would be away from the house on long drinking sprees, or if he was there he was in a world of his own and unavailable to his 'little princess'. She became quite disruptive at school, and screamed and shouted when the teachers told her off. Her mother was hard-working and lived in fear that her husband's drinking habit would be discovered and he would lose yet another job. But, despite the drinking, she adored her husband, who when he wasn't drinking was a clever, articulate, delightful and charming man. Tiffany remembered as a teenager being quite jealous of her mother's close relationship with her father, and being secretly pleased when she and not her mother had her father's time and attention.

When Tiffany was eighteen her father died of an overdose of drink and sleeping pills. Her relationships with men after that were with much older men. Jim was twenty years older than her. What she said really attracted her to these men at the beginning of the relationship was they really went overboard in making her feel totally special. She was able to make the links and see that like her father they appeared to adore her. That adoration was for her an aphrodisiac. The fact that they were married and therefore only available on a part-time basis meant that she was able to idealise them and her relationship with them. She would have conversations with Jim about how perfect life would be if only they were together all the time. But when he withdrew back to his wife and children, it was like her father withdrawing from her all over again, and she would scream and shout and become hysterical and all to no avail. In fact with Jim it made him withdraw even further. He had a volatile wife at home and did not want that in a mistress. But Tiffany was very pretty, talented, and sexy and she adored him. Tiffany was also replaying another pattern of her childhood which is why she always ended up in relationships with married men – to try and steal the unavailable man from the other woman. As a child she had been in competition with her mother for her father's love and affection. So she was hanging on to her relationship with Jim convincing herself that one day soon he was going to leave his wife. The painful part of the counselling for her was to recognise and accept that this was not going to happen. But when she was able to make the shift from saying that it was just chance that every man she fell in love with was married, to accepting why she got involved in the first place, she was then able to take charge of her life and avoid repeating the same mistakes over and over again.

SO ARE YOU A COMMITMENT-PHOBE?

Of course you deny it. There is nothing you want more than a man who loves you. It's quite ridiculous to say you are attracted by the unobtainable. But if it's happening not once or twice but has become a way of life, it really may be because you have a commitment problem of your own, or that you are constantly recreating an unresolved and still painful pattern from your childhood.

There is a pull in us all to go back to territory that we know. It is at times compelling because it is familiar, you may have hated it, but there is always the hope that this time you can make it work. If you don't realise that this is what you are doing there is a tendency in all of us to keep repeating the same old pattern. It's so much easier to spot it in others than in ourselves. How often have we seen a family member or a loved friend separate or divorce one man only to find that when she falls in love again it is with practically a replica of the former lover or husband.

If you are in a relationship where time and again you think he doesn't really love you and you are just about to end it, when at the eleventh hour, he'll send you flowers, or a card to say he loves only you, you are at your most vulnerable and you want to believe what he is saying even though it has happened countless times before, then it could be that you're used to cruelty, to being treated badly; it is really all you have experienced. So your inner self says that's all I deserve. Gerry, a pretty and talented actress, had a broken marriage and a string of disastrous relationships. Each time she fell in love, it was with good-looking men, usually actors, who were wonderfully romantic on stage, but so self-obsessed that they trod all over her needs. They would literally charm the pants of her and then not call for weeks, or she would discover that she thought she was the only one, but they had another girlfriend in some other town, they would not invite her out to dinner, but would come into the local wine bar, spend the evening giving her their undivided attention, and suggest that she went back to their house. She would go, saying to herself this time I won't go to bed with him, but in the end she did. She stayed in relationships that continually hurt her, and she kept hoping that the man would change and treat her well. All she had ever known as a child was neglect and lack of interest, so to her any show of interest kept her in the relationship even if it was not sustained but it was at least some form of attention, which as a child was in chronically short supply.

It can be very addictive to some women to play the part of rescuer or reformer. You know he is a cad, that he's more unfaithful than President Kennedy and President Clinton put together, but you convince yourself that with you he will be different. Make no bones about it, he may well encourage you in this thought, after all it is to his advantage, for there he has you hook line and sinker – that is until he gets bored and is off to pastures new. The reality is he does not want to be rescued from himself, he is happy as he is and he is certainly not going to make you happy. Well not for any sustained period, of that you can be certain.

By learning to recognise your self-destructive patterns you can protect yourself from going down the same old path time and again. It is hard to escape patterns that have been built up from childhood so you stick with an unsatisfactory relationship because you think you have the power to reverse, but the smart thing to do is to not get in there in the first place or, if that is not possible, to recognise when you are there and if things don't change to know how and when to get out.

ARE YOU ADDICTED TO MEN WHO ARE MAD, BAD AND DANGEROUS TO KNOW?

Lucinda had had many disastrous love affairs before she was able to recognise that she was always falling for the elusive mate. 'I was terribly attracted to Peter from the very first time that we met,' said Lucinda, an attractive solicitor in her mid-thirties. 'I was doing some rather difficult work for a large corporate client. When I walked into the boardroom there were three men sitting around the table, looking rather tense. They greeted me rather formally and one looked at his watch and said irritably, we are just waiting for the director of corporate affairs to join us, but I am afraid he is rather late. Moments later Peter arrived. As he crossed the room towards me, smiling and full of energy, he seemed such a contrast to the rather grey and worn men around the table. He took my hand and held it for a moment, slightly longer than was strictly necessary. I felt that shock of adrenaline shooting through me and felt sure he could tell the effect he was having on me. He was interesting, intelligent, amusing, and undoubtedly good-looking and very sexy. He was the sort of man, if you took him to a party every other pretty girl in the room would be eyeing him up and down. What really attracted me to him was I knew he would be dangerous to know. He made it clear from the start he wanted to meet again so I was not particularly surprised the next day when his secretary rang and said could I manage lunch the following week as there were some more things he felt we needed to discuss that had arisen out of yesterday's meeting. Neither was I totally surprised when she rang again two days later and said that Peter was terribly sorry but the lunch had to be cancelled as he unexpectedly had to fly to Hong Kong for a few days. The next time he rang himself. I made some caustic comment about was it his secretary's day off so he had to make his own lunchtime appointments, but he was utterly charming and very apologetic and suggested lunch the next day and I accepted

'Even on the first date he talked about how great we would be together. But his job meant that three quarters of the year he spent jetting round the world; he also lived miles from where I lived. So I knew that with the combination of the two, the relationship would flourish for him, on romantic weekends, candle-lit dinners and possibly occasional exotic holidays together. But for me, there would be the days and weeks in-between when our relationship would be reduced to telephone calls with me wondering who he was with halfway across the world or afraid to go out just in case I missed his telephone call. He was, as they say, my type, but I have had so many broken love affairs that I realised that this one would be likely to end up the same way. I think I'm addicted to men who as Lord Byron was so famously described by Lady Caroline Lamb are "Mad, bad and dangerous to know". These sorts of men start off making me feel like dancing on air and it inevitably all ends in tears, mine that is, not theirs.

'It was one of those meetings where I felt totally absorbed by him, I just did not notice anyone else in the restaurant. I remember walking out into the early spring sunshine, we stood talking for a minute or two and then he called a taxi for me as I had to get back to work. As the taxi drew up he leaned across and kissed me, just lightly on the cheek, but again that tingling feeling went right through me. He called me a week later and invited me to the theatre, but I refused. It was one of the hardest things I've ever done.'

She asked herself what she wanted and what she was not going to get from this relationship. 'I realised that though I could have a wonderfully exciting time with him, my antennae also told me that this man was not looking for a committed relationship.'

Lucinda had achieved the first step in taking charge of her life. She had looked at the situation, assessed what this man had to offer and because of past bitter experiences had realised that the excitement of a relationship with him came at a high price. One she was not prepared to pay again. She had also looked at herself and recognised that she was continually falling for exciting, unpredictable and uncommitted men who were going to let her down in the end.

The hypnotist Paul McKenna treats lots of people who are addicted to things like food, cigarettes, alcohol and also has some clients, mostly women, who go to him to be hypnotised out of destructive behavioural patterns. He has worked a lot with phobias and says: 'Maybe you were bitten by a dog as a child, so you have a file in your mind that says: see dog, create fear. It is there to protect you. That's the same with any dysfunctional behaviour: underneath, there's a positive intent. In destructive relationships, it means you are getting something from them. There is safety in things being the way they were. The mind has to confirm what it knows to be right. We seek the teeth that made the wounds.'

If we are stuck in dysfunctional patterns we have to learn how to let go of the old patterns and establish new and better ways of behaving.

It's hard to escape patterns that have been built up since childhood. You stick with the relationships because you think you have the power to reverse it. That's not a way of getting rid of the pattern, it's a way of further impressing it. Obviously if someone hit you over the head with a mallet time and time again, you would leave them.

I am not pretending this is easy, but by exploring what our childhood patterns of behaviour were we can gain more understanding about our adult way of relating to those we fall in love with. With this understanding we are more able to form the sort of relationships we want and discard those that cause us so much hurt and unhappiness.

ARE YOU ADDICTED TO BAD GUYS? AND HOW TO AVOID THEM IN FUTURE.

- You love the unpredictable, risk-taking is a turn-on, uncertainty keeps you hooked.
- Secure, stable, safe, reliable, dependable men to you spell boredom and you think it is the kiss of death to a relationship.
- You are addicted to high-drama relationships, the highs are fantastic, and the lows hellish, but it's always pure pleasure when you and he are making up.

If you are happy with living life in the fast lane, enjoying high adrenaline relations and you don't want to take time out to look at why you are attracted to bad guys – then fine. But if you have arrived at a time in your life when you would like things to be different, look at the reasons for this addiction, so you can avoid repeating the same old pattern.

- **Hidden Fear:** We sometimes avoid committing ourselves to a romantic relationship because of the fear that in doing so it will mean the sublimation of our own identity and our needs to the needs of another person. **Solution:** A committed relationship does not have to be about sublimation but it is about not having our needs met all of the time. But then if we think we can anyway that is fantasy land. Negotiation and give and take are what long-lasting relationships are based on.

- **Hidden Fear:** If we have little self-love, and therefore fear we are not lovable enough, we often get involved with romantic and unpredictable men, because that is a way of keeping relationships at arm's length. That means we can keep at bay the fear that if they really got to know us, they would not like what they saw. **Solution:** Work is needed on your self-esteem, so that you feel that you are a worthwhile person. That way you can learn to trust a man enough to allow him to get close to you. You can then allow yourself to look for faithfulness and security and commitment and avoid the bad guys who will love you and leave. So sign up for a self-esteem course, or counselling.
- **Hidden Fear:** I need a high-voltage relationship otherwise how will I know that he cares? This is likely to be because you were on the receiving end of too little love and attention as a child. Because of this, you become the disruptive naughty child to gain attention, which you did, as you were continually in trouble, so you learnt that any attention, even if it was the wrong sort of attention was better that none at all. **Solution:** Accepting that constant rows, or breaking up and making up relationships, may have short-term excitement, but in the long haul, the bad bits will increase and the good bits diminish. So take steps to avoid them in the first place. Avoid getting involved with abusive relationships, because that is what they often are. Consider counselling or psychotherapy if you need a little extra help to help you identify your behaviour pattern and avoid such emotionally abusive men.

10

When You've Married a CPM

How do I love thee? Let me count the ways.
I love thee to the depth and breadth and height
My soul can reach, when feeling out of sight
From the ends of Being and ideal Grace
I love thee to the level of every day's
Most quiet need, by sun and by candle light.

Elizabeth Barrett Browning, 1850

A MARRIED CPM

Perhaps the most difficult of all to understand is the Married CPM (MCPM). He appears to have conquered the marriage hurdle and made a commitment to you, because after all he has proposed, you have accepted, you have had the big day and you are now sharing a life together. Or at least that is what you are trying to do.

Many men, even though they marry, carry into marriage their fear of commitment. Through the wooing and courtship stage they may have been able to keep these fears reasonably under wraps and it is only after they have taken those wedding vows that a sense of panic sets in. So you are now sharing a life together, or at least that was what you thought you were trying to do, only you are finding that in very important areas of your life he just is not there for you. There are so many other things, as well as you, competing for his time and attention: work, networking, his friends, his hobbies, his dedication to sport, surfing the net, an affair or serial unfaithfulness and more.

He may opt out in a number of ways. When the new baby arrives he is hardly there as he is struggling up the career ladder. You need support when the children are ill, but it's always you who has to sort out emergency childcare. You both work hard all week but it's him who spends the weekend playing sport. You want to spend time together in the evening and he is glued to the television, studying papers for tomorrow's meeting, or rebuilding his prize vintage motor car in the garage at the bottom of the garden. It slowly begins to dawn on you that though you are married to him, he spends relatively little time with you physically and emotionally.

So you complain to your friends that your are married to a Male Chauvinist Pig. Well, you could be, but equally you could be married to a man who fears commitment. A man who is so uncertain how to handle up-close and personal relationships that he is continually involving himself in other things or other people. He does this so that he does not feel overwhelmed by too much togetherness, or because of his unresolved fears of feeling trapped – marriage is for ever, and for ever is a very long time.

In men who fear commitment a sudden loss of sexual interest in the woman who was once the object of their most ardent desire is classic commitment phobic behaviour. For no reason that you can understand you suddenly seem to have lost your appeal. But it is not your fault, the core of the problem is that the man in question is struggling with his fear of commitment, he cannot allow himself to love too much or become too vulnerable, so he sets about distancing himself emotionally and sexually so that he is then more able to end the relationship.

For some it can start on honeymoon and for others it is more of a slow-burn situation. The married man who is commitment shy has many strategies for fending off these feelings of panic and convincing himself that he is not as trapped as he fears.

This sense of feeling trapped is what causes his behaviour to change. His panic is often so intense that, a bit like a wild animal suddenly caught in a cage, he rushes mindlessly around causing havoc to the woman he has married. Instead of seeing you as you really are, his need to distance himself from you means he frequently casts you in the role of the big bad wolf who is about to devour him.

HOW A MARRIED MAN CREATES DISTANCE IN A RELATIONSHIP

- He starts to find fault with you, he criticises the way you look, the way you dress, the way you cook, the way you behave at parties. The many things about you he once loved now seem to drive him up the wall.
- He finds excuses not to make love. He is too tired, too busy, too stressed. Instead of going to bed together he stays up watching the late-night show.
- The most classic way of creating distance in a marriage is to become involved with another woman. This may be anything from a one-night stand to a more intense affair. Then he can convince himself that if he can enjoy sex with another woman he can't really be as in love with you as he thought, so that makes him feel safer and the panic subsides.
- Work becomes an acceptable mistress in his eyes. He is not being unfaithful but he is much more involved with his work than with you. The more arguments and rows you have the more he escapes to his office, so you see less of him, and the more you complain the more involved with his work he becomes, so that eventually his work takes far higher priority in his life than you.
- He uses sport, either watching it or playing it, or allows his passion for a particular hobby to take over most of his waking hours when he is not at work. Whichever it is, it is distancing and it effectively cuts you out of much of his life as the time you actually spend together is very limited.

All these strategies give him a feeling of freedom, of having more space. He has established a distance between you and him and then he can breathe more easily again. So then back comes the man you fell in love with, his old charming self, or practically. But then when he feels too close or trapped again his bizarre behaviour rears its ugly head once more.

As women we often unconsciously collude with the commitment phobic man's behaviour. We meet an attractive man, he goes all out to get us. We fall in love and he gives us every impression that he loves us just as much as we love him. So when his attitude to us starts to change we are confused. When he is more withdrawn or begins to criticise us or our behaviour we start to think what is happening? What has gone wrong? And we are soon asking ourselves: What have I done to bring about this change?

In the main women are far more likely than men to search for where they have gone wrong in relationships. We have been programmed though nature and nurture to see the taking care of relationships as central to our role. So it is all too easy for us to accept it as our fault when those relationships go wrong. This is particularly so when it comes to loving a man who fears commitment. If we jump in and blame ourselves for what has gone wrong it gives the man ample opportunity to agree with us.

The married CPM has gone further down the line than one who cuts and runs from a relationship at an earlier stage. Yet he is still a man in conflict, but part of him is often very motivated to have a committed relationship and this can be achieved if he can overcome his feelings about being trapped and seeing you as his captor. If he does not understand what is happening and why he is behaving the way he does, he can end up destroying the relationship, which is what Sebastian did when he married Emma.

EMMA'S STORY

Emma is one of those very beautiful women who when she walks into a room every man and indeed woman there immediately notices. Her long thick blonde hair frames her face with its high cheekbones and a lovely skin. She is very feminine, intelligent and witty, she is loved by her girlfriends and lusted after by men. At thirty-nine she is a younger version of Farrah Fawcett-Major but probably more vulnerable. When she met Sebastian she was in her early thirties. She had fairly recently come out of a four-year relationship with a man she had loved but whom she knew she did not want to marry. She began: 'A great friend of mine knew I was a little down and invited me to dinner. She said, "I want you to meet Sebastian, I think you will like him and you have a lot in common." She asked him to give me a lift to the dinner party as my car had broken down.

'I had dressed very specially for the evening. I suppose it was a way of making me feel good about myself. The doorbell rang and when I opened the door Sebastian was standing there. I just thought "wow" he was physically so beautiful, very tall, very dark, very handsome. He seemed a big man in every way. I was so stunned that we both just stood there beaming at each other. The dinner party was amazing as there was this very strong physical attraction between us all evening. He was so good-looking and also highly educated. His use of English was phenomenal. I found him intellectually very exciting. After the party he brought me home and I invited him in for a drink and we just talked for hours until about two or three in the morning and so he stayed the night.

'That night we made love and it was very good. He rang next day and each day after that; a week later he took me out to dinner and asked me to marry him. I wasn't really surprised. It was a very intense attraction and because we had so much in common it was quite overwhelming. I did have a flicker of doubt but I put it down to my own insecurities. I blamed myself. I have had committed relationships, but I've always shied away from marriage. I saw this as a character flaw of my own. I had been engaged twice but never married. I thought maybe I've got a problem. But I was wrong. I think my doubts were a warning voice, but I did not see it at the time.

'The morning after the first night we spent together, I remember thinking it was very odd because he spoke in a very soft voice which wasn't his normal speaking voice and he said "Take great care." I don't know why he said that. The thought ran through my mind "this man is going to get on my nerves." Then I thought I'm just being stupid.

'When he proposed it was so romantic and I thought it's now or never. If I back away from this there's something wrong with me. But part of me had serious doubts. There was an inner battle and it was all happening so fast. I thought how do I know that this is the right person for me, but the other side of me said, yes he couldn't be more perfect, so what's your problem? I was a bit of a free spirit and I liked the living-together relationships with the two men I had lived with. I regarded myself as having had two husbands, emotionally.

'The night Sebastian proposed we were on an absolute

high and we spent the night together. The next day was one of those beautiful winter's days with a thick frost and clear blue sky. It was the day before my birthday, which I was planning to spend with my parents in the country, so I suggested to Sebastian that he came with me, so he drove me down. I hadn't told them anything. The best thing, I thought to myself, was just to arrive. It was getting quite dark when we turned up and my mother thought he was a cab driver I'd picked up at the station. I said, "Mummy, this is the man I'm going to marry," and she dropped the presents she was carrying. It was the first time in my life I'd ever seen my mother speechless.

'My parents took it very well, my father produced lots of champagne and we had a lovely supper together. Six months after the proposal we got married. I think I spent a lot of that time in a daze.

'I did have second thoughts at Easter, before we married. This man I loved completely freaked me out. He was suddenly horrible, it was like being with another person. We went to stay with some friends of mine in Tuscany. He actually behaved so badly that I gave my engagement ring back. He was rude and unpleasant to everyone. The crunch came at the end of the holiday, they'd been incredibly generous, lent us the car, given us super dinners and it was all laid on because they were my friends. I said to Sebastian, "We must get them some flowers and gifts." He said: "They're rich. They don't need it." I said, that's not the point. I don't care if they're multi-millionaires, I've never stayed for a whole holiday without leaving a gift. Look how generous they've been. I want to do something, it's not gracious.

'We went down to the village where I bought flowers and gifts and he refused to contribute. I took my ring off.

He looked very shocked. I said, "It's off. I don't want to marry you." I was terribly distressed and crying then. There were hours of silence, but then he said he was sorry and he talked me round.

'He'd been married before but it had only lasted a year. I don't really know what had gone wrong, I think it was the fact that he was very young then. The way he put it sounded okay. I was later to discover he always fell out with people. We had a lovely wedding, we got married at a register office and then had a blessing which added a dimension that made it a very special occasion. Then we had a reception with lots of friends.

'I did not see it at the time but there were warning signs and the honeymoon was one of them. He was supposed to be arranging the honeymoon and I was absolutely horrified when ten days before the wedding I discovered nothing was organised. So we bought one of the Sunday papers, went through last-minute ads and found a fortnight in Corsica. When I asked him why he had done nothing he said he'd been stressed out.

'We didn't make love on our wedding night, nor in the morning. My first day as a married woman and we had not made love. I did not understand it, I felt quite depressed. We were staying in a fabulous old Corsican cottage in a tiny village. It was very quiet and it was bliss. There was even a scented jasmine growing round the door. It was gorgeous. He was enchanted by the place. In the week leading up to the wedding we had not made love, he kept saying how tired he was and that he had been working very hard. At first I thought okay, but I was a bit surprised. For the first few days in Corsica we did not make love I didn't panic; I thought, just relax, give him time. But round about day four, with this big moon, hot nights, this huge gorgeous antique brass bed with roses painted on the enamel it started to freak me out. I went for a long walk by myself and later that evening I seduced him.

'It was very strange having sex with him that night. I'll never forget it because it was chilling. When I looked at his face, it was like he wasn't there. His eyes weren't there. I remember looking into his eyes when we were making love and it was like he wasn't there. It had never happened to me before in all my sex life with anyone. I didn't understand. I kept thinking he's not there, he's not there. And yet all the right things were happening. I remember all of a sudden my whole body went frigid because I felt I was having sex with a doll or something, but not a person and certainly not my husband. I thought, let it pass, we've been having an incredibly stressful time, having to organise so much for the wedding, but we only made love twice on honeymoon and both times it was instigated by me.

'Love-making had been so good before we were married, I did not understand why he didn't want to make love. He never fully explained why, it was only in a rare moment of great honesty at the end of the marriage that he said: "Oh, this has always happened! It happens once I am really with someone, then I lose interest." He said it had started because his first wife wanted a baby but he didn't.

'Not long after we returned from honeymoon we went to a dinner party with friends of his. It was a big party and I did not know a soul. We were all sitting around the table and I was laughing at something somebody had said when suddenly Sebastian brought the entire party to a standstill. He said very loudly to someone sitting at the other end of the table from him, "Do you know, my wife has the libido of a truck driver." The whole room fell quiet and he continued, "She's insatiable, utterly insatiable." The way he said it wasn't kind or complimentary, it was implying I had a big problem. I didn't know where to look or what to say. I left the room and went to the loo and burst into tears. When I returned people were talking normally again as if nothing had been said. It was quite hideous and we had only been married a few months. He rarely initiated sex and eventually he ceased to respond to any of my advances, however subtle. Even if I just wanted to show him some simple affection he rejected it. We often used to eat out at a local restaurant. They told me long after my marriage broke down that they used to call us "The beautiful couple". Little did they know what was going on in our marriage. Once when we were walking home from the restaurant when I still had some confidence and before I had put on weight, I saw a doorway and said let's go and kiss there. I found the idea very erotic. He said, "Emma, erotic fantasy has no part to play in a marriage." I said, "I'm only asking you to kiss me in a doorway." I said, "You look so handsome." Then he told me he did not like French kissing, it made him feel claustrophobic.

'I became a very unbeautiful woman. I just cooked and cooked, made bread and jam and made huge meals and put on about three stone and lost all interest in my appearance. He then endlessly criticised my appearance and said my body wasn't good enough. My breasts were too small and my stomach was too round. He said I was fat and therefore he couldn't make love to me. I'd weighed about eight stone twelve on my wedding day. Eighteen months into my marriage I was eleven stone.

'He then started on my mind. He started to say that I

wasn't very well read and I didn't know enough to have intelligent, educated discussions with him. When we first met he told me it was wonderful to meet someone who'd read the same poetry as him and that we had everything in common and now he rejected all of that. The physical thing was the worst, not just the sexual rejection but any little everyday affection. I always had to ask for a hug. He never did that spontaneously.

'He pretended to like women, but he had this thing that women were bitches, and out to get him and somehow trap him and destroy his essence. He told me once that women were like vampires and would take his energy and he would never be able to replace it. He used to say things like, "Oh you know what it says in the Chinese texts about a man's semen is his life force and if he loses too much of it he becomes depleted."

'I did not know what was happening because when he was not being absolutely dreadful to me he could be gentle and sweet and amusing and there were times when we had fun together and it was almost like it was in the beginning. Then suddenly it would all change. I would look at him and realise he wasn't there, just like it was when we first made love on honeymoon.

'We had been married about a year and we moved into a very pretty house that we had bought together. We had only been there a few days when he turned to me and said, "I've had no desire for you at all. I've tried to pray, I've prayed to God to be able to love my wife, but I can't." I said perhaps we should have counselling, but he refused.

'I was so confused I thought if I could get pregnant maybe it would bring us together. By some miracle I did get pregnant. But three months into it I woke up in agony and the bed was flooded and I was miscarrying. I said to Sebastian please help me to the bathroom and call the doctor. He wouldn't even get out of bed and said, "Why must you make such a fuss?" I cried, "I am losing my baby." He just lay there, it was the last straw. In the morning I went to see my gynaecologist. It was all over by then. That was the cruellest, most sadistic thing I have ever experienced. I look back now and I wonder why I stayed in the marriage. I didn't know who I was any more.

'He wouldn't talk to me about the miscarriage he just said, "Obviously it wasn't meant to happen." Then he said there must be something wrong with me. It was shortly after that time that he started seeing other women.

'Everything about me had collapsed. He had almost destroyed me. The other woman business was almost incidental by then. It was about three months after my miscarriage. We were staying in a hotel with several other friends and I awoke in the middle of the night and he wasn't there. I got up and opened the bedroom door; I saw him coming out of the room of one of the other women. He said they had only been talking and that I was overly demanding, and the stupid thing was I believed him.'

LOOK AT YOUR RELATIONSHIP THROUGH THE EYES OF YOUR BEST FRIEND

If you think you are in a relationship with a man who is so frightened of commitment that he is intent on destroying the relationship it is important to try to step back and see what is happening. Imagine you are your best friend who cares about you deeply, see the relationship for what it really is, and not what you are wanting it to be. Your best friend would not make excuses for his behaviour because she would see how much you are being hurt by it, and her view is not clouded by loving the man who she sees is treating you badly. If you are finding as Emma did that you are changing from a happy, confident, outward-going and loving person, to someone who is unhappy, undermined, and suffering from low self-esteem then something is seriously wrong. Don't ignore these warning signs and if possible try and spot them earlier. They really are indications that something is very wrong with the relationship. If that is the case changes will have to be made.

If, like Sebastian, the man you are involved with is a worst-case commitment phobic, creating some space and distance between you will not be enough. The relationship is probably doomed. The problem is that he can't make a permanent commitment in either direction. He does not know whether to stay or to go. The pendulum swings in both directions and he does not seem able to make a decision. The problem is he does not want to take the responsibility of taking the decision. He is hoping he can abdicate the responsibility and that something will happen that will sort it out or that you will get so fed up with him that eventually you will take the decision for him and end the relationship.

The problem for you is that so often you still love him, or at least you love the person he once was. You keep hoping that he will be like that again, so you stay in there putting up with his appalling behaviour long after you should have got some professional help for you both or ended the relationship. Being involved with such destructive behaviour threatens your own peace of mind and even your sanity.

Emma agreed to talk to me for this book because she hoped that her experience would help other women, who may be experiencing similar situations, to get help. She hoped that it might prevent other women from sinking to the depths of despair and unhappiness that she did in her relationship with Sebastian.

If you are stuck in a very unhappy relationship where all your friends are urging you to get out, because they think he is treating you so badly, think twice before you reject their concern. Like Emma's friends they may be seeing a lovely and vulnerable woman become someone they hardly recognise.

We often stay in problematical relationships because in some curious way the present relationship has very strong links to our past. For Emma when she started to look at what they were, she was able to see that in many ways her relationship with Sebastian was a re-enactment of her relationship with her mother, who had been highly critical and undermining of her. She was repeating a childhood pattern.

It was not what she wanted but it was familiar to her, and of course as I have said before, it is easier for most of us to stay with the familiar however unsatisfactory than break through into something new.

Emma's parents had a very volatile relationship which absorbed a lot of their energies so Emma and her brothers were rather pushed to the sidelines. 'When I was very small,' Emma said, 'my mother used to tell me relentlessly how plain and how stupid I was.'

As Emma moved into her teenage years she became her mother's confidante. Emma explained,' My role was to listen to her about her problems and about my father's countless mistresses. I had no other role as far as she was concerned.'

By the time Emma was sixteen she was startlingly pretty and she was getting lots of attention from men. Her mother's jealousy increased. She said to Emma, 'I don't know what's wrong with all these men, why on earth are they looking at you? It must be because you're showing off your legs.'

Two years later Emma was eighteen and was offered a job modelling in Milan. When she told her mother, she said – sounding absolutely astonished – 'YOOOOUUU? surely not YOOOOUUU?' then added, 'Perhaps they like different sorts of looking women over there.'

'On my wedding day,' Emma said, 'I remember it very clearly, that was the priceless one. My mother who was there as I was getting ready had said nothing and when I asked her how I looked she said, "I suppose you look as good as it would be possible for you to look." I did actually turn on her and told her she was supposed to say I looked beautiful. She said, "Hm. Well you look nice."' By marrying Sebastian she had indeed married the critical parent figure. 'Yes,' said Emma smiling sadly.

'I do love her, she can't help the way she is. I accept her like that. It would be nice to have a mother. But I have no idea what that's like.'

Throughout much of her life Emma has tried to gain her mother's approval, without success. So when Sebastian told her that she was not what he wanted intellectually or sexually she was on sadly familiar territory. So also she tried endlessly to get him to show her he loved her. If her self-esteem had not been so damaged she might have been able to see that the problems lay more within Sebastian rather than herself and therefore would not have put up with such abusive behaviour or have stayed in the marriage so long.

IT WAS 'GOODBYE SEX' ALTHOUGH I DIDN'T REALISE IT AT THE TIME

Sebastian continued with the affair, all the time denying that he was having one, so much so that Emma thought that she was going nuts, for all the evidence pointed in that direction. Eventually she could take no more and she asked him to move out for a little while. He went abroad with this girl for a month but claimed he had gone on a retreat to think about their marriage.

Emma said, 'When he got back he accused me of having an affair with this woman's husband and he was furious over this supposed infidelity. We talked and talked and I said I still loved him. We went to bed and had the best sex we'd ever had. But it was "goodbye sex" although I didn't realise it at the time. I begged him to try and make a go of our marriage. We made love again in the morning and then he sat up and said: "I don't know how you can touch me after I've been with somebody else." I was so shocked I slapped his face. I said, "I love you and that is why I hope we can try again."

'Over the next seven months he came and went several times. He said he was confused and that he was thinking about us and that he wanted us to be able to sort things out. What saved me was I re-met an old boyfriend. I started an affair with John and it was the most comforting, it was familiar territory. A so-called girlfriend of mine who was after Sebastian told him I had slept with this other man and he came round in a fury and said, "I hear you've been seeing John again. That's it. You've broken your wedding vows, you've been unfaithful." I said, "But so have you." He looked at me coldly and said, "That's different."

'He shouted at me: "You've blotted everything. You've spoiled everything," and he left. For the whole of that year I carried on wearing my wedding ring. I was having sex with him on and off. The sensation at that time was one of hanging on by my nails from the edge of a cliff.

'I lay in bed for three days crying and crying. I couldn't eat. I almost wanted to die. I never rang anyone. My cats walked over me while tears were running down my cheeks. It galvanised me and I went and bought food for them. I thought I might as well have some toast myself. It was the worst point in my life.

'I had a dream of that Pre-Raphaelite painting of a veiled woman in a field of poppies. The painting came alive in my dream and the woman was beckoning to me. And I walked towards her through the poppies and then I panicked and thought if I follow her I will never waken. And I woke in an absolute sweat at four a.m. and my heart pounding and thinking I've come very close to going. The cats got me going. It was good. I would have turned around without them but they did help a lot. There were no thoughts in my mind. I was just a body of misery, no sound in my head. It was then that I filed for divorce.

'Sebastian remarried immediately the divorce came through, in just the same way. Meeting some woman and marrying her within six months. His first wife was the sister of a woman he had lived with. He told me after a year of marriage he realised he'd got the wrong sister so he left her. He's now left his third wife.

'Sebastian has a life-long mistrust of women and in the end he has left every one of them. He was born as a result of his mother having a brief fling with an old friend. His mother's marriage survived that but eventually broke up three years later. She took Sebastian with her and went to live in Paris where she married a Frenchman. There she had two daughters in quick succession. Sebastian grew up surrounded by women and he would describe his mother and sisters as they grew older as a dark force. He said his ex-wife and girlfriends were all like dark devouring angels. He experienced women's sexuality as very threatening. He said it was like a magnetic sexuality that men would be attracted by, despite their better judgement.'

For Sebastian his particular panic button ignited once he was married. The panic set in on the first night of the honeymoon and intensified as the marriage continued. Sebastian lost sight of Emma as a person, so he felt at liberty to be unkind, and to behave so badly.

Once married he saw a sexual relationship with a woman as threatening and devouring. He saw women like the female spider, who as soon as the male of the species has mated with her, promptly eats him unless he can outwit her and make a very hasty retreat.

It's taken Emma a long time to recover from her relationship with Sebastian. Only in the last two years has she felt completely herself again. A few weeks ago she dreamed of Sebastian for the first time in over two years. She said, 'I was walking down a road and he was standing in a building and I just glanced at him and walked on. I didn't run. Finally that's how I feel now. I don't have to run away from him any more.

'I've now got a new boyfriend I met in the summer. I'm still protecting myself. I still believe in marriage as a commitment and a very relaxing thing to do. The ultimate relaxation. The next marriage wouldn't be nest-building, I'm not dewy-eyed any more. It might be with someone much younger, even in separate homes. I know it's safe with my boyfriend because he'll have to leave the country to return to his own country soon. I love him. I feel very much alive. I feel like a woman again. I feel appreciated as a woman and that my femininity is not a problem, but something to be valued and treasured. It's been quite amazing to start enjoying all that again.'

KNOWING WHEN AN MCPM SPELLS DANGER

There are times when it's healthier to end the marriage or relationship than continue with it. This was certainly so where Emma and Sebastian were concerned. It is very important to be able to recognise the signs if you are in a relationship with a man who fears commitment so badly that there is little or no chance of him changing. That way you are more able to end that relationship before it becomes too destructive. If you have been in one but it is now over, by going back over what happened and trying to identify when perhaps you should have got out, which was probably a lot sooner than you did, you can also learn from past experiences.

THE HOOK THAT KEEPS YOU THERE

The contrast from how he was at the beginning of the relationship, impulsive, loving and in hot pursuit contrasts so starkly to when the relationship is not really viable or reaching its end that it is not really surprising that you feel totally confused. That being so the likelihood is that because you can remember vividly how lovely it was and how much he seemed to love you, you will be there bending over backwards to make it all right again. Emma did this on numerous occasions, after being continually rejected on honeymoon, after the very public humiliation at the dinner party, the criticism of how she looked and her intellect. The cruel way Sebastian treated Emma when she was having a miscarriage and when she discovered him with another woman, and so the list went on. But she is no different from many other women who get involved with such men. You hope against hope that things will be different, that they will improve. And there is the rub, the reality is that often they do. But the improvement does not last. It is just enough to reel you back in and play with you as a fisherman does when he has the excitement of trying to land an extra large fish he can truly boast about to his friends.

This cat-and-mouse game wreaks havoc with your emotions. One moment you feel that he loves you and if you try a little harder everything will be all right, the next you are thrown into anxiety and despair because things seem just as bad or worse than before.

Along with his erratic behaviour he will leave all sorts of clues that he is thinking of ending the relationship but he can't make a commitment to that either. He may feel ready to end it, but remember he is also likely to be feeling torn in two directions, his need for a committed relationship alongside his fear of having one.

He may also feel guilty, though that will depend on whether he is prepared to acknowledge any responsibility for how he has changed or whether he is insisting on putting all the blame on you. Look how much Sebastian came and went in the final throes of their marriage and how little recognition there was of the havoc his behaviour was causing to Emma. This is a very typical scenario because the man cannot really be up-front and tell you how he feels, so he looks for ways of behaving that will damage the relationship.

The three most common ways he uses of sabotaging his relationship with you

- Criticising you, putting you down and picking fights over the tiniest thing.
- Getting involved with another woman, being careless about you catching him out and then denying it hotly.
- Wanting more time without you, continually working late at the office, maybe suggesting he takes a holiday alone, or moving out temporarily, and he will probably justify this by saying it will give him more time to sort himself out or decide what he wants to do about the relationship.

He is in the throes of terminal indecision of wanting you and not wanting you. Of deciding to leave one minute and then changing his mind the next, telling you he needs to find himself or that he needs more space but that he still cares about you.

How to respond to the Yo-Yo behaviour of a worse case MCPM

- Stop thinking about him and his needs and concentrate on your own needs. That is to take care of yourself. Despite all his promises he has patently not taken care of you or your feelings, so it is up to you to take care of yourself.
- Do not be drawn into giving him yet one more chance when you have already been there a hundred times before. He is not going to change because it's the 101st time.
- Summon up the strength to end the relationship for your sake and for your own survival and sanity.
- If you don't end the relationship, the likelihood is that eventually he will. Taking some control back into your life for perhaps the first time for months or more likely years is an important first step on the road to recovery.

Not all men who fear commitment fall into the worst-case scenario category like Sebastian. Many more men marry and are genuinely surprised and confused by their erratic behaviour. They do not really understand why they are blowing hot and cold. They may even express surprise if you suggest that they have a problem with commitment. They know they love you, they feel they want to be with you but the problem is that they appear to want to be with you a lot less that you want to be with them. It may also be that when you want to turn to them for emotional support they find it hard to give. They are committed in so much as they have married you but they are emotionally unavailable.

GETTING THE LOVE YOU WANT

If a man has married, then in the main it does at least show good intent. He wants this relationship with you. His problem is he is finding so much closeness and intimacy hard to handle. So it may be that you are approaching this relationship from opposite ends of the arena. You want intimacy and togetherness and he wants space and independence. You want to talk about the relationship, he finds he has something he urgently needs to do. You want to spend time together, he is always at work, on the golf course or glued to sport on television.

If some of these things are all too familiar to your relationship it could be because the man in your life is handling his fear of commitment by being emotionally unavailable or physically absent from the marriage a lot of the time. As I said at the beginning of the chapter there are many ways that men choose to create space and distance in a marriage. Sometimes this is done consciously and at others quite unconsciously which of course when challenged makes it easier to deny. There's the critical partner/parent who constantly puts you down, the lover who withholds sex, the unfaithful spouse, the workaholic or the sports fanatic. All are classic ways of avoiding commitment and keeping an emotional distance in the marriage.

First it is important to realise he doesn't want out of the marriage, though from his behaviour you might find this hard to believe. It's a case of learning to understand what he does want, and how both of your needs can be met to a satisfactory degree. I stress I am not for one minute suggesting that you constantly subjugate your needs to his as a way of keeping him in the marriage. No, not at all. For one thing you would soon start to feel very resentful and secondly it would only be tackling the symptoms while the problem would still be there alive and kicking.

What you need to do is discuss with him how you are feeling, what your needs are, and ask him what his needs are. Really listen to what each other is saying. Then you can start to negotiate some changes so that you achieve a better balance between your desire for intimacy and his for space and independence.

Here is an exercise to help you understand your needs and those of your spouse.

LEARNING TO MEET EACH OTHER'S NEEDS

Take a piece of paper each, and without seeing what the other is writing make a list of five things you want from the other person; don't write something too general, like YOU: 'I want him to love me more,' HIM: 'I want great sex.' You both need to be very specific about your needs. Secondly, start by looking for small changes, otherwise it will feel too overwhelming and the task will not be accomplished, for example:

YOU

- When you come in from work, to give me kiss and a big hug, tell me you love me or that you are glad to be home.
- One evening every week for you to be home by seven, and you read the children a bed-time story while I get supper.
- To spend half an hour in the evening telling me about your day and listening to mine, sharing the highs and lows together.
- To go out for a meal just the two of us once a month, and take an interest in what I am wearing.
- To ask your parents to have the kids for an occasional weekend, so that we can have uninterrupted time to make love, which does not have to be when I am tired at the end of the day, or a rushed quickie in the morning.

HIM

- For you to initiate love-making more often.
- For you not to nag if I play sport on Saturdays, as long as we spend all day Sunday together.
- To give me half an hour to unwind when I get home from work, so I can just have some transition time on my own between work and home.
- For you to agree to invite our friends around to supper, say, once a month.
- To wear some pretty underwear, like you used to do before we were married.

These are just suggestions – what is important is that you each make your own list of five things.

Then share your lists with each other. To start with agree on one thing each from your list that you would most like your partner to do for you. Each week try and build in one more thing from your lists. They should be as near as possible of equal value. Hopefully after one week you will notice a little change, and after five weeks if you keep to this task, you will be much better at fulfilling each other's needs.

Most importantly don't forget to tell each other how much you appreciate them, when they do something to please you. The more we feel appreciated the more we want to give in return.

One of the things that had turned sour in Matt and Val's marriage was that he did not really understand the demands that three small children made on her, and Matt did not feel Val appreciated how hard he worked for her and the kids.

MARRIED TO THE JOB

Matt would always arrive for his counselling session on the dot. A few minutes earlier you would hear the wheels of his gleaming BMW squeal to a halt as he arrived at speed swishing into the car park. This was followed by a banging of doors as he got out of the car and tore across the tarmac, talking all the time into his mobile phone, which would be promptly switched off as he burst into the room and sat down on a chair opposite his wife. This was his counselling hour and he was going to give it all he'd got. That is how he approached his work, and it had certainly made him a very successful sales director for a large multinational company at the age of thirty-four. His marriage, he admitted, was rather less successful.

Val his wife, a slim and pretty woman with short blonde

hair, originally had to drag Matt screaming and shouting to counselling and it was only because their marriage was in such deep trouble that he eventually agreed to come.

They had been married for nine years and had three children of eight, seven and four. The communication between them was at an all-time low. If you had asked Matt he would say he was committed to the marriage, after all, he was still there wasn't he, working hard for all of them. The picture that emerged was one where Matt was driven by hard work and success, but as he was to admit, he was emotionally an island. He was fiercely independent and unaware of how desolate and angry this left his wife feeling. He loved Val, but saw her as the one with all the problems. He said her family was very dysfunctional, her parents' marriage had been one of verbal violence and abuse with a father who had a drink problem and was work shy and a mother who had given up the struggle to bring up her five children to the extent that Val, the eldest daughter, had from an early age to take responsibility for her young siblings. While his parents had a happy marriage, he and his older sister had an idyllic, secure and trouble-free childhood. But things are rarely quite what they seem.

Val became pregnant within weeks of returning from honeymoon. She had hoped to have several years without children as she had a job she enjoyed and she was only in her early twenties. But Matt was over the moon. He could not wait to be a father and wanted lots of children. So babies followed in quick succession. The reality of fatherhood was slightly less appealing. He loved his children, but he found little time to be with them as he became more and more involved with his work. This meant long hours and several house moves as he wanted to provide well for the growing family. He was there at the children's birth but Val said with his mobile phone in one hand and his latest sales figures in the other. She became increasingly resentful as Matt never seemed to understand quite how demanding three young children and the constant house moves were. The solution to the problem as Matt saw it, was to hire in some extra help with the children which he did but that was only part of the problem solved. The more Val turned to him for help and support the more he ran in the opposite direction. After the second baby, Val developed mild post-natal depression. Even more help was hired and she saw even less of Matt. As time went on Val withdrew emotionally and sexually from Matt.

Matt, like many successful high achievers had a high sex drive. At the beginning of the relationship sex had been particularly good but, eight years on, sex was a battleground, with Matt constantly making advances, and Val in retreat like the Russian army in the Napoleonic wars, disillusioned, angry and defeated.

It was really only when Matt was able to understand what the last years had been like for Val that she was able to let go some of her bottled-up anger.

Her unexpected early pregnancy meant that much as Val loved her children, another part of her resented the responsibility for them falling on her shoulders all over again. She had virtually been a surrogate mother to her own siblings, so that as a child she was weighed down with responsibilities for her brothers and sister from an early age. She had wanted more time between leaving behind the responsibilities forced on her as a child, and embarking on her own family. Val never felt that Matt ever appreciated quite how much hard work babies were, especially three in quick succession, and though when he was there he was a very good father, much of the time he was absent. Failing to get her point across to Matt in private she resorted to barbed comments wrapped up in humour at dinner parties. Her favourite story, which she used to recount, was about the husband who one night was given a lift home from work by a colleague. The husband got out of the car and opened his garden gate and began to walk up the drive. His children rushed out of the house in great excitement and threw their arms around their father. The colleague remarked to the wife what a heart-warming picture it was that the children were so pleased to see their father. The wife remarked icily, 'They are always like that with strangers.'

Val also felt that Matt had never wanted to know what it was like for her to have given up her job to be at home with the children. It had been a joint decision but she felt he showed little understanding about how much she missed her job and the good feeling it gave her. Also how Matt's success made her even more aware of where she might have been and what she might have achieved if she had still been at work.

As Matt started to look a little more into his own upbringing he was able to admit that his own parents never talked openly about their feelings. Everything had to be seen to be all right, anything that was difficult or uncomfortable was brushed under the carpet. The work ethic was the only acceptable way of gaining their approval. Both Matt and his sister had worked hard and done well at school. But his sister who was seven years older than him had dropped out of university. She had started to go around with unsuitable men and became involved with drugs – though this was never mentioned to her parents – and she moved from one badly paid job to another, much of the time scraping a living on the dole. This was never discussed at home, it was just as if it was not happening. If friends asked his parents how his sister was they were told that she was fine, and enjoying university or her job. Finally when she was in her early thirties she had a nervous breakdown and spent many months in hospital receiving treatment. Even when Matt was in his twenties none of this was ever really discussed by his parents in front of him, though he would hear them arguing about it when they thought he was not around. His parents continued to try and help his sister out financially throughout her breakdown and poorly paid jobs, but her behaviour and her breakdown were a taboo subject.

Matt realised that when Val had wanted his time and understanding, or showed any signs of neediness, a picture of his emotionally unstable sister would set alarm bells ringing, and rather than respond to her needs he would bury himself in his work, just as he was encouraged to do as a teenager when his sister's behaviour was causing his parents distress. He dared not really commit emotionally to Val because his hidden fear was that women were too demanding and emotionally draining.

As Matt realised what he was doing and was able to become more responsive to Val's needs she in turn started to unfreeze. She also needed him to recognise what a good job she was doing as a wife and mother, and to give her much more praise and encouragement. As a child she had been continually criticised by her out-of-work and drunken father who was also never there for her. When Matt understood her needs he was able to respond, for he thought she was a fantastic mother – he had just failed to tell her so. He also did practical things that made a real difference. He started to alter his schedules so that at least two evenings a week he would be home by seven, and the weekends were for Val and the family. They went out together more, just the two of them which gave them time to talk about what really mattered to them. Matt encouraged Val to go out and do things that she enjoyed like badminton and art classes, and she started planning to do some retraining courses so that once the youngest child was at school she could go back into the workplace.

It became very clear to Matt that he had allowing work to encroach more and more on his relationship with Val. The more she complained the more he threw himself into work. Why, after all, did he want to return to a nagging or emotionally demanding wife? There was no pleasing her, was how he justified it to himself.

As Val felt closer to Matt and realised that he really cared about her, she also began to desire him sexually again. All of this did not happen overnight but over many months with both of them trying hard to open up the lines of communication that had virtually broken down.

If this sort of situation that Matt and Val were struggling with is familiar to you, try sitting down together, and doing the exercise on 'Learning to Meet Each Other's Needs', page 344.

TWO'S COMPANY, THREE'S A CROWD: THE MCPM WHO HAS AFFAIRS

One of the most classic ways that a man uses to avoid emotional commitment is to have an affair. By having a secret and illicit relationship, it enables him to withdraw a little from you, into a world that you do not share. An affair is a reaction to mounting panic or his feelings of being trapped in his marriage. The very fact that you don't know what is going on makes him feel more independent. His sense of freedom is increased by his sexual relationship with another woman. He is in fact using them to reduce his fear of commitment. The problem often is that he does not recognise why he is behaving in such a way.

If it is a one-off affair, and if the affair is discovered and he really regrets what he has done, how much he has hurt you, and how through his actions he has put the marriage at risk, then he can learn from this, and make every effort not to repeat this pattern. It is particularly helpful if he understands what is driving him, because that insight and understanding means that he is far less likely to do it again. It is very helpful if there has been an affair, if you can persuade him to have some joint counselling; it is not only supportive to you, but it can help a couple look at the reasons that led to the affair, and help them rebuild their marriage if that is what they both want and basically he is likely to want that as he does not want to lose you.

More damaging to marriage is where the man has a series of affairs, or flings like President Clinton or a long affair with a mistress running concurrently alongside his relationship with his wife, as it was alleged that Prince Charles did with Camilla Parker Bowles. Princess Diana pointed this out so poignantly in that incredible *Panorama* interview with Martin Bashir, when she said, "Well there were three of us in this marriage, so it was a bit crowded.' When asked 'What evidence did you have that their relationship (Prince Charles and Mrs Parker Bowles's) was continuing even though you were married?' Princess Diana replied, 'Oh, a woman's instinct is a very good one.'

This is what Stephanie also felt about Dominic her husband; from time to time she thought that there was another woman in Dominic's life. Yet every time she confronted him, he brushed it aside saying she was just being ridiculous, or she was imagining things. But eventually there seemed to her too many tell-tale signs. In desperation she hired a private detective. She gave him a description of her husband, the address where he worked, and the wine bars and restaurants he was likely to have lunch in. Shortly after she returned from her holiday with her daughters she received a letter from the detective.

Dear Mrs S.,
Re. Observation of Mr Dominic S. on Wednesday 3rd September
Further to your instructions, I arrived at your husband's office at 12 noon on Wednesday the 3rd September. I enclose my report which indicates certain times and events that took place.
12.00: Arrived at office of Mr S.
12.45: A man left 21, Chancery Lane. He was tall, slim, early to mid-forties, dressed in a dark striped well-cut suit, pale yellow tie and cream shirt. He fitted the description and picture that you had given to me of Mr S.
1. 00: Mr S. arrived at restaurant 'Rouge et Noire'. Many people going in and out as busy lunchtime. I did not go in but sat outside at pub across the road.
3.05: Mr S. left the restaurant with a woman similar age to your husband – about fortyish, slim, well-dressed, dark medium-length hair. They seemed relaxed and were talking animatedly. They crossed the road towards

me, he took her hand, they walked along the road a little then he called a cab. I followed in another cab and they went to a smart block of flats in Waverley Road, Kensington. They remained in the building for about one and a half hours.
5.15: Same man came out of the flats alone and hailed a taxi cab.
There seemed little point in following him further. Total hours spent in observation five and a half. Plus time of one hour each way to and from site and taxi fares.
Yours sincerely,
Arthur Wiseman

Stephanie felt it was pretty conclusive evidence. She dressed carefully, took a train to London and a taxi to her husband's office. She walked past his rather flustered-looking secretary who was surprised to see her and straight into his office. Dominic got up from his desk and said, 'What a surprise, darling. What are you doing here, is something wrong?' Stephanie replied, 'Yes something is very wrong, I know you are having an affair.' Dominic started to say, 'Don't be ridiculous, you mean you've come all this way to tell . . .' His voice trailed off as Stephanie took the letter out of her bag and began to read it out loud. Dominic went absolutely white, he knew he could no longer deny having an affair. They returned home and talked all afternoon and late into the night. Stephanie was distraught much of the time and, though Dominic was very sorry about the affair, he was absolutely furious that Stephanie had hired a private detective, to spy on him as he called it.

So one warm late September afternoon they walked into the counselling room. Stephanie sat on the edge of her chair, her arms folded around her body as if she was hugging herself; she was an ultra-slim, pretty woman, in her early forties. Dominic sat on the edge of his chair and he stared angrily out of the window. The tension between them filled the room like a bomb just about to be ignited.

It emerged that the affair had been going on for the last seven years of their twenty-year marriage. Over the next few weeks as they each told the story of their marriage Stephanie cried and raged with hurt and anger. Dominic would sit moving uncomfortably in his chair, there was always a long pause before he was able to speak.

He said he loved Stephanie and he did not want the marriage to end. He said he was happy in his marriage, and that he had not thought that his relationship with Lizzy, the other woman, would threaten his marriage. He said they only met occasionally and he never intended to leave Stephanie for her. Stephanie was irate. 'Why,' she screamed at him, 'did you then get involved, how could you do this if you loved me?' She turned to him with tears streaming down her face and said, 'It means everything we have shared together over the last seven years is now tainted by your whore.'

Stephanie said that there had been many times in the marriage when she had not been happy, and when Dominic had not been there for her. When the children were small, when her father had died, whenever there was a a family problem it was always she who had to sort it out, Dominic always seemed to have to be somewhere else. As they went back over how they saw the marriage, like many marriages it was two very different stories. Stephanie said she remembered when they were just married Dominic had said to her, 'Now we are married we are going to live as individuals.' She said 'I did not understand what Dominic meant at the time, but I knew that something about that was not what I wanted. I wanted to be close to him, I wanted to be a real couple.'

Dominic realised over the months of counselling that his cold unloving mother and his withdrawn and remote father may have made him uncomfortable and uneasy with intimacy and closeness, and Stephanie realised that the more he withdrew from her, the more panicky she became, and the more demands she made on Dominic, which drove him further away. But she also began to see that she could survive without him, that she had choices about whether she wanted to continue in the marriage or separate and live on her own. She became more confident and independent but they were also for the first time really able to talk about how the marriage had been for both of them, and how they wanted it to be in the future.

To begin with Stephanie needed to express a lot of anger not only over the affair, but over how she felt she had missed out on the closeness and support that she had longed for in the marriage. This was painful for Dominic but he learnt to express how he felt more and more. He struggled not to run away from sensitive and emotional issues, and as both of them listened to each other they started to grow closer together.

Dominic was able to see that by having 'a secret affair' it had created a distance between him and Stephanie. Dominic was also able to see that part of the attraction of the affair was that by having two women who loved and wanted him, he was compensating for the lack of love from his mother. He also saw how he was torn between wanting a close loving relationship with Stephanie and his fear of fully committing himself to her. For deep down he feared that if he loved her too much, one day she might reject him as his mother had done all those years ago, and he did not want to experience that pain all over again. So as a sort of insurance policy he had another woman waiting in the wings.

HOW TO HANDLE A CPM's INFIDELITY

Infidelity is very attractive to the commitment phobic married man, because it's a way of telling himself that he is not really trapped. Here he is playing the field, just like a single man. He may move from affair to affair, because of course he does not want to commit to the woman he is having an affair with any more than he wants to fully commit to his wife, in fact rather less so. So he keeps his affairs as light-hearted as possible. If the woman in question tries to move the affair into a more committed relationship then the chances are that she won't see him for dust.

Alternatively he calls all the shots in how he conducts the affair as Dominic had with Lizzy. He only saw her once or twice a month, never at weekends, not even a stolen few days away together. She was under strict instructions that she must never contact him at the house, and only in dire emergency at his office. Also she was relatively safe as she was married, though unhappily, and he gave her no encouragement to get out of that marriage; if she had, he would probably have terminated the affair.

If you discover your spouse is having an affair it is devastating, it sometimes means the end of the marriage, but it does not have to be, and more marriages survive affairs than end in divorce.

If you both love each other, and you both want the marriage, and he finishes the affair, it is possible to rebuild the relationship. It is important that he is able to let you express all the hurt and anger that you are feeling. That he accepts that you need to ask questions such as: Who was she? How long has it been going on? Where did you meet? How often? Why did you have an affair? How could you do this if you loved me? He will probably be reluctant to talk too much, because of his feelings of guilt, because it's uncomfortable for him, because he thinks it is only making thing more painful, but talk you must. It is natural for you to want to go over things again and again, before you are able to re-establish trust, self-esteem, and forgiveness.

But if there has been a series of affairs and each time the affair has been discovered he has promised never to do it again, only to sally forth once the dust has settled, then that may be a different story; how often can he really expect you to forgive? If you go on accepting him back, it is as if you are condoning the affairs, and it is very self-destructive. In those circumstances if he refuses to take responsibility for his own behaviour, he is unlikely to change, so you may decide enough is enough, and tell him that you are going to end the marriage and mean it.

THE OTHER ETERNAL TRIANGLE

Another classic way that a man avoids commitment to the woman he loves is when there is another woman on the scene. The other eternal triangle – that devastating emotional stranglehold of the other woman – no, not the mistress this time, but his mother!

When a man marries, his first loyalty should be to his wife and children (when they arrive on the scene). Most mothers want their sons to grow up, fall in love and marry and have children of their own. So there is a natural loosening of the bonds throughout their teens, where the young man growing up is encouraged to be independent, to move towards living his own life and taking responsibility for his own decisions. But some mothers can't bear to see their sons moving away from them. They see this natural process of moving into adulthood as losing their son's love, or losing their control over him. So rather than helping him to become a mature and independent young man they dominate or manipulate their son so that he remains tied to their apron strings.

This is done in a variety of different ways. It may be through bullying and controlling, or playing the helpless card, where the son feels that he has to be at his mother's beck and call. Alternatively from an early age he has learnt to constantly walk on eggshells for fear of upsetting her, making her ill or sending her into hysterics. If he has not been able to break free from her demands or emotional blackmail and establish a relationship with her which is loving but independent of her, it is very difficult for him to form adult loving and committed relationships.

When a controlling, dominating or clinging mother sees another woman appearing on the horizon of her son's life she starts to panic. If she feels that this is going to be a serious relationship, or worse that you are a potential marriage partner she sees you as a threat, someone whom her son will love more than her, rather than as well as her. This is not always at a conscious level and she would probably hotly deny her behaviour if it was pointed out to her. But the result is the same: she consciously or subconsciously wants to alienate you from her son's affections.

So she will often be critical of her son's girlfriends, create uproar or become even more demanding. The more the man is under her thumb, the more he will give in to her demands to the detriment of his relationship with his wife or girlfriend. The result almost invariably is that once living together or married you the new daughter-in-law feel that his mother is always interfering in your life. It is very threatening and undermining to a marriage if the husband's first loyalty is to his mother, because that inevitably is at the expense of his relationship with you. As a woman you feel that your spouse is more committed to keeping his mother happy than he is committed to you. The man feels like piggy in the middle and that he is constantly pulled in two directions. That is how George felt when he met and fell in love with Katrina.

THE MOTHER-IN-LAW FROM HELL

Katrina was twenty-one when she met her husband, George. He was eleven years older than her, deep in debt and struggling to set up his own business. After a few months they started living together. George was clever and hard-working but had borrowed rather a lot of money to get the business off the ground and consequently was having difficulty balancing the books.

Katrina gave up her job and threw herself into helping

him, and with two pairs of hands things improved greatly and the debts receded.

They soon decided that they wanted to spend the rest of their lives together, and though Katrina did not realise it at the time that is where her problems began. Buoyed up and very excited she went with George to see his parents to tell them that they were planning to get engaged. When they arrived at George's parents' house, Katrina was slightly surprised when George said he wanted to talk to his mother alone. Katrina went out into the garden; she was just about to return to the house when she heard raised voices. George was desperately pleading with his mother over and over again to approve of the forthcoming engagement, constantly beseeching her to give them her blessing. She heard him say that he could not bear to get engaged unless his mother approved. Katrina froze as George's words drifted across the lawn. It was only after much pleading on George's part that his mother finally and reluctantly agreed.

His mother it appeared had quite a list: she disapproved of the age gap, she thought Katrina's clothes were much too trendy, that she was a townie and not interested in country sports, and that George had not known her long enough. But Katrina was very much in love with George and as things quietened down she put these concerns to the back of her mind and threw herself into organising the wedding. It was once they were married that the problems really started.

Every Sunday they were expected to do the two-hour drive to see his parents for lunch. When they tried to leave to have some time on their own, his mother became hysterical, demanding that they stayed longer. While she shouted and screamed at them, George would endlessly try to pacify her saying how upset it made him to see her in tears. Meanwhile her husband would remonstrate with George and Katrina for being so cruel by not giving in to her wishes.

Katrina said, 'It got worse and worse, his mother seemed to want to interfere in every area of ours lives.' Then George said he wanted to move out of town. 'I was quite keen to move into the country,' said Katrina. 'I was pregnant with our first child and I thought it would be nice to bring her up in the country, that was until I discovered that he wanted us to move to where his parents lived. We argued and argued about it for months. Eventually he wore me down. I loved him and I did not want to lose him so I agreed.'

But things deteriorated even further after the move. George's mother now had them on her doorstep. Much to Katrina's distress George gave his mother a key to their house, so that she would frequently call round, and just let herself in, even if neither of them was there.

Katrina would arrive home to find little notes or messages on the answerphone from his mother. One would say that the dishes needed washing or his shirts had not been ironed well enough, or the windows needed cleaning. She would often leave food in the fridge, saying take-away foods where not good for George. 'His father was no help. He always backed his wife in whatever she did.

'I kept asking George to tell his mother he did not want her coming round when we were out,' said Katrina. 'I really minded that she felt she could just walk into our house whenever she felt like it. It just didn't feel like my home. It was worse after Flora our daughter was born, my mother-in-law would just walk in and sit down and stay for hours. I didn't mind for a short time, but I did not want her there for hours on end. In the end I tried to talk to her about this, to explain I needed some privacy. She exploded and said I was thoroughly ungrateful and she was only trying to help. It got straight back to George who accused me of being rude to his mother. Which I hadn't at all. George and I had a huge row.'

'On Valentine's Day George sent me a lovely bouquet of flowers, in my favourite colours, pale yellow and cream, with a very loving message. When his mother saw the flowers she said she thought Valentine's Day was overrated. Then a few weeks later on his mother's birthday George sent his mother exactly the same flowers. That was bad enough, but in his card to her he had written the same message that he had sent to me. I could hardly believe it, I was absolutely gutted. I had been so pleased with the flowers and the message, but all of that was completely taken away.'

George's mother continued to rule him. He made some attempt to stand up to her, but he always capitulated under her onslaught. By now George and Katrina's marriage was in serious difficulties because of his mother's continual interference in their lives. Katrina still felt she loved George, but she also felt that he was more committed to his mother than to her and their daughter Flora.

After yet another major row Katrina said she could take no more and told George that she was going to file for divorce. He was devastated and begged her to give him a second chance. Katrina pointed out that he had already had second, third, fourth in fact countless chances. But each time she asked him to stand up to his mother for her sake and for Flora's he backed down. She told him that she had never felt that he had committed himself to her. His loyalty always seemed to be with his mother. After much pleading Katrina agreed not to divorce as long as George agreed to go to counselling or psychotherapy, and also that they would move house. She made it very clear that she no longer coped with being on his mother's doorstep. Some time ago they had talked about moving to live in Dorset and George agreed that is where they would go, which would put a distance of some two hundred miles between them and his mother. He agreed to both of Katrina's requests and he set about getting professional help.

Over the next six months George struggled with his very mixed feeling towards his mother. To start with he was wildly protective, but as the weeks passed he was able to see that he was also very angry with her, that he had felt controlled and bullied by her throughout his childhood. He also realised that she used guilt as a very powerful weapon with which to attack his defences. His mother's hysterical outbursts made him feel quite paralysed. He feared that unless he gave in to her, she would just go on and on. Her tears made him feel that it was all his fault and that he was responsible for hurting her. He realised that he was also behaving like his father, who long ago had given up any attempt at standing up to his wife, so he just took her side as a way of getting a peaceful life. So now George, like his father before him, did the same thing.

Slowly George started to claim his independence and his own life back. When he was able to make changes

Katrina was very supportive. It made a huge difference to her, when he stopped blaming her for being unreasonable, and was able to see that so many of the problems between them were caused by his mother's unreasonable behaviour and not hers. Every step of the way his mother objected, she screamed and shouted and cried. When they asked her to return their key, she said she did not want to see them ever again. George, with Katrina's help was able to say that it was important to them that she telephoned them before she came round to see if that suited them. She refused to do this and said in that case she would not come at all. It was touch and go as to whether George could stand up to her, he nearly gave in countless times. But her absence gave him a breathing space and allowed him really to do some work with his counsellor on his relationship with his mother. But it was a good eighteen months later before he felt able tell his mother that they were putting the house on the market and were moving.

His mother's behaviour did not really change much, she was now talking to them again, but swung between ranting and raging and being cold and sullen. But George's relationship with Katrina improved enormously. The closer he felt to Katrina the more able he was to withstand his mother's antics. By the time they came to move he was just as keen to as Katrina and able to tell his mother it was something they both wanted. It was really the first time in their seven-year marriage that Katrina felt 100% supported by him.

HOW TO GET THE LOYALTY YOU NEED

George's mother was pretty much the mother-in-law from hell. Not all such dominating mothers are as bad as she was but it is far from an isolated case. It is something that frequently comes up in counselling. When a man has been brought up with a very dominating and controlling mother and a weak and passive father it is difficult for him to learn to be able to stand up to her. It was only when Katrina finally presented him with her intentions to divorce that he was really able tackle his problem with his mother. He loved Katrina and he was scared of losing her. It is possible to change, but as with all change it has to come from the person themselves, they have to be prepared to try and change, you can't make someone else change, but you can, as Katrina did, make it clear what your needs are, and what is acceptable or not acceptable behaviour. It is then up to them.

Katrina learnt how to communicate her needs to George, and George loved her enough to try and understand how his relationship with his mother was threatening their marriage. He was then able to learn to stand up to his mother, to withstand her unreasonable demands. Only then was he able to fully commit himself to Katrina and Flora.

If you are in a similar situation where you feel his loyalty to his mother comes before his loyalty to you, it is necessary to make it clear to him what is happening and how this is hurting you and undermining the marriage. It can help to do a list of needs as I described earlier in the chapter, only this time it is specially related to the problem of his relationship with his mother and how it is having a negative impact on your marriage. For example:

Difficult mothers-in-law

Each of you makes a list of three things that you argue about most when the issue of his mother arises. For example: what happens at Christmas; how fed up you are with having his mother to lunch every Sunday; how she is able to upset plans you have already made. Put the one that matters most to you at the top and the least important at the bottom:

Your List of Needs

- That you don't cancel the arrangement we have made as a couple or a family when your mother rings and says she wants you to go round to see her.
- That his mother doesn't come to lunch every Sunday but only once a month.
- That she does not come to stay every Christmas as she has done since you were married, but instead you have her for alternate Christmases.

His List of Needs

- That she comes to stay every Christmas. I can't stop that now.
- She is in her sixties, so if she suddenly needs me to go around to see her, I can't say no.
- That we have her to lunch every Sunday. She expects that.

Discuss this together and agree on a compromise. I admit it won't be easy because by this stage you are both likely to be fairly entrenched in your views, but it is important to work out an agreement together. That is possible and necessary if you want a more loving and fulfilling marriage where you feel loyalty and commitment to each other

THE ART OF COMPROMISE – FOR EXAMPLE:

- Your husband's sister could be asked to have her mother for Christmas every other year. So you could both talk to his sister about this and give your husband moral support. That way your husband does not have to worry about his mother being on her own, and his sister could face up to doing her share of 'looking after mother'.
- You agree that if it is a real emergency, he does drop your plans and goes round. But otherwise he tells her that you are already doing something, and arranges another time when he can go over. In return, you don't moan at him for that.
- To go from having his mother around every Sunday to just once a month would be too big a change to ask of your husband. He would feel very bad about hurting his mother. But you could agree that one Sunday a month is mother-in-law free and that week he goes round to see her one evening during the week. That way she can have him all to herself, which she would probably enjoy.

Remember that the man you are married to finds it very difficult to stand up to a mother who has controlled or dominated and bullied him for much of his life. She may even have resorted to emotional blackmail to get what she wants. Making small changes to start with can make a big difference to your lives. It also reduces the arguments, helps him to see that he can learn to stand up to his mother, and that by doing so neither she nor her world falls apart. He will see that it is a relief not to feel constantly pulled in two directions and that if you tackle the problem together then his relationship with you has the potential to improve enormously.

When Guilt Rules

Libby, a delightful and easy-going woman in her mid thirties, was married to Idris who was recently divorced. They had been married three years and Libby was slowly going up the wall. Each year driven by guilt Idris insisted that they take his ex-wife with them when they went on holiday. Not because he wanted to, but because of a combination of guilt mingled with his ex's attitude of 'what about poor little me?' which made him feel obliged to include her in their holiday plans. Libby with a little encouragement stood up to her husband, and said enough was enough. No more ex-wife on holiday; reluctantly Idris agreed. Within a year his ex had made different holiday plans, and the following year, she remarried, much to Libby's delight and Idris's relief.

The compromises suggested above are just an example of how you can negotiate for change. There were many ways that these two lists of needs could have been resolved. For example if you were the woman in that scenario you could have agreed to go to your parents-in-law for Christmas, if you partner agreed that your in-laws did not come on holiday with you.

Nobody can make another person change if they really don't want to, but with a man who fears emotional commitment, it's frequently not that he does not want to change his behaviour, but rather more that he is afraid to. Much of the time he may be feeling fed up or frustrated by his problem, or he may not really recognise why he behaves the way he does. But if he loves you and wants the relationship what he probably can see is that something is wrong, and that he has a part to play in contributing to the conflict between you. If he is willing to do something about the problem you may well be able to do this together. Alternatively you could encourage him to seek professional help, either in individual therapy to start with, or in joint counselling. I know from my own experience as a counsellor of working with couples in such circumstances change is possible, but you both have to be prepared to work at it.

ROMANTIC LOVE

As a woman when you fall in love and get married your hope and expectation is to have your need for closeness and intimacy met through intimate conversations with the man you love. Unfortunately problems occur because many men don't have the same needs as women do for intimate talk. The result is that because of these differences both of you then experience a degree of frustration or even anger. You feel frustrated because the man in your life does not have the same need to talk as you have. For the man he feels frustrated because he listens to what you want to talk about and then comes up with a solution to the problem, and that annoys you, because you were not looking to him to provide solutions, but to understand how you were feeling, and he feels frustrated because as he sees it you have asked for his advice, and then rejected it, so what was the point of talking about it anyway?

There is no reason really why a man should become like a woman, even though we may think that he would be happier, that he would gain so much more by having the ability to really talk about feelings, and how could he not see the sense in changing? There is in all of us 'the Selfish Gene' so naturally it would also suit us very well. But it is more a question of meeting each other halfway. When a woman describes her husband as her best friend, that is usually because he is meeting her intimacy needs, so if a man is prepared to try and meet the woman's intimacy needs a little more, by recognising how important it is for her to create the intimacy bond through talking, and how frustrating it is if he is solution-focused, withdraws or stonewalls her, by being unavailable or unresponsive to her needs, that does create greater harmony. In turn if you try to accept that his need for relationship talk is less than yours he too can have his needs meet. It is a question of trying to meet each other halfway. This is where the CPM and his spouse have to be prepared to struggle quite hard to achieve this balance.

Men and women, as I have said earlier in this book, can also feel differently about sex. Most women need emotional connection and intimacy for good sex. Whereas men are able to separate intimacy from sex more easily. So the more important component in women's romantic images is emotional attachment, while in men's it's the erotic aspect.

These differences mean men and women enter relationship with different ideas and expectations of how their relationships will be.

One way where this is frequently highlighted sexually is where a man will use sex to get close and make up after a row; a woman will feel, 'How can he expect me to make love when we have had a fight and not talked for the last twenty-four hours?'

Married Talk/Relationship Talk: By doing this exercise together it will enable you to look at what your expectations were when you first married, some of the stresses that are now getting in the way and how you would like things to be.

Keeping Love Alive

a. Each make a list of: What your hopes and expectations for yourself and for your relationship were when you first married. Share this together and talk about the good times, what you found attractive about each other and what your expectations were.

b. Make a list and discuss: What are the top three things that you now find the most difficult or stressful about your spouse/partner or the relationship?

c. Then Discuss: How could you each start to make some changes so that both of you feel that your partner understands your needs and is prepared to make adjustments in their own behaviour to meet them?

The first step. Talk together and each agree in the coming week to do something manageable that you think your partner would like you to do for them. Don't at this point tell them what it is, or ask them what they would like – that is for you to work out. It could be buying her a bunch of her favourite flowers, or taking the children out, so that she could read a book or have the luxury of a long relaxing bath. You could, for example, cook him his favourite meal, or suggest that he has a lie-in instead of coming Saturday morning shopping with you.

At the end of the week, discuss it, and see if your partner noticed what it was that you did to please them. Don't criticise your partner if they did not realise what you had done, or if they did not get it quite right for you, but show appreciation that they tried. The next week each of you ask your partner to do something for you that you would really like – it must be of equal value. By the third week you will then perhaps feel ready to move on and tackle the things that you would like changed, that you both identified in the exercise above.

It is surprising how, by starting to make small changes, the bigger and more important ones also start happening. That is because, if you both feel that your spouse or partner is trying to do something kind or loving for you, it is likely to result in you wanting to do something for them equally loving in return. It is a question of being made to feel valued, so that you then feel you want to show your love and appreciation in return. One swallow does not make a summer so it's important to make this way of responding to each other a normal part of everyday life.

11

From Romantic love to Enduring love

Love one another, but make not a bond of love:
Let it rather be a moving sea between the shores of your souls.
Fill each other's cup but drink not from one cup.
Give one another of your bread but eat not from the same loaf.
Sing and dance together and be joyous, but let each one of you be alone,
Even as the strings of the lute are alone though they quiver with the same music.
Give your hearts, but not into each other's keeping.
For only the hand of life can contain hearts.
And stand together yet not too near together:
For the pillars of the temple stand apart,
And the oak tree and the cypress grow not in each other's shadow.

Kahlil Gibran *The Prophet* 1923

GETTING THE COMMITMENT YOU DESERVE

If you are in love with a CPM remember you have to be self protective. You have to value yourself, your needs, your desires, your way of life. If you don't, then he certainly will also fail to do so. Don't jump through hoops or bend over backwards to be the woman you think he wants you to be. Be you, and tell yourself that you need to be loved the way you want to be loved. Take time over building a loving relationship because then you are in a much better position to get the commitment that you deserve.

THE RECOVERING ADDICT

The CPM is addicted to loving and leaving. He is often controlled by his fear of commitment. Just as gamblers, alcoholics and sex addicts cause mayhem by inflicting their chaotic lifestyles on those closest to them, so can CPMs make life hell for the women they love. However, change is possible, even though it can be a long road for the recovering addict.

THREE STEPS TOWARDS CHANGE

- To start with a CPM takes flight when he does not understand what is driving him. To be able to change this pattern he has to fall in love with a woman enough to want to change how he behaves.

- Secondly he has to be prepared to look at the underlying reasons why he finds committed relationships too hot to handle. If he is not able or prepared to do that, he at least needs to recognise that he is the one with the problem, not you.
- The next step is to admit to himself that he would like things to be different, and for him to take responsibility for making some changes.

All change is scary, from feelings of nervouseness to something so frightening that we are either immobilised and dare not make a move in any direction or we take flight hoping that if we run hard enough the problem will be left behind.

But remember for many CPMs it's not that they don't want a committed relationship with the woman they really love, it's that they are afraid to have one. So that fear can make them sabotage their relationship, or end it altogether. But if they really love you, the fear of losing you can begin to outweigh their fear of commitment. A man can start to recognise that he has left a string of broken relationships in his wake and wish that it were different. Alternatively he may have fallen deeply in love once, twice or more before, and now with the advantage of hindsight see rather more clearly that it was he not she that screwed up. That insight can enable him to begin to make the shift from running away from love to examining his own behaviour and see how he can do it differently. Let's recap:

Falling for a CPM is a high-risk affair. Being madly in love is wonderful, passionate and romantic, but it is such an emotional state that it also becomes dangerous and risky.

It means being vulnerable, it means the possibility of being hurt, disappointed, tormented, rejected. Remember the CPM will pull out all the stops when he is in hot pursuit of you. He is passionate, eager and romantic, he seems to desire you more than anyone else in all the world. He wants to sweep all caution to the winds, and more than anything he wants you to join him on this romantic journey. So the number one rule for you at the beginning of a relationship with a CPM is to *keep your feet on the ground*. You need to stay realistic and recognise that it is up to you to *slow the pace* if you want your relationship with him to stand a chance. This will not be easy, but then your relationship with a CPM will not be easy either.

FROM 'ROMANTIC LOVE' TO 'ENDURING LOVE'

Falling in love feels so wonderful because it is such a heady, dizzy, floating on air sort of experience. At that very 'in love' stage you become intensely aware of the person you love, thoughts of them fill all your waking and dreaming time. It is sometimes difficult to move from this very romantic in-love stage, where you view your loved one as practically perfect in every way to the deep, more enduring love that ongoing loving relationships are built upon.

The more you are wedded to the ideal of romantic love, the more difficult it is to make a long-term commitment to another person. Because then, when the perfect loved one becomes slightly less perfect, you become disillusioned. When you have to deal with the loved one and all their frailties rather than your idealised version of them, that is when someone who is hooked on 'romantic love' starts to doubt their own feelings.

For a CPM who tends to be very romantic this transition can be difficult. If he comes into the category of worst-case CPM it is even more difficult for him to make that transition. That is until he reaches a stage in his life where he is able to stop running and check out what he is doing to cause all his relationships to fizzle out. When he can stop blaming you when things go wrong, and accept that all relationships have their ups and downs, then he is in touch with reality. When he can accept that there will be times of passion and times of unhappiness and that this is a normal part of all relationships, then he is ready to move to a deeper and more committed relationship.

YOU NEED TO SET THE GUIDELINES

Remember that a CPM is a man torn in two directions, with part of him longing for a loving relationship and the other part downright scared of one. That does not mean he can't make a commitment, though it might do, but it does mean it is much more of an uphill struggle for him than for other men.

So remember 'The Five Golden rules' that I wrote about in Chapter Four on page 116.

Five golden rules to remember are:

- Don't rush into a relationship because he seems wild about you. You set the pace.

- Refuse to jump into bed with him. He won't die of unrequited passion. If he gives up on you because you resisted his sexual advances, he would have done so anyway once you had been to bed with him, which would have hurt more.
- Listen to your basic instincts. Keep in mind the things about him that worry you.
- Look at his track record. If it is one of broken hearts don't assume that he will be different with yours.
- Keep your feet on the ground. Don't convince yourself that because he seems so emotionally open, that he really understands himself or for that matter you. He probably doesn't.

It is essential in a relationship with a CPM that you set the guidelines for the relationship. Only by taking time to get to know each other properly can you both build secure foundations for the future of this relationship. It is equally vital that you learn to recognise if you are involved with a worst-case CPM so that you can have the courage to get out of that relationship before he is able to do too much damage.

Selina is a thirty-six-year-old divorced woman with a seven-year-old daughter. She has a good job, owns her own home and drives a smart car, but her emotional life is a mess. She wrote:

> *Last year I met and fell in love with a man the same age as me. Charlie and I spent every weekend together, we went away on great holidays and he adored my seven-year-old daughter. This man made us a family and we adored him, and Charlie said he had never*

been happier. Then a few weeks ago, shortly after we returned from a lovely holiday he walked out without saying a word. My daughter and I are devastated, and he refuses to talk about 'us'.

In her letter Selina also told me a little about this man: 'He has always been a loner, he has no male friends, only renting rooms, never putting down roots. He has constantly walked away from jobs, and all of his previous relationships have lasted less than three weeks.'

Every one of those characteristics in Selina's letter is a warning sign in itself. Added together they are certainly in the worst-case bracket. If only Selina had allowed her head to rule her heart and realised that everything about this man screamed non-commitment. She wrote of her devastation saying, 'Now our lives are so empty. I can't even bear being in my own house. I have lost so much. Why did he do this to us?' All too often when you fall in love with a CPM you make the mistake of thinking that with you he will be different. If he is a worst-case CPM it's almost 100% certain that you will be wrong.

A WORD OF WARNING – A WORST-CASE CPM

If your think you are involved with a CPM who comes into this category then the best thing you can do is protect yourself and end that relationship. The CPM who is totally caught up in the search for a perfect love frequently sabotages the relationship with the woman he loves. That way he is then free to move on in search of another new and perfect love.

The sort of woman who will fit his internal romantic image, who will provide total bliss and happiness, where all doubts and questions about himself will be answered. So it is really important for you to be able to recognise 'a worst-case CPM' like Charlie.

BE YOUR OWN BEST FRIEND

Be your own best friend if you think he is a worst-case CPM. Try and stand outside the situation, and ask yourself this: If this were happening to a very loved friend of mine, what would I want to say to her about how this man is treating her? The chances are you would be saying 'Why are you allowing this man to treat you so badly? Why are you putting up with this?' Or if you have split up with him or nearly split up and are thinking of trying one more time, you would be saying 'Why are you going back to him when the chances are he will hurt you all over again?'

What tends to happen is that our family and friends and those who love us are saying just that. But there you stand, your ears closed to their words of warning, even defending the indefensible behaviour of the man who is hurting you so much. The more they press you to see sense, the more you run to his defence. It's you and him against the world now. He has found his protector in you.

So remember, don't kid yourself that he will change through the love of a good woman. He won't, or the odds are so very heavily stacked against you, that you would be almost certain to lose.

THE HEART OF THE MATTER

The heart of the matter is that the worst-case CPM is incapable of giving more commitment to you because he is still devoted to someone who takes priority over you, someone he loves more than you and that is himself. So take your good advice and finish the relationship.

- If you need to remind yourself how to identify him then go back and reread chapter four.

MOVING ON

The majority of CPMs do not come into this worst-case category and like the rest of us they are able to make the transition from the heady in-love stage to a committed, loving and sustaining relationship but the task for them is a little harder than for other men. Consequently if you are in love with a CPM that will have its impact on you too. But knowing how to handle your relationship with him, and how to protect yourself is a basic requirement when involved with such a man.

TAKE CONTROL OF YOUR LIFE

If you feel you have lost control over your life it's important to reclaim it, and if you haven't, it's equally important to retain it. The most significant rule of all is that you have to take care of yourself, to protect yourself from being drawn into his world and abandoning yours. It is natural when you fall in love to want to make yourself absolutely desirable to the man you love, to fulfil his vision of you, to please him, to be interested in the things he is interested in, to overlook some little niggardly doubts about the relationship, or what he is like as a person, just because you are so in love. But with a CPM it is particularly important that you don't allow yourself just to be swept blindly along.

You have your life, your friends, your work, your interests, things to do like going on that mountaineering holiday in the Himalayas you were planning, the Cordon Bleu cookery course you had signed up for. Whatever you do don't abandon them. Do not let your life circulate around him.

This is for two reasons:

- Firstly: If you let him become the centre of your life, your number one priority, then everything else is pushed to the sidelines. If he does leave then the loss will feel so much greater, because your life and your support systems will have been eroded in the name of love.
- Secondly: One of the very things that is attractive to a CPM is your independence, so don't abandon it.

Independence and love are not mutually exclusive. Being your own woman, having your own life, are attractive to him, even if he tells you differently and makes you feel he wants your world to circulate around him. Remember a CPM does not like clinging and dependent women or claustrophobic or smothering relationships. He will only panic more if the woman in his life invades his space and expects him to sacrifice too much of his own independence for her. He may give you the impression that he wants it but what he hates most of all is if you make him feel that you love him so much that you can't live without him. Instead, let that be the feeling he has about you.

CHECK OUT WHAT HE MEANS WHEN HE SAYS 'I LOVE YOU'

The language of love is more than simply saying 'I love you', important though that is. What you need to be sure of is that you are speaking the same language. When he says 'I love you' does he simply mean that is how he feels about you at that moment, whereas when you say 'I love you' you mean: 'I am committed to you and I want a future together.' Is his idea of long-term planning about where you are going to spend Christmas together, whereas you are so much in love that you want to be together for always.

You owe it to yourself to be honest with yourself, and if you have doubts don't try and convince yourself that all is well when the signs indicate otherwise and are there for you to see. So don't bury your head in the sand or you will end up becoming your own worst enemy. Don't make assumptions, remember that when you talk about love and the future that you make sure you both mean the same things. Don't fall into the trap of thinking because we have been going out for some while, or because we have been together a long time, he should know what I am thinking. Because the only way you can be really sure he does know is to express your thoughts and feelings clearly. Time and time again men and women fall in the trap of the woman thinking: 'He loves me so he will know what I want him to do and say.' Whereas men think the woman they love will tell them what she thinks, feels and wants. When you don't, he complains: 'The trouble with you is I just don't understand you. How can I know what you want if you don't tell me?'

By this I am not suggesting that you propose marriage, though in this age of equality there is no reason why you shouldn't. Most women it seems, still want the men to do the proposing. So he needs to know that you believe in a committed relationship and that when you really fall in love you want to marry and settle down and also want to have children with him. He needs to know where you are coming from, what long-term desires you have for your future. You need to know how he views all of these things, what his hopes and dreams and plans are for his future. Then you need to move on to how you both feel about each other in this respect.

MAKE SURE THAT HE LOVES YOU AS YOU WANT TO BE LOVED

As your relationship progresses you need to know how he feels about you and what sort of relationship he wants for you both. Don't let it be a guessing game. If a romantic holiday in Greece with no strings attached is all you want, fine. But if you are in love and you want more than that then you both need to know how you think and feel about each other. You also both need to know what you want from the future, and whether that future means the same thing to both of you.

Remember, this is not a man who doesn't want a committed relationship with the woman he loves, but that a CPM is a man who is afraid to have one. The first step on the road for CPM recovery is for him to accept that he has a problem, the second is that he should be prepared to do something about it and the third is for him to realise that he will not achieve success without a struggle. The CPM needs to recognise that if he does not want to lose you he has to work at overcoming his fears. He needs to know that if he is not prepared to give you the commitment you want, you will find someone who does. That is because your desire is to be with someone you love and who loves you in return. Someone who like you wants love and commitment that will last for ever. That is, after all, a very reasonable desire.

If he is struggling to overcome his fears but needs a little extra help, suggest to him that he seeks some professional help. This could be either through counselling, cognitive therapy or psychotherapy. Remember you can't be his therapist but others can.

Bibliography

POETRY

Elizabeth Barrett Browning, 'Let Me Count the Ways', *The Book of Happiness*, Michael Joseph, 1959.

Bhartrhari (7th Century), 'In Former Days', *Love Poems*, trans. John Brough, Everyman's Library Pocket Poets.

Lord Byron, 'Don Juan', *Poems, Prose and Letters*, Collins, 1971.

Kahlil Gibran, 'Love One Another', *The Prophet*, Alfred A. Knopf, 1923.

Jean Kerr, 'It Was Hard to Communicate With You', *Mary, Mary*, Act II, 1960.

R.D. Laing, 'If She Did Not Love You', *Sonnets*, Michael Joseph, 1979.

Dorothy Parker, 'Social Note' and 'A Telephone Call', *The Collected Dorothy Parker*, Penguin, 1989.

William Shakespeare, 'Sigh No More Ladies', *Much Ado About Nothing*.

Ella Wheeler Wilcox, 'Blind', *The New Quotable Woman*, Elaine Partnow, Headline, 1993.

RESEARCH/SURVEYS

Laureen Snider, Department of Sociology at Queens University, Kingston, Ontario, 'Towards Safer Societies', *The British Journal of Criminology*, Winter, 1998.

Dr Catherine A. Surra, Department of Human Ecology, University of Texas at Austin, 'Commitment Processes in Accounts of the Development of Premarital Relationships', *Journal of Marriage and the Family*, February 1997.

Dr Maryon Tysoe, *The Good Relationship Guide*, Piatkus, 1998.